"A gripping account of life inside an eating disorder and how one individual escaped through the bonds of motherhood, *Insatiable* is an inspiring personal memoir of turning struggle into triumph."

—Ira M. Sacker, M.D.,
author of *Regaining Your Self* and *Dying to Be Thin*

"This is a deeply felt, moving account of turning obessions into passions, of becoming free to meet love on its own terms. Written in an original style and propelling structure, *Insatiable* reveals the heart of a young woman struggling to face her demons. The triumph is that she managed to become whole." —Natalie Goldberg,
author of *Old Friend from Far Away* and *Writing Down the Bones*

"Erica Rivera has written a fierce, difficult, honest book about living with—and almost dying from—food disorders and anorexia. As readers, we experience the painful, intimate details of a life taken over by the author's desperate struggle to make herself so thin she becomes barely a shadow. We see the enormous cost of this illness, and feel gratitude and a sense of hope as Ms. Rivera takes on her demons and finds her way back to a life worth living."

—Deborah Keenan,
author of *Willow Room, Green Door: New and Selected Poems*

insatiable

a young mother's struggle
with anorexia

ERICA RIVERA

BERKLEY BOOKS, NEW YORK

THE BERKLEY PUBLISHING GROUP
Published by the Penguin Group
Penguin Group (USA) Inc.
375 Hudson Street, New York, New York 10014, USA
Penguin Group (Canada), 90 Eglinton Avenue East, Suite 700, Toronto, Ontario M4P 2Y3, Canada
(a division of Pearson Penguin Canada Inc.)
Penguin Books Ltd., 80 Strand, London WC2R 0RL, England
Penguin Group Ireland, 25 St. Stephen's Green, Dublin 2, Ireland (a division of Penguin Books Ltd.)
Penguin Group (Australia), 250 Camberwell Road, Camberwell, Victoria 3124, Australia
(a division of Pearson Australia Group Pty. Ltd.)
Penguin Books India Pvt. Ltd., 11 Community Centre, Panchsheel Park, New Delhi—110 017, India
Penguin Group (NZ), 67 Apollo Drive, Rosedale, North Shore 0632, New Zealand
(a division of Pearson New Zealand Ltd.)
Penguin Books (South Africa) (Pty.) Ltd., 24 Sturdee Avenue, Rosebank, Johannesburg 2196,
South Africa

Penguin Books Ltd., Registered Offices: 80 Strand, London WC2R 0RL, England

This book is an original publication of The Berkley Publishing Group.

This book describes the real experiences of real people. The author has disguised the identities of some, and in some instances created composite characters, but none of these changes has affected the truthfulness and accuracy of her story. Furthermore, the publisher does not have any control over and does not assume any responsibility for author or third-party websites or their content.

FIRST EDITION: October 2009

Library of Congress Cataloging-in-Publication Data

Rivera, Erica.
   Insatiable : a young mother's struggle with anorexia / Erica Rivera. — 1st ed.
      p.   cm.
   ISBN 978-0-425-22987-3
   1. Rivera, Erica—Mental health.   2. Anorexia nervosa—Patients—United   States—Biography.
   I. Title.
RC552.A5R56 2009
362.196'852620092—dc22
[B]
                                    2009019160

PRINTED IN THE UNITED STATES OF AMERICA

10   9   8   7   6   5   4   3   2   1

Penguin is committed to publishing works of quality and integrity.
In that spirit, we are proud to offer this book to our readers;
however, the story, the experiences, and the words
are the author's alone.

Acknowledgments

First and foremost, I must thank my agent, Jamie Brenner, for believing in me as a writer and for being a relentless advocate for *Insatiable*. Without your unconditional support, candid feedback, and steady guidance, this book would not have been possible.

Thank you to Denise Silvestro for her keen editorial eye and for giving me the freedom to shape this manuscript.

Thanks are also due . . .

. . . to Natalie Goldberg for being the momentum behind my writing, for teaching me how to "write down the bones," and for reminding me that I "don't need to be so good." You are my literary guru and I am forever indebted to you.

. . . to Madelon Sprengnether for taking a chance on me, to Deborah Keenan for pushing me toward creative nonfiction, and to the *Star Tribune* for publishing my first clips.

. . . to Bill Addison for kicking my rear into gear; were it not for your encouragement, *Insatiable* might still be in my file cabinet.

. . . to Kevin S. Moul for capturing my soul with his camera.

. . . to Shannon for calling me on my shit.

. . . to Kelly Kiernan and Caribou Coffee for caffeinating me and providing me with a creative refuge.

. . . to all the members of my personal pit crew who were instrumental in my recovery and continue to keep The Machine running smoothly.

. . . to all my friends and fellow writers who inspired and uplifted me throughout the many drafts of this book.

. . . to all the men mentioned in this manuscript. Thank you for loving me when I felt most unlovable. No act of affection, no matter how small, went unappreciated.

. . . to Tito for keeping my feet warm during the many hours at my desk.

. . . to my father, stepfather, and brother (the best men in my life) for lightening the mood with your laughter when I lingered too long on the dark side.

. . . to my mother. Before you get mad, remember that this book got me out of your basement and paid for the remodeling! We'll write the happy memories in the next one.

. . . to all those whom I have inevitably forgotten to thank: though your name is not mentioned on these pages, there is infinite gratitude for you in my heart.

I dedicate this book to my daughters, to whom I owe my life. May the rest of my days be spent making up for the time anorexia stole from us. (Disney World, here we come!)

insatiable

chapter one

Mendota Mad Dogs

december 2005

I'm not supposed to be here. I'm not supposed to be sitting in the waiting room of the eating disorders ward at Mendota Hospital. I don't fit in with the sunken-face, ash-complexioned toothpick girls drowning in baggy sweats. The two teenyboppers seated across from me aren't even old enough to drive; their mothers, clutching leather Coach purses with delicately manicured hands, sit beside them and peer at the other patients from under feathery bangs. The mothers are almost as thin as their daughters.

I do not belong. I am twenty-four, a soon-to-be divorcée, and a mother myself. I'm not starving myself in a passive-aggressive attempt to delay the onset of adolescence. Hell, I'm not even starving. I eat all the time. One hundred percent whole foods, too. I'm probably the healthiest woman on the planet.

Granted, I haven't felt up to snuff lately. Since I started my health kick this fall, I've noticed a few odd symptoms. Most notably, my period is MIA. I don't mind so much—it's nice to have a sabbatical from messy ol' Aunt Flo.

There's also an annoying ache in my ass that makes it uncomfortable to sit for more than thirty minutes and to chauffeur my clients around at work. That's another issue—I've been so damn exhausted lately that I've been calling in sick to Teen Transformation (TT), the residential treatment center where I work part-time.

There's also an incipient weakness in my arms; my limbs go limp like noodles at a moment's notice. I can't carry my purse, let alone lift my twenty-month-old daughter, Lola, from her crib or my almost three-year-old daughter, Julia, from the toilet. Okay, that's a stretch—I'm too pooped to potty train for now.

Speaking of which, I've regressed. Every few nights, I awake in sheet-soaking puddles of piss. I also pee uncontrollably when I exercise, though often I'm so sweaty I don't notice the stinky swamp between my legs.

My eyesight is fine, but words don't process. This instantaneous illiteracy, aka Teflon brain, makes it impossible to study, and forced me to take a semester off from my master's program in professional counseling.

For now, I'm functional, but this strange cluster of symptoms reminded me of an adolescent flirtation with an eating disorder. I consulted my shrink, Dr. Garrison Trader, on my stay-slim strategy of laxatives and excessive running. Garrison met my confessions with the same blank-screen silence as with everything else I told him. Garrison didn't think I was disordered, but my nutritionist did. At her suggestion, I decided to get a second opinion.

The receptionist at Mendota hands me a stack of papers bigger than a graduate school application and a sharp no. 2. Hooray for questionnaires! I love psychopathology and all the tools used to diagnose it. I'm the dork who volunteers to complete customer satisfaction surveys, census forms, and college course evaluations without compensation. The feeling of filling in those little bubbles satisfies my need for definitive answers. This is right, this is wrong. This is normal, this is not.

I begin.

Have you been deliberately trying to restrict the amount of food you eat to influence your shape or weight?
Affirmative.
Have you tried to avoid any foods that you like in order to influence your shape or weight?
Can't have your cake and a six-pack, too!
Has thinking about food or its calorie content made it much more difficult to concentrate on things you are interested in; for example, read, watch TV, or follow a conversation?

My attention wanders before I even finish reading the sentence. My mind is busy playing its favorite game: tally the calories! Tall light frappuccino, 120 calories; asparagus omelet . . . Oops—what was I doing? Oh, yeah, eating disorders assessment. I'll have to re-read that last question.

Have you definitely wanted your stomach to be flat?
Who doesn't?
Have you felt fat?
Have I ever felt *thin*?

The questionnaire continues, pages and pages of statements I must rank on a six-point scale. Most are not about weight and diet-ing at all but about self-worth, familial relationships, guilt, and disappointment. I skew my answers toward the more severe end of the scale so the experts won't think I'm wasting their time. The docs are going to laugh at me, I know it. I'm not frail enough to belong to the exclusive club of Skinny Minnies.

I'm on the last page of the questionnaire, meant for the "Support Individual." I don't have a support individual. In fact, no one—not even Garrison—knows that I'm here.

"Do I have to fill this one out?" I ask the receptionist.

"Didn't you come with a support person?"

"No."

"Who do you live with?"

"My daughters."

"Fill it out according to whoever you consider family."

I don't have a family; at least, that's how I feel. My husband fought for joint custody and succeeded with a sixty (me)/forty (him) split of visitation time. I had a boyfriend—he even proposed—but after a weekend playing house, he bolted. My mom and dad are around to babysit, but not much else.

I scribble N/A on the top of the page and hand over my papers.

Back in my seat, I smooth my hair down. I look extra put together for my appointment: blond bob curled under, pastel makeup, a knit sweater with faux-fur hood and dark jeans. I used to look completely coordinated all the time, but lately, I haven't felt like dressing. It's easier to lounge in workout clothes all day, in case the opportunity arises for impromptu exercise.

"Erica?" an attendant calls.

Finally. I've been here two hours and I haven't seen even one white-coated expert yet.

As she leads me down a long hallway, the attendant whispers, "You'll meet with the psychologist first."

I hate Lesley right away. She is blond, mildly pretty, and has clothed her soft, rounded torso in a pink mohair sweater. She is me, plus forty pounds and a PsyD.

"So," she says, crossing one thick thigh over the other, "what's going on?"

"A nutritionist suggested I be assessed for an eating disorder."

"Why do you suppose she did that?" Lesley inquires.

"I've lost a little weight lately and she was concerned."

It's not my weight—123 pounds on a five-foot, eight-inch frame—that worried the nutritionist; it's my body fat ratio. At 12.4 percent, I have half the padding of the average American woman.

"How do you feel about your body?" Lesley asks.

"It's all right, but I'd like to be a little **thinner**."

"How much thinner?"

"A hundred and ten pounds."

"That's all?" she asks in the sassy tone of a teenager.

"I don't want to look . . . *sick* or anything. Definitely not under a hundred and five."

"What percentage of the time do you think about food, weight, and body image?"

All the time. All. The. Fucking. Time. But that's because I don't have much else going on in my life.

"Ninety percent," I say.

"That's a lot."

I shrug.

"Any major life changes lately?"

"Just a contentious divorce, a broken engagement, trying to finish my master's degree, massive credit card debt . . ."

"Anything else?"

"Isn't that enough?"

Lesley suppresses a scowl.

"You're quite a runner."

"Yup. Seventy miles a week."

"What are you training for?"

"Nothing. I just like to run."

"That must be hard on your body."

"If I didn't run, I'd go crazy," I say.

Lesley and I lock eyes.

"Maybe you need to go crazy."

The silence is stifling. After a moment, Lesley looks down at my file.

"I see you're on Wellbutrin."

"For depression."

Another slight stretch of the truth. I started taking the medication for depression, and for a few months, it helped. Then the effect faded and the despairing doldrums resumed. I still pop the anti-

depressant daily because Wellbutrin is an upper and a superb appetite suppressant.

"You realize that Wellbutrin is contraindicated for women with
eating disorders."

"In English, please?"

"It means you could have a seizure."

But if I stop taking it, I'll gain weight, and then I'll *really* be
depressed.

"I'm not going to stop," I say. "I need it to get by."

"The belief at Mendota is that eating disorders bring on depression.
If we treat the eating disorder, the depression will go away, too."

I shake my head. "The depression comes first. When I'm depressed, I lose weight. Being thin makes me feel *better*."

Lesley crosses her arms. I cross mine. The face-off is under way.

"What happened to your hands?" she asks, motioning to my
ruddy, red knuckles.

"Dry skin."

"Do you wash your hands often?"

"I dunno . . . maybe twenty times a day?"

Her eyebrows shoot up. "That's excessive."

Great. Now she's trying to peg me with obsessive-compulsive
disorder. I may be a lot of things, but I am not one of those freaks
who lines up her shoes and measures the distance between each pair
or who flicks the light on and off a hundred times before she can
leave the house.

"I have two children in diapers," I say. "I have to wash my hands
a lot."

Five diapers per daughter, per day, plus my multiple attacks of
diarrhea, plus peeing. Twenty times a day is a conservative estimate.

Lesley nods.

"How serious do you think your eating disorder is?"

"I don't have an eating disorder."

"Really?"

"At least not a diagnosable one."

"Do you know what the criteria are?"

"Not off the top of my head, but I know I don't meet them."

Lesley takes a deep breath and recites the requirements from the *Diagnostic and Statistical Manual of Mental Disorders* (DSM): "Refusal to maintain normal body weight for age and height; intense fear of becoming fat, even though underweight; disturbed body image; denial of seriousness of current low body weight; amenorrhea."

She pauses, and a self-satisfied—no, a *sadistic*—smile breaks out on her face. She must love sending youthful bodies like mine off to fatten up in the hospital against their will.

"Erica, you have every single symptom."

I don't know which edition of the DSM she's using, but it must be as ancient as she is.

I grit my teeth and mutter, "I'm just trying to get control over one area of my life. That's all."

Strike one.

MENTAL STATUS EXAM

Erica is an impeccably groomed 24-year-old female . . . She is coifed and manicured from head to toe. She sat rigidly with her hands folded in her lap. Her hands are chafed and red. Affect is bright despite a report of severe depression and multiple stressors. She appears disconnected from her feelings. She has minimal insight into the severity of her eating disorder . . . no evidence of delusions or hallucinations.

—LESLEY WAGNER, PSYD, LICSW, LP

Lesley sends me down the hall for the medical portion of the assessment. On the examination table, there is a folded gown bleached so stiff it could stand up on its own. The gown swallows me like a paper bag and the fabric infects my entire body with the urge to itch. My skin has been ultrasensitive lately, so dry it flutters off my body in dandruff-like flakes. The hair on my head has been falling out, too, while the long white hairs on my arms seem more abundant than ever.

The longer I sit, the sicker I feel. The bones in my ass ache as if there were two machete blades beneath me. Lesley's interrogation has left me beaten to a pulp, psychologically speaking. Until this moment, I have not felt too thin; now I'm starting to wonder if I'm as healthy as I seem. A tiny tremor spreads down my limbs.

Knock. Knock.

"I'm Dr. Stone," a brunette in a white coat says as she strides through the door. She is plump, as I've noticed most of the practitioners at Mendota are. Her dark eyes scan me up and down. "Would you like a blanket?"

A scoff escapes me. A blanket? How infantile am I?

"No."

"Some patients get a little cold."

"I'm fine," I say, though frozen is my default state. I've always attributed my incessant chill to the Minnesotan winter weather.

I lie down and Dr. Stone does a full-body prod. Her fingers palpate my throat, dig deep beneath my ribs, and dance across my chest. She stands back and annotates her findings in my chart.

"Have you noticed a decrease in breast tissue?" she asks.

"No," I say. Though my boobs no longer fill my bras, I assume my small chest is typical of long-distance runners.

"Any vomiting?"

"No."

Though not for lack of trying . . .

"Any syrup of ipecac?"

"No."

But thanks for the tip!

"Chewing and spitting?"

"Excuse me?"

"Do you chew food and then spit it out?"

I barely hold back a giggle. What sort of freak would chew food and not swallow it?

"Are you serious?" I ask.

"Some patients do it to avoid ingesting calories."

"Sounds stupid."

"So that's a no?"

"No."

"Diet pills or diuretics?"

"No."

Is this treatment or a crash course in how to be bulimic? If I ever decide to cross over to bulimia, I'll know the tricks of the trade.

"Constipation?" Dr. Stone asks.

"When I don't take laxatives."

"How often is that?"

I'm going through several boxes a week, but I say, "Three pills every other day."

"Do you think you could stop on your own?"

"I'm going to stop," I say. "As soon as the bloating goes away."

"You're setting yourself up for a heart attack if you don't."

A heart attack? Yeah, right. My heart is a powerhouse. How else to explain my superhuman athletic endurance?

"Stand up, please."

I do. Familiar black polka dots explode before my eyes like fireworks, then fade away. My legs go lazy, as though I just stepped off an amusement park ride.

"Dizzy?" Dr. Stone asks, pressing her fingers to the inside of my wrist.

"Yeah . . ." I say suspiciously. Did my pulse give me away?

I sit back down and Dr. Stone tests my reflexes with her mallet. Tap. Tap. No motion. My damn right knee won't respond.

"Relax," she says and taps again. This time when the rubber triangle makes contact with my knee, the leg kicks.

"What happened here?" Dr. Stone asks, indicating my thighs. The lower half of my body looks like a Dalmatian's coat: pale white skin spotted with black-and-blue bruises.

"I bruise easily."

"Did you fall?"

"No. I'm just . . . clumsy."

"Mm-hmm." She runs a finger over my feet where my Sauconys have rubbed the skin raw. "And this?"

"Running shoes."

"It looks painful."

I shrug. What can I say? These are the inevitable side effects of skinny.

"Have a seat," Dr. Stone says, indicating the plastic patient chair. Dr. Stone has not told me my weight, pulse, blood pressure, or body mass index (BMI). I want to know my numbers, but I can't read sideways as she scribbles her notes.

"Do you pray, Erica?"

Since when do doctors conduct spiritual checkups?

"Uh . . . I guess so," I say.

"What do you pray for?"

"That my daughters are well?"

"Do you pray for your health?"

"No."

Dr. Stone takes a deep breath.

"Erica, my recommendation is for inpatient treatment."

The statement hits me like a sledgehammer. Every internal function—heartbeat, breath, hunger pangs—stops. If anorexia were an airplane, I'd be the passenger watching the nosedive into the ground from a window seat. Of all the possible assessment outcomes, I never fathomed this.

The fear kicks my brain into gear, and the consequences of hospitalization come roaring into consciousness. I'll miss Christmas, Julia's birthday, New Year's. I list all the phone calls I'll have to make: to my ex, my parents, my brother, my boss. If I'm not released by January, I'll have to withdraw from school.

Suddenly, tears held hostage for so many months spurt from my eyes.

"No, no, no!" I whimper, drawing my knees into my chest, rock-

ing myself, clenching my fists. I want to bolt from the chair—
hospital attire be damned—and race down the hallway and into the
streets. I want to sprint barefoot to my daughters, scoop them up,
take them to bed with me, and hibernate beneath the covers until
this all goes away.

Verbal incontinence overtakes me.

"My daughters!" I scream. "Christmas! School! My job! I'm so
busy, I can't possibly . . . Oh God, my daughters!"

Even I am surprised by my outburst. Who knew I cared so
much?

"I'm worried about your daughters, too," Dr. Stone says, her
voice as soft and sweet as a pigeon's coos. "I'm worried that you can't
take care of them. What if something happened while they were
with you?"

I imagine myself splayed, face down, on the stained beige carpet
outside my bedroom. I imagine Julia in her pink pajamas, creeping
up to me, reeling at the stench of vomit. I imagine Lola toddling up
behind her and trying unsuccessfully to wake Mommy up.

For an instant, the acquiescence is on my lips. Yes, the hospital.
The hospital would be good for me. Nurses in pastel scrubs, tennis
shoes squeaking across clean floors, meals on trays, and juice with
peelable plastic tops.

"Don't you want a break, Erica?" Dr. Stone's voice is far away
now, barely an echo in my ears.

I *do* want a break, but not from my entire life. I just want to silence that nasty voice in my mind, want the worries to stop spinning, want to quell that annoying ache in my ass. I just want my
body to let my brain be.

"Wouldn't you like a rest?" Dr. Stone asks.

Yes, yes, a rest. I want to lie down. I want to take a catnap. Sleep
on the idea. Sleep, yes, that's what I need. I just need more sleep.

I take a deep breath and quiet my crying.

"If I go to the hospital," I force myself to say in an even tone, "my
soon-to-be ex-husband will take my daughters away from me."

"That sounds extreme, Erica."

"It's not. He fought me once for custody and the divorce isn't finalized yet. There's still time. He could use this as leverage against me. Please, I'll do anything. I'll eat whatever you want. I'll stop running. I promise."

But even as my lips release the words, inside I know it's bullshit. Nothing comes between me and my running. I'm beyond caring about my health—my focus has shifted to maintaining my freedom. I will say anything to get out of this situation.

"What are you thinking, Erica?"

"I think I want to go home."

"I'd like you to finish your evaluation first."

"You're going to have me committed, aren't you?"

"We can't commit you, Erica. You're over eighteen. Besides, we don't have a bed available today."

I wipe my eyes and look at Dr. Stone. If she didn't have such a friendly face, I'd spit in it.

"Please," she pleads. "Meet with Allison, the dietician, and I'll discuss your concerns with the team."

Strike two.

IMPRESSION

1. Anorexia nervosa, purging subtype.

2. Amenorrhea.

3. Hypotension.

4. Hypothermia.

5. Leukopenia.

6. Laxative abuse.

7. Lanugo hair growth.

—EILEEN STONE, MD

I may be starving, but I'm not stupid. With inpatient treatment hanging over my head, I won't incriminate myself any further. My strategy upon entering the dietician's dungeon: downplay my wacky food habits as much as possible.

Allison is a petite, bronze-skinned woman with exotic facial features. She looks like a woman I might swap childcare with—that is, if she weren't The Enemy.

"Describe a typical day of food for you," she says with a poised pen.

Easy enough to regurgitate, as I eat the same foods to maintain my daily 1,500-calorie intake.

FOOD ITEM/AMOUNT

Pre-Run Snack: Whole-wheat tortilla, one slice turkey, 1 tablespoon guacamole.

Breakfast: Two scrambled eggs and 1 cup asparagus.

Snack: Low-fat string cheese, 1 celery stalk, 6 black olives.

Lunch: 2 cups salad, 3 ounces tuna or chicken, ¼ cup pistachios.

Snack: Apple and 1 tablespoon almond butter.

Dinner: Two cups steamed vegetables and 1 cup shrimp.

Snack: Apple, 6 ounces fat-free yogurt, ¼ cup almonds.

"Is there anything you won't eat?" Allison asks.

I think: milk, juice, full-fat dairy products, fattening condiments, cereal, oatmeal, granola, crackers, trail mix, bread, buns, bagels, pancakes, waffles, muffins, doughnuts, pastries, cakes, pies, ice cream, Popsicles, chocolate, candy, fruit snacks, potatoes, carrots, corn, peas, pineapple, grapes, bananas, melon, and raisins.

I say, "Junk food."

"Can you be more specific?"

"Sweets."

She nods and scribbles.

"Do you binge?"

"Once a week."

"Describe a binge."

"A medium Blizzard from Dairy Queen."

"Just one?"

"Have you seen how big those are? They've got at least eight hundred calories!"

She nods and scribbles some more.

"Do you avoid eating out?"

Yes, with a passion. I will postpone, cancel, and excuse myself from every meal-centered commitment possible.

"I don't avoid it," I say casually. "I just don't have anyone to go out with."

Another nod. More scribble scribble.

"Now, part of our program involves following a meal plan. How do you feel about that?"

"I don't like it," I say.

The rebellious Erica has awakened. I do not do well with rules, unless they are self-imposed.

"Regardless of whether or not you like it, would you be open to trying one?"

"As long as I don't have to eat bad carbs."

"We work off the Food Pyramid, which requires six to eleven servings of grains a day."

"You've got to be kidding."

"I'm sensing some resistance to the meal plan."

"You can say that again."

Allison slaps her manila folder shut. "Well. I think I have all the information I need. Why don't you take a seat in the waiting room?"

Strike three.

* * *

The other stick insects and their mothers are gone. I slink down in a stiff chair across from a basket filled with Nutri-Grain bars, peanut butter crackers, and chocolate chip granola bars. Hmm . . . chocolate. Before I can even salivate, a voice in my head drowns out my desire.

Bad carbs! Bad Erica! Bad! Bad! Bad!

I pull a packet of mixed nuts from my bag instead. Before I dig in, I pick out the peanuts one by one and chuck them into the garbage can. I've been reading up on the Paleo diet for runners; peanuts aren't really nuts, they're legumes, and therefore, it claims, unnatural for human consumption.

Halfway through my peanut extraction project, a tall, voluptuous blond appears in the doorway.

"Erica?"

The woman leads me to a corner office. The lights are dimmed and pastel inspirational plaques cover the walls. She motions to a puffy, plush armchair. My ass is very happy.

"I'm Katie, the director," she says with the perky attitude of a department store saleswoman. "I'd like to discuss our program with you."

What the hell. I've already invested half the day in this assessment. I might as well hear the spiel.

Katie talks as though she were selling me a car, cheerily counting off the components of the inpatient program: Supervised meals, occupational therapy, family visiting hours, open-door bathroom policy.

"What was that last one?" I ask.

"You have to leave the bathroom door ajar while you use it."

I shudder at the idea of someone listening to me shit, especially under the influence of laxatives.

"Can I exercise?" I ask.

"No."

"Not even walking?"

"Once your weight has stabilized, you may participate in stretching classes."

"Stretching?"

"We believe in replacing exercise with occupational therapy—to
show you that you can be successful in activities that don't involve
your body."

I imagine a sloth-like existence making pot holders from ugly
rolls of yarn.

"How long would I have to stay?" I ask.

"That depends on how fast you gain weight."

"Ballpark."

"Two weeks, maybe more."

"How old are the other patients?"

"Most are younger, but we'd put you in groups with women
your own age."

I imagine Britney Spears wannabes having rib-counting con-
tests. I imagine group therapy sessions involving corny affirmations
like "My body is my temple." I imagine sipping my coffee in a hospital gown while flipping through *Teen Beat*.

Like a mind reader, Katie says, "No magazines on the ward, by
the way."

"No magazines?"

"And no coffee."

That's it.

Hospitalization sounds more like being held hostage. Jesus
Christ, I *work* in a treatment center where *I* direct the damn check-
in group, enforce 9:00 P.M. bedtimes, redirect inappropriate conversations, and restrict caffeine intake. The difference is that at work, I
get to leave at the end of the day.

I cross my arms in defiance. The experts are wrong about me. I
don't need inpatient. I don't need anyone. I am an adult, not an

anorexic. More precisely, I'm an athlete. I didn't *try* to get this skinny; it just happened. Maybe I took my health kick a tad too far—but swinging to and from extremes is my nature.

"We'll have a bed for you next week," Katie says.

"I am *not* going into the hospital."

"Why not?"

"One: I'm not that sick. And two: I have a life."

If I'm hospitalized, everyone will think I have an eating disorder! They'll think I can't handle the responsibilities of single parenthood, the rigors of graduate school, and maintain my figure all at the same time. There goes my Wonder Woman image.

I flash a saccharine smile. "I'll do the outpatient program."

"We're not offering you outpatient treatment, Erica."

"Why not?"

"Because you need round-the-clock care."

"I don't! I can get better on my own. I know I can."

"That's a risk we're not willing to take."

"Wait a minute. I come in—on my own—to get checked out, you make me take all those tests, tell me I could walk out of here and drop dead from a heart attack or have a seizure, and then you give me an ultimatum? All or nothing?"

"Inpatient is all we can offer you."

I want to bite Katie's head off.

The professionals may have a file as thick as a doctoral thesis on my condition, but they don't know a thing about me. The worst thing anyone can do to Erica Rivera is back her into a corner and demand that she submit.

"So you're not going to help me? Not even with a therapist?"

"You said you already have a therapist."

"I do, but—"

"We'll send him your records," Katie says. She extends an impeccably French-tipped hand. Her charm bracelet jangles. "Here's my card. Call me if you change your mind."

"I won't."

She maintains a sparkling smile but her eyes shoot darts at my face.

"We'll see," she says.

And . . . you're out.

PLAN

It is highly unlikely that Erica . . . would be able to receive enough support in an outpatient program to really affect recovery.

—EILEEN STONE, MD

Back in the waiting room, I grab my Gap vest from the coat rack. I glare at the snack basket again.

Fuck it. I might as well start fattening up now. I take the crackers, flip over the package, and cringe at the calorie count. Here goes. The crackers slide out of the plastic wrapper. I split one in half and peel back the imitation peanut butter, imprinted with little air bubbles, and place it on my tongue. Yuck. The peanut butter is tasteless and the crackers are stale. So not worth the caloric damage. I toss them into the nearest garbage can.

I can design my own treatment. I created this problem; I can solve it. The timing couldn't be more perfect: with Christmas—and its obligatory family feasts—a week away, I've been not only urged but threatened with confinement if I don't gain ten pounds.

I need a caloric splurge to jump-start the weight gain, so I make a pit stop at Starbucks. I order a chocolate chunk cookie as big as a tricycle wheel and a grande caramel frappuccino.

"Do you want whip on that?" the friendly barista asks.

"God, no," I say. It's not like I want to get *fat*.

Anorexic habits die hard. As the barista blends my drink, I reach into the crinkly bakery bag and break the cookie in two. Before the first blissful bite passes my lips, I drop half of the cookie into the garbage; pastry portion control.

I down my frappuccino in a few syrupy gulps and meander my way across the mall to Barnes & Noble. In the journal section, a small, red leather book catches my eye. The cover is smooth and thick, stamped in the middle with a delicate heart. I crack open the journal and marvel at the crisp, clean pages.

Garrison has been urging me for weeks to use his "thought surfing" technique to deal with my emotions. I'd blown the recommendation off as glorified journaling, but maybe he was on to something.

That's it! I will *write* my way through this eating disorder. I will heal myself with words. I will use my journal to catalog my miraculous recovery.

I'll kick this thing lickety-split.

chapter two

Edible Memories

september 1987

As far back as I can recall, food has been my memorial compass. My first food memory is of doughnuts—thick, squishy, gooey doughnuts; pastries so fresh the glaze drips in sugary streams onto my tongue.

I am six, accompanying my parents to pick up my brother from preschool. Across the courtyard, there is a bakery where puffs of flour burst from the rooftop all day long. It is a south Minneapolis secret that every Thursday after 3:00 P.M., a knock on the back door earns you a free sample.

The screen door creaks open and an unshaven baker in a dirty apron stands on the other side, flooded in fluorescent light, and presents a tray of perfect puffy pastries. These freebies are not the toothpick-portioned samples of grocery stores on Saturdays; these pastries are as big as my two-year-old brother's face.

The illicitness of it all—sneaking through the alley, the secret knock, the handover of the doughnut as though it were an illegal drug—makes the orbs of glaze and grease and yeast even more delicious. No, not delicious. Divine.

Fast-forward one year and I'm watching my father as he shifts from side to side, absorbed in the choreography of cooking. The pot beckons to him with its boil, and he responds by pouring a bag of No Yolks egg noodles into the water. Clouds of steam blossom from the stovetop, coating the surrounding cupboards with a steamy sheen. The ground hamburger bleeds through a foam tray on the counter, its scarlet trail dribbling into the sink. When the meat hits the skillet, it sizzles, and my father pushes the crumbles back and forth with his spatula until they reach a precise shade of brown. He lifts the skillet and deftly drains the grease into a jar already half-filled with coagulated fat.

"Why not just eat it?" I ask as the thick white stream spills into the jar.

"It clogs up the arteries," he says.

"So why not put it down the drain?"

"Clogs up the sink, too."

The noodles, cooked until they look like slimy ribbons, slide onto three plates—for him, my brother, and me. The leftovers steep in cool water so they won't lose their al dente texture.

My father tends to the sauce, where the recipe holds its mystery. A gray bubbling bog speckled with slivers of something red—tomatoes? peppers? chilies?—simmers atop a tiny flame.

I assume my father invented My Favorite; after all, he never cracks a cookbook's spine or refers to a file of index cards. Everything he makes is by memory. It will be years until I see a photograph of a similar dish in a magazine, beneath the headline "The Best Beef Stroganoff." I will balk as I study the accompanying recipe—what a boring name for such an extraordinary meal!

But for now, in my seven-year-old eyes, my father is the only chef on earth. He is conductor of the kitchen, orchestrating the dinner preparation so that each component reaches its culinary conclusion, its peak temperature and taste, simultaneously. I never want the cooking to end; as soon as the plates are full, we disappear inside ourselves. My brother and I eat elbow-to-elbow in front of *The Simpsons;* my father eats alone at the kitchen table.

My father shops for groceries on Friday nights. I am his eager companion, anticipating the outing like my friends do roller-coaster rides. As my father steers the cart up and down the aisles of Randy's Foods, I hop on and off the cart whenever a hologram-covered cereal box catches my eye. My father doesn't buy generic *anything*; he chooses foods on quality, not quantity.

My father simply loves food; no excess, no obsession. I study him every night as he dunks a pair of cookies into his coffee. His favorites are Pepperidge Farm Milanos, the shortbread wafers with melted chocolate in the middle. How can he eat just *two*? Why not the whole bag? I can't wait to be an adult and have access to all the sweets I crave.

Cooking is my father's form of communication. A stereotypically stoic man of Norwegian descent, my father is as mysterious as his sauces. What stories are buried in the sugary, buttered folds of lefse? What tales, as long as spaghetti noodles, are left untold? What disappointments does he disguise in cheesy tunnels of manicotti? What sorrows drown in bottomless cups of black coffee?

My mother is simply different—or rather, *in*different—about food. Seemingly allergic to the kitchen, her culinary abilities rarely surpass grilled cheese sandwiches, scrambled eggs, and Kid Cuisine microwave meals. A blank check weighted down with the salt shaker is her passive-aggressive hint that my brother and I are on our own for lunch. Shane and I duke it out over fried chicken from Chow Express, hoagies from Carbone's, or Bigfoot Pizza from Pizza Hut.

After the delivery man's drop-off, my brother and I open the red-and-white checkered boxes like Christmas presents. We argue over who gets the drumsticks, jettison the wings, and are too embarrassed to say *breasts* much less eat them. Shane makes mashed potato volcanoes erupting with gravy, while I devour white rolls so doughy they stick together in six-packs.

Mornings, en route to Montessori school, meals on the go are the norm. My favorite is an apple Danish from the McDonald's drive-through window. My brother prefers ham and cheese croissants from Super America, where the cashiers know us by name.

My mother never eats with the rest of us, if she eats at all. She nibbles like a bird at odd hours, creating cringe-worthy creations by topping everything with cottage cheese. In restaurants, she surprises me with her unpredictable orders—multicolored nachos, mounds of garlic mashed potatoes, bloody cheeseburgers. Ordering and eating, however, are two different actions. Watching my mother eat—or avoid eating—is excruciating. She is the master of The Shuffle: Her stay-slim trick is to rearrange her meal on her plate to make it look as though she had eaten. Her soup spoon lollygags in the bowl; her fork picks apart her entrée.

"I'm stuffed to the brim!" she always says after a total of two bites.

Her stomach must be the size of a walnut.

Doggy bags were invented for my mother; while her dining companions have barely begun to munch, she's already dishing half of her food into a foam box.

My appetite is far from ladylike. I go head to head, stomach to stomach, with the hungriest of men and often outeat both my father and my brother. While I stay slim thanks to soccer, my brother blows up to Sumo wrestler form. He stuffs himself with trays of Oreos, devours hot dogs by the dozen, and tosses towers of Cheez-It crackers down his throat. He totes two-liter bottles of Pepsi everywhere, knocking back the entire syrupy brown beverage by the end of the day. When he exhausts his pop supply, he overdoses on milk from quart-size cups. Party-size bags of Doritos and Cheetos disappear at random from the cupboards, and jars of Gedney pickles—juice included—rarely remain in the fridge for more than twenty-four hours. Even the emergency supply of Chef Boyardee cheese ravioli dwindles unexpectedly.

The only food Shane won't eat are SnackWell's cookies.

"I don't want reduced fat, I don't want low-fat, I don't want nonfat!" he screams one day when he finds his Double Stuf Oreos replaced by sugar-free Grasshoppers. "I want regular fat!"

And he gets it. Shane's body balloons until the only clothes he can wear are sweat suits from the Target men's department.

chapter three

The Body Battle Begins

My mother works as a nurse at Fairfield Hospital. She prepares ter-minally ill children for surgery and entertains them during epic hospital stays. My mother works too much, too erratically; swing shifts, overnights, doubles. When she isn't working, she naps.

The only time I get one-on-one interaction with my mother is when I'm sick. By my eighth year, my Friday night routine is no longer grocery shopping—it's trips to the pediatric emergency room. The raspy tickle in my throat usually starts in school, then surges into pulsating pain by midafternoon. Summoned by my third-grade teacher, my mother leaves work early to fetch me. An-ticipating a lengthy delay, we hit the drive-through at Wendy's on the way to the hospital.

As I run down the hall toward the ER, I high-five the stuffed, six-foot Big Bird. His feathers are falling off and his beak is smudged with fingerprints. Each week he has a new affliction; today his thumb is wrapped in medical tape. Happily absorbed in the cable TV cartoons of the ER, I dip my French fries one by one into a chocolate Frosty.

"Come on back, Erica!" a nurse trills. The staff knows me well; I am sick so often that the clinic has tested every family member—even our golden retriever—to reveal the carrier of the illness that plagues me.

I put on the crinkly gown in the examination room, and the doctor with the Donald Duck voice shoves a swab down my throat.

I gag.

We go home.

I chug down my penicillin, a nauseatingly sweet potion I've developed a fondness for. Walgreens makes the thinnest, smoothest mixture that coats my aching throat with bubble-gum flavor. The first—lukewarm—dosage is the worst; I like my medicine chilled.

I psych myself up for another weekend quarantined in the den with my pet parakeets; in my infirm state, I am excused from floor-scrubbing, dish-washing, dog-walking, and all those other annoying Saturday morning chores. I read voraciously during my sickbed stints. My mother brings me chicken noodle soup with saltines, glasses of pulpy orange juice, and Minute Maid ice pops.

After six bouts of strep throat, our health insurance plan approves my mother's pleas for a tonsillectomy. My adenoids will be removed too; I can't even pronounce the word, much less figure out what they're for. They must be one of those nonessential body parts, like the appendix.

It's fun, this chronic condition business, until the day of the surgery arrives. The operating room is so sterile it stinks. I am prostrate and trembling; my teddy bear hospital gown is scratchy on my skin. Fluorescent lights blur the masked faces floating above me. I audition anesthesia scents from the Lip Smackers line and decide on orange. A hard plastic cup comes down on my mouth and nose; a machine thumps and hums behind me.

The steady drone of Dr. Brandt, the surgeon my mother has a crush on, echoes through my ear canals. Every sound is filtered and far away, like listening through a can.

"How many fingers do you see?" he asks. His hand seems to be shaking; my eyes fight to land on a number. I open my mouth to answer but before the words emerge, the world around me fades to black.

When I come to, woozy on painkillers, I try to speak but it feels like a tennis ball is wedged in my esophagus.

The highlight of my two-night stay in the hospital is the unlimited Popsicles, though it hurts so much to talk that I'm at the mercy of the meal service attendant for flavors.

A week post-op, my mother prepares to leave me and my best friend, Cassie, home alone. Thanks to my tonsillectomy, she's out of personal time off and has to tour "some fucking clowns" (as she calls them under her breath) around the hospital.

Cassie and I entertain ourselves as little girls do; we raid my mother's closet, and then waddle around in ill-fitting shoes and polka-dot dresses that droop on our ironing-board bodies.

As the afternoon sun fades, the familiar ache in the back of my throat returns.

"Take some Tylenol," Cassie suggests. I sift through the spattering of pills in the medicine cabinet and come across a box of chewable children's Tylenol. I crunch two pasty discs between my teeth, but when I swallow, they feel like little shards of glass. I cough. And cough. And cough.

"What's wrong?" Cassie asks.

My mouth fills with saliva—at least, that's what I think it is—until I spit long scarlet strings into the sink. My heart races inside my chest; blood floods my head and fills my mouth.

The next thing I know, my mother is at my side and we are rushing down the hall toward the ER again. This time, I do not high-five Big Bird.

"This is very unusual," the attending physician says after my exam. "It appears the scabs were aggravated by something and have been torn apart. I'll have to cauterize them to ensure they stay shut."

I gulp. I do not mention the Tylenol before the doc knocks me out.

When I wake up, it is evening and I am in my parents' bed. A bowl of tomato soup congealing on the bedside table sends a wave of nausea crashing into my belly.

"Mom?"

My mother is on the opposite side of the room, rolling socks and tossing them in a laundry basket.

"Hmm?" she asks.

"My stomach feels funny." The queasiness crests; I clamp and contort my face as though I could prevent what is about to happen. "Mom . . ."

We trip down the stairs; I turn the corner, but before I make it to the bathroom, a flame of blood shoots from my mouth and splatters across the door, the toilet, the tile floor. My father storms in, swoops me into his arms, and sprints toward the car. My mother runs to the house next door, knocks, and shoves my sleepy brother into the neighbor's arms.

My father guns our beat-up Ford; I'm in the backseat, my head out the window like a dog on a summer afternoon. I don't know what I'm puking onto the pavement—Juice? Popsicles? Bile?—but I leave an acidic stream all the way down Lake Street.

The bouquet of light bulbs above the examining table blinds me. Masked people in scrubs circle around.

"She's vomiting blood," my mother says.

"Are you sure?" someone asks.

On any other day, my mother might be exaggerating; but tonight, she is spot-on. She is uncharacteristically strong, assertive, and wild eyed. This is a bona fide emergency and my mother is in her element.

"I'm sure," she says.

As though on cue, my gut spins like a blender inside my body and I barf all over my lap. I gulp down a few big breaths. I barf again. My stomach deflates and expands as though an invisible enemy were punching the bloody puke out of me. Scrubs shuffle and tennis shoes squeak on the floor, bringing me basins shaped like kidney beans. I fill them all with bright red sludge reminiscent of cherry pie filling.

My body is completely out of control.

The second hospital stay is more of the same: parents sleeping in shifts, Popsicles, phone calls from relatives, missed school days. When I return home, I receive a gargantuan Hallmark card from my classmates wishing me a speedy recovery. I can't stop staring at the thirty loopy signatures; I feel like a celebrity.

My fame as sick girl is short lived. The stitches heal and I never have strep throat again. My mother's attention returns to the Really Sick Children. Even I can't compete with cancer patients.

"What's wrong with your parents?"

Cassie turns to me and cocks her head. A bundle of amber curls falls across her forehead.

"What do you mean?" she asks.

Cassie's parents are rocking in a blueberry-hued recliner across the living room. They tease and tickle one another, giggling like high school sweethearts.

My parents don't touch; they're rarely in the same room together. "Ships passing in the night," I once heard my mother say.

The only canoodle I've ever seen between my parents is frozen in a photograph. Amid a wintry wooded background, my mother and father face each other in profile. Their heads are covered in knit caps, their cheeks are ruddy and chapped, and their eyes blaze with desire. Their noses touch and their lips are spread in mutually love-struck smiles, but they aren't kissing. No PDA for my parents, not even in photo albums.

I turn back to my friend. Doesn't Cassie know that such squir-relly behavior is for hormonal teenagers and flawless movie stars?

Married people don't make out in front of their kids; it's akin to molestation.

"Never mind," I say and turn back to the television. I won't break the news that her parents are freaks.

My family doesn't talk about bodies.

After her morning shower, my mother opens the bathroom door to release the steam. I watch, furtively, from the hallway as she examines her reflection in the mirror. She does not smile, does not caress her body lovingly as she coats her skin with Jergens. When she pulls on her panties, her stomach hangs loose over the elastic waistband. Her underwear is ugly, oversize, always boring beige or ivory, not like the lacy lingerie in JCPenney ads. My mother owns a few frilly pieces but they come out of the closet only for weddings, funerals, and high school reunions.

On those occasions, my mother paints her face in bright pastels and rouge. And when she does—what a beauty! Most mornings, she walks to her car still combing her wet hair, barely a layer of mascara on her lashes.

Family members and strangers alike often exclaim "What a resemblance!" when they see my mother and me together. As a moody preteen, I'm expected to cringe; the surprise is when my mother does the same.

I don't just have my mother's face; I have her body, too. We share the same padded hips, the rounded thighs, the kangaroo pouch of a belly. When I see the abrasive way she turns away from herself in the mirror, how can I think of my body as anything but flawed?

I learn to hate my appetite in Girl Scouts.

My friend Renee suggests a week-long canoeing excursion with a dozen other Girl Scouts. Renee is a hard-core camper, but I'm lukewarm about roughing it in the northern Minnesota wilderness.

"It's not really camping at all," Renee reassures me. "There are cabins and showers, even a cafeteria."

On a sultry July afternoon, we arrive at the camp and meet our counselors: Mindy and Muffy, two twenty-somethings as ditzy as their names suggest.

After a week of preparation for the sixteen-mile journey down the Mississippi, we arise with the egg-yolk sun. We gobble up bowls of steaming oatmeal, are fitted with life jackets that reek of dog-day water and dead fish, and take our places in the banana-shaped boats. When the sun switches sides from east to west, we beach the canoes on a sandy patch of land.

"We'll stop at the top of the hill to eat," Mindy says.

Reclining like lizards on rocks, we dig into Ziploc bags stuffed with Ritz crackers, squares of pepper jack cheese, and a few slimy discs of salami.

"More, please!" I yell down the line after the snack fails to quiet my rumbling stomach.

"We'll have dinner when we get to the campsite," Muffy reassures me.

The trek to the campsite seems to last longer than the canoeing does. After the tents are erected, I poke my head into the counselor's tent to check on the supper status. Mindy and Muffy are seated cross-legged on the ground, magnifying mirrors on their laps, mascara wands in hand.

"There's a men's group one campsite over," Mindy gushes. "We're going to say hello."

By the time the flirt birds return, we are all famished. Our mouths moisten as dinner boils in a pot above the campfire. Mindy and Muffy drop a small lump of noodles and a spoon of tomato sauce onto each of our plates.

"That's it?" I ask, looking down at the measly serving of spaghetti.

"Uh . . ." Mindy says, eyeing Muffy for support. "We forgot one of our food packs, so that's all we have for now."

Beneath the starless night, tucked inside the downy folds of my sleeping bag, I stare at the roof of the tent. My co-campers snore and wheeze and sniffle beside me, but I can't sleep. The gnawing hunger deep in my gut terrifies me; it is a sensation so fierce it sears and scorches my insides until I can't imagine any substance assuaging my appetite. My stomach gurgles, thunders, and rattles inside my body; my intestines somersault. How did I end up here, with camp counselors so careless they remembered their Great Lash and forgot the goulash? This is my first lesson in female priorities: beauty, first; eating, dead last.

The rest of the canoe trip is more of the same: too much physical activity and too little fuel. By the time we return to the Girl Scout camp headquarters, we are rabid. We rush into the mess hall and straddle the benches with newly slimmed yet unsteady legs. The cooks present the biggest taco buffet I've ever seen.

We attack the platters on the table and fill our plates with crispy taco shells, steamy ground beef, shredded lettuce, chunky salsa, and fistfuls of cheddar cheese. It is an eating orgy; our crunching, our chewing, our slurps and swallows echo through the mess hall.

"Slow down, girls!" one of the cooks insists as she replenishes the bowl of ground beef. "There's more than enough for everyone."

I can't slow down. I eat until my belly bursts from beneath my T-shirt, until I have to unbutton my jeans shorts, until I groan with overindulgence.

My body doesn't trust adults to nourish me anymore. No gastronomic guarantees. Every stomach for itself.

chapter four

Familial Upheaval

The bomb drops around my twelfth birthday.

Ashley is my best friend by default because she lives across the alley from me. She's short, stick thin, and one year my junior. Ashley has smooth skin the color of cookie dough and a raucous laugh, and is so limber she can remove her Pearl Vision glasses with her toes.

Ashley and I consider ourselves entrepreneurs and test out our wannabe business ventures regularly. Now that our beauty salon, bookstore, pet-sitting, and babysitting empires collapsed, we've moved on to greeting cards. We're in the middle of a fresh batch of birthday cards in the study when my mother opens the door.

Something on my mother's face makes my ears buzz. I hear the announcement in muted fragments; *Dad* and *divorce* in the same sentence is enough to send me into a tailspin. Ashley is still standing beside me, stunned silent.

My legs react before my brain. I dash upstairs and stop in the hallway outside my room. The sole family portrait we have hangs on the wall in a gold-rimmed frame. I zero in on the four beaming faces. In my red dress, I look like Little Orphan Annie.

Stupid girl, I want to growl at my former smiling face. *You and your picture-perfect life. You have no idea what's coming to you.*

I must mutilate the memory of this happy family.

I smash the photograph on the floor and stomp on the frame. Between the shards of glass, I retrieve the photograph and tear the image to pieces. The ripping sound of the thick Kodak paper is surprisingly satisfying.

My brother appears at my side, snot and tears dripping down his chubby cheeks.

"Did she tell you?" I ask.

He nods. I am angrier because he is not.

"Don't you get it?" I scream. "Our family is finished!"

Nonsensical words burst from my mouth; my brother stares back at me bug-eyed.

"I'm going to get Mom," he says.

"Mom is a liar! Mom is a traitor!"

Shane scampers off down the stairway. What a baby.

The realization that I am totally, completely alone floods me.

In an instant, I'm running, arms pumping, chest heaving, barely breathing. I sprint through the kitchen, down the back steps, across the yard, then the alley. I crawl behind a bush on the side of Ashley's house where the scent of Downy dryer sheets wafts up from a vent beside me. I pull up fistfuls of grass from the ground. I curse at the fiery sun. But I refuse to cry.

To my surprise, the sky does not open up and swallow me. How can the world look so normal when my family has just been shattered to pieces?

The divorce process is hidden from my brother and me. On the surface, nothing changes. There are no screaming matches, no legal battles. The shit has hit the fan and is dripping down the walls, but my parents pretend they can't smell the stench. Family disintegration, it seems, is as natural as gravity. Our family's silence says: This sort of thing happens; just keep going.

When the divorce is finalized, my father takes on the mortgage and my mother moves out. She spends the summer bouncing from one temporary dive to another, from a spare bedroom in our neighbor's house to a rented basement across the lake.

One day I open the door to the study and find it has been converted to a bedroom. My mother is back . . . because she has breast cancer.

There isn't a formal discussion of her diagnosis, no pomp and circumstance—not even around life-threatening illness—in my family. There are no heart-to-heart chats, no corny illustrated books to help my brother and me understand the disease. Just because my mother is sick doesn't mean an emotional reunion à la Hallmark movie of the week.

Medical terms I can't pronounce, much less understand, buzz between family members. Benign? Malignant? Beats me. *Mastectomy* is the word I hear most often; apparently, it comes in singles and doubles, like fast-food hamburgers. When my friends inquire about the upcoming operation, I say, "They're taking off a boob or something."

My family is so noncommunicative about the ordeal that I believe Everything Is Fine. Tumor removal is akin to a cavity filling.

After the surgery, my father takes my brother and me to the hospital for a visit. Sun shines like a thunderbolt through the window of my mother's room, washing out the faces of medical personnel who hover and discuss her case in hushed voices. My mother is drugged and drowsy; her head rolls from side to side on a stack of pillows. She's too weak to speak, but I'm not worried—Mom looks like she always does: sleepy. It's as though I had interrupted another one of her naps.

When my mother comes home, she shuts herself in the spare bedroom. She's home 24/7, but she's more distant than ever. She shuffles like a ghost in floral pajamas to and from the bathroom. There's talk of another surgery, something called "reconstruction."

The silence and secrecy surrounding it all is disconcerting. The one comfort I have during my mother's recovery days is food. One afternoon, someone rings the doorbell; when I open the door, I find a wicker basket on the porch. If there's a note, I don't bother to read it; I just want to eat.

The scent of tomato sauce envelops me as I unload an Italian spread of Romaine salad, a loaf of garlic bread wrapped in foil, and a warm pan of lasagna on the kitchen table.

I know my family won't sit down to dinner, even if it is as tenderly prepared as this, so I serve myself a hearty square of lasagna, a heap of salad, and two slices of bread. I tuck into the pasta while watching the tire swing twirl from the oak tree out back. The tangy marinara, the crispy crust of bread, the slip and slide of noodles over my tongue is like an edible embrace. Today, lasagna feels like love.

My father and brother finish off the leftovers later. Knowing my mother, I'm sure she never tastes a bite.

When my mother receives a clean bill of health, my parents implement a rotating-parent-in-residence program. Mom in. Dad out. Reverse and repeat. Like a babysitting service, I rarely know whom to expect when I arrive home from school.

When I complain about the confusing arrangement, my mother says, "We're doing this so you and your brother can stay stable."

I feel anything but.

My mother moves into a friend's house across the lake. Soon she is dating.

She has a type; I think of them as "Greenpeace guys," aging intellectuals with an excess of social conscience. These are the kind of guys who attend war rallies on weekends, who spend their vacations volunteering in third world countries, who are unashamed to own multiple cats. They are physically unremarkable men with well-trimmed beards and gentle voices.

The initial introduction to Jay interrupts a Nintendo game, so my brother and I barely give him the time of day. That night, Jay looks as generic as any of the other men we'd met, in a button-down shirt and black jeans.

Shane and I are both surprised when Jay is the one who sweeps our mother off her feet. Around my fifteenth birthday, my parents do the residential switch-a-roo again. Now Jay and my mother move in; my father moves out.

"Who's that?" Cassie's mother asks when she drops me off one afternoon. Jay has just pulled up in front of our house on his Harley-Davidson.

"My mother's boyfriend," I grunt.

"You don't say," she says, flipping down the mirror and reapplying her tomato-shaded lipstick.

From an outsider's view, Jay looks like a catch: he is several years younger than my mother, has a tight, toned body from his work as a carpenter, and sports a rebellious ponytail beneath his motorcycle helmet. He's often compared to Dustin Hoffman—albeit with long hair and a hog.

After Jay replaces my father in the master bedroom, another side of his personality emerges—that of a hunter and rifle enthusiast who kills time watching old Westerns on the couch in his skivvies. His sneezes shake the chandelier, he breathes laboriously, and his two favorite words are *wow* and *whoa*. I often watch Jay as he sucks on his cigarettes on the porch, his silhouette muddled by clouds of smoke, and wonder what in the world my mother is doing with a man who's so . . . *not* my father.

On the other hand, having Jay around the house isn't all bad; he awards me the keys to his Chevy Celebrity when I ace my driver's permit test, treats my tense shoulders to rubdowns, has an encyclopedic knowledge of cinema, and can fix anything.

The most impressive feat of all: He makes my mother happy.

Jay and I share a common love of food. Like my father, Jay nurtures through nourishment; he single-handedly revives formal dining in our household. Our three-pronged family doesn't know how to have dinner; without my father in the house, we've survived on the every-man-for-himself style: "Cooking" is code for microwaving, we sit wherever there's space (the piano bench or an overturned bucket are popular perches), and the predinner prayer is a mockery of religion, à la "Rub-a-dub-dub, thanks for the grub. Yay, God!"

When Jay cooks, the guts-and-glory side of family dining emerges, complete with screaming matches, slamming cupboards, rattling pots on the stove, smoke spiraling from toaster coils, and the occasional slice of white bread flying through the air like a Frisbee.

"This is why I don't like family meals," my mother says during one exasperating dinner prep. "It brings up all my childhood memories."

Stories about my mother's father, Stuart, are legendary. Though my mother and her siblings laugh about it now, Stuart was an unpredictable and often violent man who disciplined with belts, used shotguns instead of fishing poles to catch muskie, and once hurled a whole turkey at the wall because it was too dry. In time, Stuart came to prefer to drink, rather than eat, his meals.

What distinguishes Jay is that he makes an effort. After the culinary chaos calms, Jay unearths his mother's fine flatware from the china hutch, sets the table with gold-rimmed goblets, and polishes the silverware. Before the four-course feast begins, Jay, my mother, my brother, and I all join hands and thank the heavens for allowing us to eat together. For a few moments, I feel like I'm part of an intact family. Even Martha Stewart would be impressed.

That summer, my love life heats up as much as my mother's.

I audition for and am cast in a production of *Fiddler on the Roof* at a community theater company. I'm immediately smitten with one of my cast mates—coincidentally, the only villain in the play.

Jeremy has Iowan farm-boy good looks—honey-hued hair, skin the color of toasted oats, and eyes as blue as the Midwestern sky. The fact that he's twenty years older than I am only fuels my *Lolita*-like fantasies.

"You do a great German accent," I tell Jeremy one afternoon as we await our cue. I lean against the stage and jut out a hip, looking as alluring as a pubescent teenager with bad skin and braces can.

Our introduction leads to casual conversation, during which I discover that Jeremy lives only a mile from my house. When the first of many cast parties is announced later that week, Jeremy offers to be my ride home. When I ask my mother if it's all right, her face lights up like she's hit the jackpot. She hates to have her sleep interrupted, especially to drive out to the suburbs at two in the morning.

For me, the party is just pretext for the main event: the drive home, alone, with Jeremy. He's a rare breed of adult: one who asks for my opinion—on everything from politics to public radio—and actually listens to my answers. I'm so hot for him that when he looks at me, I feel all fiery and tingly inside.

"Don't take me home yet," I beg Jeremy on the drive home.

In response, he cocks a blond eyebrow, steers into a vacant parking lot, and relaxes his foot off the accelerator. I roll down my window and the sound of the Mississippi River surges in.

"I really like talking to you," I say.

"Likewise," Jeremy says. "You sure don't act your age."

Jeremy unbuckles his seat belt, then mine.

"I don't think we'll get into any accidents here," he says.

I shift in my seat, my thighs stuck together with sweat. The furthest I've gone with a guy was a French kiss at a New Year's Eve party. I'm hornier than hell and even more turned on by the illicit—make that illegal—nature of our affair.

Jeremy brushes my bangs off my forehead and strokes the back of my neck. An electric current shoots down my spine.

"Can I kiss you?" he asks.

I nod coyly. Jeremy leans in and his insistent mouth presses against mine, our tongues twisting awkwardly around my braces. Jeremy's kiss is so different from the slobbery, high school kid smooches I've had; Jeremy knows exactly what he's doing.

"I should take you home," he says after a few minutes of sucking face. "Your parents are going to be worried."

I tiptoe into my house just before sunrise; when I awake twelve hours later, my mother is hovering over my bed.

"Are you drunk?" she asks, squinting as she searches for alcoholic evidence on my face.

I *am* drunk: drunk on the power of seduction, drunk on the possibility of sex.

"Oh, Mom," I moan. "Nothing happened. I fell asleep at the party."

I'm a good girl. My mother knows I've never smoked a cigarette, never had a cocktail, never slept with a man. She trusts me—perhaps more than she should.

The *Fiddler* cast likes to party and get-togethers are scheduled every Friday and Saturday night after the performances. My mother lets me go, her anxiety assuaged by the presence of my trusty chauffeur, Jeremy.

What she doesn't know is that sometimes Jeremy and I attend the fetes; other times, we head straight to his house.

It isn't long before Jeremy introduces me to oral sex.

"Are you close to coming?" he asks the first time he goes down on me. I am spread-eagle on his bed, his face between my legs.

"How do I know?" I ask.

"Believe me, you'll know."

But I don't. The longer he does . . . whatever it is he's doing down there, the more weirded-out I feel. What do I smell like? What do I taste like? I'm disgusted with my body and all its uncontrollable oozing and twitches. I'm so self-conscious, an orgasm is impossible.

After an admirable effort, Jeremy gives up on making me come and drives me home.

Jeremy and I date all summer on the sly, perfecting the art of "everything but." He takes me out for Italian appetizers, lets me tag along on his voice-over auditions, and even introduces me to his parents when they visit from out of town. I know he's seeing other women—adult women—because he tells me so, but when it's just him and me, sitting in his car beneath the starry summer sky, I feel like we're the only two people in the universe.

When the run of *Fiddler* comes to a close, I offer up my virginity to Jeremy in hopes of hanging on to him long term. An attorney by trade, he isn't willing to risk the legal repercussions.

"Do you know how hard I studied to pass the bar exam?" he gawks when I bring up the possibility of popping my cherry.

Soon our affair fizzles and Jeremy dumps me for a flutist he can legally fuck.

Shortly thereafter, I retire from acting and take up ballet instead.

"You're too tall to do this professionally," a high school class-mate tells me when we take our places at the barre for dance class. "You'll never make it beyond the corps."

It's true; my body isn't built for ballet. Elevated on tiptoes, I measure six feet—too tall to be paired with a man. My balletic po-tential, even at age fifteen, is limited.

My height is just the beginning. My contemporaries are two years my junior and still have prepubescent twigs for bodies. Aes-thetically, every ballet position looks better on slim bodies, and girls with clean lines get more feedback. A poke in the butt is the ultimate compliment, a shift of the chin reassurance of grace. I ache for a tweak from my instructor's long, spindly fingers. Being ig-nored is an insult, a sign that my form is beyond correction.

Ballet fits with my black-and-white worldview. There is a

Right Way and a Wrong Way to execute the steps, rigid sequences to memorize, obsessive attention to detail. The body has one purpose in dance: to be sculpted. Perfection is possible if I work hard enough.

"See the difference?" my instructor, Lena, says as she passes by me on the barre. Lena is a former professional ballerina with a flamingo figure, a sharp chocolate bob, and a stern voice. She taps my knee half an inch outward and tilts my ankle fifteen degrees north.

The floor-to-ceiling mirrors are meant for this corporeal criticism. I fixate my gaze on the reflection before me. I *do* see the difference, like snapping the final puzzle piece into place.

My womanly figure is holding me back in ballet. I have B-cup breasts and broad hips; in comparison to my peers, who maintain ironing-board physiques, I look out of place.

My toothpick peers are offered positions in The Company, promoted to assistant teachers, and invited to advanced technique classes. To make it big in the little world of Lake City dance school, I have to overhaul my body.

"You could lose twenty pounds, sure," Dr. Diet says as her eyes scan my body.

Dr. Diet's thin frame is draped in a nauseatingly floral dress with shoulder pads and lace collar. Her tight brown curls dangle over the edges of her tortoiseshell glasses.

"Let's see your food diary," Dr. Diet says.

She rolls her chair toward me until our knees touch. I pass her a scraggly piece of notebook paper that details the last three days' worth of meals:

Breakfast: Grape-Nuts, honey, and milk.

Lunch: Grilled cheese and tomato soup.

Dinner: Spaghetti with meat sauce, green beans, and buttered crescent rolls.

I've fudged a bit on the details—a cookie omitted here, a bowl of ice cream erased there—so I don't appear a total pig.

"Looks pretty balanced," Dr. Diet says. "But there's enough room to make cuts. For example, how much cereal do you eat?"

I shrug. It's not like I measure the stuff. "A bowl?"

"How big is the bowl?"

"Normal size?"

Dr. Diet frowns. "If you were eating Cheerios, it wouldn't be an issue. But Grape-Nuts is very concentrated, so you might be ingesting close to a thousand calories in one bowl."

I nod, though the science is over my head. I've heard of calories, but never counted them. A thousand of *anything* sounds like a lot.

"Try switching to packets of oatmeal," she says, scratching a giant check mark across the breakfast section of my diary. "For portion control."

Point taken: Grape-Nuts bad.

"Now, let's cut the crescent rolls."

"But that's my favorite part of dinner!" I protest.

Dr. Diet shakes her head with a smile. I have so much to learn, like enjoyment is irrelevant when it comes to weight loss.

"You can ease into it," she says. "Eliminate the butter for a week, then eat only half a crescent roll, then a quarter, until you taper off altogether."

I slump in my chair. This losing weight thing is no fun.

"Eat less, exercise more, and count calories."

Dr. Diet passes me a handful of colorful pyramids, meal logs, and serving charts.

"Being thin requires sacrifice," Dr. Diet says as she escorts me to the door. "There's no way around it."

Though Dr. Diet recommends restricting to 1,200 calories a day, I take weight loss to the next level. In my trademark overachiever style, I cap my daily calories at an even 800. In a month, I lose ten pounds.

Though the diet makes me feel miserable, I persevere. I like how

I look. The weight dissolves as though an unseen ice sculptor were chipping away at my body. I marvel at the twin ladders of ribs across my torso, the gap between my thighs, my half-moon stomach. My sunken bone structure adds years to my face; which, at fifteen, is what I long for.

No matter how difficult dieting is, the rewards are tenfold when I admire myself in the mirrors at the dance studio. In see-through tights and itty-bitty leotard, my silhouette is so streamlined it attracts attention from all the fellow dancers.

"How'd you do it?" they inquire.

"Easy," I say. "I stopped eating."

They think I'm joking, but the truth is the less I eat, the less I crave. Once I downsize, it's impossible to go back. Even the smallest meals make my belly blow up like a balloon; I believe I will burst if I ingest a normal meal. One slip—a slice of cheesecake, a bowl of cereal, hell, a box of raisins—will send me spinning into obesity from which I will never return. A neon warning sign that says DO NOT OPEN THIS PACKAGE flashes before my eyes. I understand that if I do, something—annihilation? world destruction?—very, very bad will happen.

The easiest way to stick to my diet is by eating the same things every day:

Breakfast: 1 packet plain oatmeal, 1 envelope Equal sweetener, ½ cup fat-free milk, ½ cup orange juice.

Snack: Carrots and fat-free dip.

Lunch: Apple and rice cake with 1 teaspoon peanut butter.

Snack: 6 ounces fat-free yogurt.

Dinner: 1 cup green beans, 1 slice fat-free cheese.

My family doesn't seem to notice the incredibly shrinking Erica. My mother and Jay are busy planning their wedding; my brother, now a middle-school social butterfly, is rarely at home; I see my father only on the weekends to go to the movies.

The major dietary land mine in my life is high school. Five days a week I fight the temptation of pepperoni pizza and curly fries in the cafeteria, the well-stocked doughnut-sale stand, the colorful call of the vending machines.

Resistance is a bitch in that environment, so I surround myself with fellow food shunners. By sophomore year, all my girlfriends are on the same starvation kick. It's an unacknowledged competition: Who has the fiercest willpower? Who zips through her day on the least amount of fuel? Over the course of a semester, we dissolve into a flock of underfed chickens.

Our clique, an unnamed skinny sorority, bows down daily to the Holy Scale. Instead of algebraic calculations, we catalog our dietary sins in spiral notebooks. We drown our skeletal silhouettes in grunge garb: hooded sweatshirts and baggy cords held up by leather belts with rapidly multiplying holes. We shiver through six classes a day despite layers of long underwear; our hands turn midnight blue. Our profiles go gaunt, showcasing too-sharp cheekbones and eyeballs that roll like bingo balls inside their sockets. We talk incessantly to disguise the baritone cacophony of our hollow stomachs.

"It's Vegetarian Awareness Week," Alyssa, an upperclassman, says one day when we cross paths in the commons area. "You should convert." Alyssa is a striking Korean beauty with a Cindy Crawford mole on her upper lip and silky black hair that hangs to her waist. Her clothes are straight out of the hippie '60s, and buttons touting Greenpeace and Amnesty International symbols litter the straps of her tasseled bag. She is, by definition, Much Cooler than me. She is also a vegan—no meat, no eggs, no dairy—constantly on the lookout for recruits.

"Read this," she says. She passes me a flyer with black-and-white photos of slaughtered turkeys, their limp necks gushing blood. "And we'll see if you still want to eat meat."

The pamphlet describes in graphic detail how animals are doped up on hormones, confined to pens to prevent movement, mistreated with electric shocks, and heartlessly killed.

I *am* an animal lover, but even more, I want to impress Alyssa. Vegetarianism also seems like a good excuse to push food away at the dinner table. If accused of eating too little, I'll blame it on social consciousness. I vow that day to never let an animal carcass pass my lips again. One by one, my friends convert, until vegetarianism infects my entire social circle.

There is only one girl in my group of friends who refuses to diet. Jenna is an inch shorter and at least twenty pounds heavier than me. I envy her ability to eat a trio of chocolate chip cookies for lunch without a twinge of guilt. Jenna is comfortable in her body; she flaunts it in tight tank tops and form-fitting skirts. To me, however, her curves are intimidating; her voluptuousness screams sex. Though she is only a freshman, the most popular boys, the eighteen-year-olds with cars, jobs, and college applications, all want to go out with her.

Jenna is also into women's lib at an age when *feminist* is still a four-letter word.

"This is stupid," she tells me one day as I nibble on my rice cake. "All you talk about is losing weight. I'm not going to cheer you on while you torture yourself. Let me know when you come back to your senses. Until then, I won't hang out with you anymore."

I don't want to lose my friend, but I'm in too deep now; my competitive nature eggs me on. I want to be exceptional at something, and weight loss is it.

Meanwhile, dancers drop left and right.

The bell rings and Laura rises from her desk across the aisle from me in history class. Recently cast as the Sugar Plum Fairy in *The Nutcracker,* she is the axis of my envy. Laura is so thin her empty belly protrudes from beneath her tank top like a Save the Children poster child; her hip bones rise and fall from the waistband of her jeans like roller-coaster curves. She barely takes a step when her palm shoots up to her left temple and she crumples into a heap of bones on the ground. I've never seen anyone faint before, but Laura does so gracefully. Even facedown on the scuffed-up tile floor, her body folded beneath her desk, she is delicate, beautiful.

The teacher, ready to drop dead herself from old age, rushes to Laura's side and elevates her floppy head with both hands.

"Are you all right?" she asks, slapping Laura's pale face until she comes to.

"I had a migraine," Laura whispers. "Just a migraine."

I smirk at all ninety pounds of her. She may be thinner than I am, but I'm smarter. If her parents knew how extreme she's taken this diet thing, they'd pull her out of dance class. There is a fine balance between skinny and starving. The trick is to get as thin as possible without arousing suspicion. True diet devotees make weight loss look effortless. You're not supposed to get *caught*.

I have no worries in that department. I've hidden the weight loss beneath my ill-fitting Ragstock wardrobe. My moodiness and my isolation are nothing new; I've always been a loner. My mother even addresses me by the nickname "Stormin' Norman." As long as I rack up A pluses on my report cards, as long as I stay away from drugs and cigarettes, no one in my family will raise an eyebrow at my body.

Soon I'm too tired to be pissed off, much less social. I slog home from the school bus and head straight to bed. I do not pass the kitchen. I do not linger in the bathroom. I go upstairs and put on my pajamas. Pj's are my personal straightjacket. As soon as they're on my body, the message to my stomach is clear: I am done eating today. I pull back the covers and crawl into bed.

At first, relief washes over me like spring water. I'm as far away from food as possible. I'm safe. To get to the fridge would require walking all the way down a flight of stairs, through two heavy doors, and into the incriminating kitchen lights. Too much work for a few extra calories.

Then an invisible force tethers me to the bed. I lie flat on my back and stare at the ceiling, gripping the sheets with both fists. My jaw is so tight, I worry I will awake toothless from the pressure. My stomach feels like a rope being twisted in tighter and tighter knots.

Hang on, hang on, hang on, I say to myself. If I feel spiritual, I change my chant to *Help me, help me, help me.*

Most nights, I am so famished, the hunger pangs so crippling, I cry myself to sleep.

By spring, the diet I thought I controlled is now controlling me. Staying skinny is so all-consuming, so draining, I don't have the oomph to go to dance class. I feel like shit and I look as shapely as a knobby-kneed skeleton. All traces of womanhood have been erased. My butt is barely there, my breasts wither to mere nubs with nipples, and my period disappears.

The first blood-free month brings relief, not worry—one less embarrassing bodily function to deal with. Then another month passes, and another, and worry awakens in me. Even as a teenager, I am keenly aware that I want to be a mother someday.

So I blow my own whistle and schedule an appointment for a physical.

Though I'm fifteen, I return to the pediatrician's office I frequented when I was little. The cartoon-character décor, the pastel-painted dollhouses, and the tetra-filled aquarium in the pediatric waiting room comfort me.

"Do you want me to go with you?" my mother asks when a nurse calls me back.

"No," I moan with exaggerated angst.

The nurse leads me to a scale and flicks the metal cubes with fake fingernails.

"You're a skinny Minnie, aren't you?" she muses when the weights balance at 110 pounds. I'm five feet seven inches.

After I change into a gown printed with infantile teddy bears, Dr. Hyde arrives. She is middle-aged and wrinkled, with lush wavy hair and a serious demeanor. She performs my physical exam perfunctorily without breaking the physician poker face.

"Any concerns, Erica?" she asks as she sits down across from me.

"I don't have my period anymore," I say.

"How long has it been?"

"Three months."

Dr. Hyde crosses her arms and leans back in her chair like a detective who just received the confession she's been waiting for.

"Why do you think that is?"

My mouth responds before my brain can invent an excuse.

"Because I haven't been eating."

Dr. Hyde nods. Just nods. I've been waiting for someone, anyone, to sound the alarm. I want bells and whistles, a team of specialists to storm down the hall, break down the door, and stick an IV in me.

"Would you like to do something about that?" she asks.

Now I just nod, barely holding back the tears pooling in the corners of my eyes.

"I know someone who can help you," Dr. Hyde says.

"Does the scale bother you?" Lydia asks.

My new therapist, a stubby brunette woman with pale skin and faded freckles, studies my face as she weighs me. It's been a week since I fessed up to Dr. Hyde, and I'm about to get my head shrunk for the first time.

"No," I say. I'm on the scale morning, night, and after every bowel movement. Though this scale is digital, and therefore more sensitive than my scale at home, the bright red numbers are off— I'm only in the double digits today.

"I'm weighing you in kilograms so you don't fixate on what your weight is doing," Lydia says.

I can get around the metric system. There's a conversion chart in my biology textbook that will help me determine the damage. I etch the numbers in my brain to convert later.

After the weigh-in, Lydia sits across from me in an impersonal office with her legs stiffly crossed. She is dressed in a beige skirt and sweater set as bland as the bare walls. I know we won't bond.

"I have your results," she says, referring to the lengthy questionnaire I spent an entire morning filling in a few days earlier. She holds up a Technicolor chart with three spastic lines stretching across the page.

"This is the average woman," she says, indicating one line. "This is the average anorexic, and this is you."

The chart is as irrelevant to me as a splatter-paint creation.

"I don't get it," I say.

Lydia seems pleased; a mellow smile spreads across her face.

"You aren't thin enough to be anorexic."

Not thin enough? Doesn't all that deprivation deserve a title?

"So what's wrong with me?" I ask. It better not be bulimia. Bulimia is for fat girls.

"You have an eating disorder NOS—not otherwise specified."

This EDNOS business doesn't sound as glamorous as anorexia. It's as brag worthy as getting a B in an advanced placement class.

Lydia slides the papers, facedown, across her desk. "So this is how we'll work together," she says. "Every session you'll have a homework assignment that we'll discuss in the subsequent session."

The goody two-shoes in me stands at attention. I love homework!

"Your first assignment is to keep a food diary."

"I've been keeping one," I say with a prideful puff of my chest. I'm already kicking butt in this recovery stuff.

"This is different," Lydia says. "No calorie counting."

"What's the point, then?"

"To record the time and what you eat. I want to make sure you have regular meals that include all the food groups."

I will later learn that Lydia is a cognitive behavioral therapist, meaning she employs a systematic method to cure eating disorders. Every patient she sees goes through the same psychological assembly line.

My mother is invited to sit in on one session, though I'm not sure she believes in this head-shrinking hooey. Even if my mother did acknowledge eating issues in our family, I don't think she'd be willing to confront them now. She probably thinks I'm malingering, trying to steal her attention away from her soon-to-be-hubby.

There's so much unexpressed emotion between my mother and me, Lydia would need a bulldozer to get it out of the way. With my adolescence in full swing, the relationship with my mother is beyond strained. It's an "I love you—now get out of my life!" attachment dynamic. We're on opposite ends of a psychological seesaw; one of us is always enmeshed while the other is indifferent. When I need her the most, she's busy working or spending time with Jay; when she's available, I suddenly insist on asserting my independence. When I need her to shut up and be supportive, she talks too much; when I want advice, she's wary to offer it. We're trying to do the mother-daughter dance but we keep stepping on each other's toes.

Often I feel like I'm a child again, standing on the edge of a diving board, about to attempt some fantastic feat. I yell, "Mom! Look at me!" but by the time she realizes I'm calling her and turns to watch me, I'm mid–belly flop.

"What could your mother do to support your recovery?" Lydia asks, looking back and forth between us.

I shoot for the lowest expectation I can think of.

"She could take me to Vina," I say. "It's my favorite restaurant."

My mother sighs. "Eating out is *expensive*," she says. "Why can't you make something at home?"

"I think Erica's idea is positive," Lydia says. "It's important to honor cravings in order to prevent binges."

My mother lifts her purse from the floor and plops it onto her lap, ready for our soul-searching experience to be over with already.

"Fine," she says.

That night, she schleps me to the Vietnamese hole-in-the-wall and hands me a blank check. While she waits in the car, I order my favorites—cream cheese wontons, vegetarian egg rolls, and tofu lo mein—to go. That night, I eat my only maternally endorsed recovery meal in front of the television. Alone.

I submit to Lydia's fast-food approach to therapy. By now, eating disorders are as passé in my social circle as ponytail scrunchis and leg warmers. The perfectionist in me isn't interested in the unexciting EDNOS title; it sounds so half-assed. If I can't be successful at being sick, I might as well give recovery a shot. I complete every homework assignment. I document meals in my diary. I build the perfect food pyramid brick by caloric brick.

Around the time my therapy dwindles down, my Spanish teacher mentions a student exchange program in Spain. This trip would mean a month away from my chaotic family, an opportunity to shack up with a Castilian family on the other side of the world, and private Spanish lessons with a native speaker. The one drawback? The tuition is thousands of dollars. I take the impressive color brochure home and present it to my mother.

My mother has always bribed good behavior out of my brother and me, buying our complacency with trips to Target, rewarding dental checkups with Toys "R" Us pit stops, and encouraging swimming excursions with the promise of ice cream afterward. I hock the trip to Spain as an incentive to recover from the eating disorder, a way to divert my attention away from ballet and into academia abroad.

"Let's see what Lydia thinks," she says.

Lydia is lukewarm on my leaving the country.

"It could be motivation to get better or it could send you right back into the eating disorder," she says at my next session. "If you go, you cannot come back even one pound less than what you weigh now."

I promise to maintain my weight. My mother whips out her credit card and signs me up. I count down the days to my big escape.

Before my departure, I reunite with Jenna—my nondieting, feminist friend—at a fancy Italian restaurant. Over fettuccine alfredo, she presents me with a paperback copy of *Feminist Perspectives on Eating Disorders*. On the cover, there is a woman in a black dress, her face obscured by a wild curtain of curls, twisting a rope around her waist.

"Food for thought," Jenna says. "And the flight."

I am sixteen now and on my way overseas for the first time. As soon as I touch down in Spain, I'm aware of how painfully out of place I am. This is a country of caramel-skinned curvy women; like an adolescent Tinker Bell, my hair is white-hot blond and pixie-style short. I am aspirin pale and thin as the spatula handle that my host mother waves in the air.

"I don't know what to feed you!" the plump, jolly woman exclaims on my first night in León, a tiny town on the northwestern coast of the country. My host mother crosses her arms over her generous breasts and shakes a head of raven-colored curls.

As if my American palate isn't challenging enough, I'm still—horror of all horrors—a vegetarian. My host family knew this when they agreed to the monthlong visit, but the reality of a teenager who eats primarily pasta is more daunting than they imagined.

I was instructed in orientation to be ultra-accommodating, to never refuse a food or activity. I was also told to arrive bearing gustatory gifts—specifically, peanut butter.

"It's practically a delicacy," the program coordinator informed me.

The familiar jar of Jif is still in my suitcase; perhaps I'll have to dip into it myself, tablespoon by tablespoon, to prevent starvation.

"What is a meal if it doesn't include *carne*?" my host mother asks as she raises her tired eyes toward the heavens. Then, as though God Himself responds to her plea for divine intervention, her heavily lined brows shoot up. "You eat fish, no?"

I shake my head no.

She sighs and her shoulders crumple toward her chest.

My host mother flings open cupboard doors and slaps them shut with a series of muted thuds. She shakes a can of tomato sauce triumphantly in the air.

"You like *es*-spaghetti, yes?"

"Sure," I say.

Es-spaghetti is not the same dish served on American soil; the pasta is actually angel hair, overcooked and squishy, with a thin sheen of tomato sauce on top. No spice. No salt. No herbs or chunks or parmesan cheese topping. I slurp the bland spaghetti with a fake smile on my face; surely as soon as my jet lag wears off, my Spanish family will whisk me off to a fancy restaurant for vegetarian paella and fresh-fried tapas.

On my second night in Spain, my host mother insists on another homemade meal. After twenty-four hours to plan, she must have an extravagant surprise on the menu. She flutters around the kitchen like a parakeet with clipped wings. From my place at the dinner table, where I play cards with my two school-aged host sisters, I can hear water boiling and something simmering on the stovetop.

My host mother emerges from the kitchen in a whirl of steam and passes me a plate piled high with . . . *es*-spaghetti. Again.

Night three: *Es*-spaghetti.

Night four: *Es*-spaghetti.

You get the idea. I eat *es*-spaghetti for thirty days straight.

Breakfast varies as much as dinner does. Because I'm an early bird, my host mother leaves a big blue tin of Danish shortbread cookies for me on the table. Each morning, I munch through entire stacks of the sugar-sprinkled, pretzel-shaped delights.

At least there is lunch, my one opportunity to stock up calorically. The entire family—mother, father, daughters, cousins, uncle, aunt, and grandfather—converges at 1:30 P.M. daily for a banquet-style meal.

"*Más, más!*" they insist as bowls of squash soup and saffron rice make their way around the table. I eat my weight in bread—huge wheat boulders pockmarked with seeds and grains, still warm from the *panadería* down the block. Between bites, the women swap shameful gossip and the men engage in political debate. Everyone smokes. I feel more at home, surrounded by these semistrangers, than I ever did back in Minnesota.

Spain is a tour for the taste buds: tiny white cups of *café con leche* on every corner; *cuernos* dripping with chocolate glaze in bakery cases; *almendrados*—almond-chocolate ice cream bars—from side-walk vendors. Of course there were remarkable moments—gawking at Picasso's *Guernica*, getting sunburned on the beach, dancing at the *discoteca* with a handsome host cousin—but the food is what lodges itself in my memory.

I realize that my former dieting days shrunk not only my waist-line but my worldview. Now I'm too busy learning a new language, fumbling with customs, and flirting with foreigners to care what my weight is doing. I walk everywhere, though not out of a com-pulsive need to burn off my meals. I wander through the ancient cathedrals and pigeon-filled plazas, swinging my hips sensually be-neath my gypsy-style skirt. I understand that in order to explore, I have to eat for energy. The passion I once reserved for ballet and reforming my body is now available for more important endeavors. Instead of calories, I'm counting how many high school credits I can get for the afternoons spent studying Spanish at my instructor's kitchen table.

Traveling takes my mind off my body. Spain is like an elixir for my soul. By the time I return to Minnesota, my figure is fuller and my period reappears. The corporeal tug-of-war is over.

"Spain was good for you," Lydia says during our follow-up session.

It's true: I have better things to do with my time now, new talents to develop, college applications to prepare. I've given up ballet and no longer socialize with my former dancer friends, so the pressure to be thin is gone. My mother and Jay are about to get married, and family life will settle down.

The eating disorder ordeal is like a blip on my adolescent radar, a hush-hush affair that my family is either too embarrassed or too apathetic to address any further.

Lydia is tickled pink with my weight gain. She closes my medical file proudly and sighs.

"I think our work here is done."

chapter five

Mexican Craving

In the fall of my junior year, I enroll in a program for advanced high school students that allows me to take unlimited free courses at the University of Minnesota. The university campus is a mini-city through which twenty thousand people traverse every day. Intellectuals scurry to and fro, speed-walking through the underground tunnel system like gophers.

Despite being surrounded by thousands of people, I feel more alone than ever. I am a commuter and, therefore, am on campus only when necessary. As a sixteen-year-old amongst adults with families, full-time jobs, and fellowships, I'm out of place. My high school social circle is nonexistent, as I'm only there for one class a day.

All homework and no play make me very uptight. The YMCA, where I'm still on my family's membership, is my refuge. After a run, weightlifting, a swim, and a sauna, I stop at Cub Foods and load up on groceries with my $25 weekly allowance. Jay does the grocery shopping now, and he's a penny-pincher. If I want to eat what I truly enjoy, I have to buy it myself.

When I arrive home, famished from my workout, I prepare a

personal feast. A pot of Contadina ravioli bubbles above a blue flame, a saucepan of Classico simmers on the stove, pungent wedges of garlic bread toast to a golden brown in the oven. I polish off an entire package of ravioli, shoveling the cheesy squares into my mouth three at a time. Sometimes I'm so eager to eat I stand over the sink as I drain the pasta, the steam coating my face, and pop the piping-hot ravioli in my mouth without bothering to sprinkle it with sauce.

A familiar discontent, not unlike what I felt when my parents divorced, hums in my veins, buzzing like an electric current beneath my skin. As long as I sweat and stuff, the ache stays buried in my body.

I can hardly feed myself on $25 a week, so I take a cashiering gig at a photo shop part-time. One dull Friday night, on the brink of my dinner break, the store's doorbell dings.

"I'll get it," I moan to a coworker. "But this is my last customer."

I step up to the counter where a man with skin as brown as his leather jacket stands. His jet black hair is slicked back with too much gel, forming hardened spikes of hair. Despite the porcupine hairdo, he's dashingly handsome.

I'm sure that he's Latino, so I ask, *"¿Hablas español?"*

The man's head jerks back in surprise at my bilingualism.

"Claro que sí," he says. *Of course.*

In an instant, the Hispanic hottie and I are chatting away in Spanish. Cesar, I learn, is from Mexico City, a twenty-two-year-old student in his last semester at the nearby chiropractic college. Cesar compliments me on my Spanish. I giggle. We click.

"So what can I do for you?" I ask.

"Photos," he says. "For my visa."

I snap the standard shots with a Polaroid. The flash pops and the camera spits out twin photos. When I package the photos in a bright blue envelope, I discreetly slip in my phone number with the prints.

A few weeks later, on Valentine's Day, Cesar takes me on a date.

"Can I give you a kiss?" he asks after dinner.

I turn to Cesar, who is smiling his big, gap-toothed smile. His hands rest loosely on the steering wheel of his cramped Nissan.

"You don't have to ask," I say and lunge across the stick shift.

Our lips meet, our tongues intertwine, and when we separate, he flashes that adorably defective smile again.

"That was nice," he says, reaching behind my seat. "But this is what I meant."

Cesar places a giant Hershey's kiss in my lap.

A cute guy and carbohydrates is all it takes to win me over.

Though I'm only sixteen, Cesar and I jump headfirst into an exclusive relationship. My parents are wary about our coupling at first, but after they see what a responsible, kind man Cesar is, they welcome him with open arms.

Almost one year after the infamous first kiss, Cesar asks me to accompany him to an appointment.

"It's about my visa," he says. "It expires in April."

At an immigration law office on Summit Avenue, Cesar and I swivel side to side in matching chairs.

"I don't know what to tell you," the attorney, a petite Asian woman, says as she shuffles Cesar's documents across the polished conference table. "It's nearly impossible to get a work visa these days."

I mention the movie *Green Card* in which a French man weds a New Yorker for the sole purpose of immigration status.

"Couldn't we just get married?" I ask.

The lawyer peers over her smart black glasses. "I'm going to pretend you didn't just ask me that," she says and slaps Cesar's file shut. "As is, I can't help you with your case."

"And if we had come in already engaged?" I ask. "Could you have helped us then?"

The attorney stands, her crisp burgundy suit lending an air of intimidation to her unimpressive stature.

"Understand, that this is a *hypothetical* answer," she says and leans in closer to us. "Had you come in already married, Cesar's application would be approved."

The attorney extends her hand to Cesar and me.

"Good luck," she says.

To celebrate the one-year anniversary of our first date, Cesar and I drive upstate to Two Harbors. We stay at Superior Shores resort, in a suite bigger than Cesar's apartment. Though we both play it off as a road trip, it's really a domestic rehearsal; a test to see if we could be together, forever—or at least until Cesar receives his citizenship.

I'm torn. In my ideal life timeline, marriage didn't factor in until my late twenties. If I marry Cesar, I'll lose my health insurance and a chunk of my financial aid package at Macalester College, where I'll be pursuing my bachelor's degree come September.

But if Cesar and I don't marry, I'll lose the only man I've ever loved, the man I gave my virginity to. Cesar will go back to Mexico and resume the life he left. I'll go back to my part-time photo shop job, my textbooks, and my childish canopy bed in my mother's house.

After our weekend away, Cesar and I return to the Twin Cities on a freakishly warm February day. All along the streets, dog walkers, joggers, and stroller pushers have emerged from hibernation and are stockpiling the sunshine outside.

After Cesar drops me off, I lace up a pair of Sauconys and take off toward Lake Nokomis. My feet reacquaint themselves with the blacktop as I leap over melting piles of snow, but the rhythm of my run doesn't undo the knot in my stomach.

When exercise fails to calm my anxiety about my romantic future, I try to stuff it down with a carton of reheated fried rice, which I devour on the living room sofa while watching *Titanic*. The house is empty; my brother is with my father, Jay is visiting his kids in Wisconsin, and my mother . . . well, where could *she* be?

Perhaps she's treating herself to a massage or soaking in the Jacuzzi at the YMCA. Remarriage hasn't been as blissful as she'd envisioned. Lately, my mother seems worn down; she's been napping incessantly again, just like she did before my parents' divorce.

Her absence tonight doesn't alarm me, but it is odd that she hasn't left a note on the kitchen table letting me know when she'll be back. As I sink into an MSG-induced stupor, the front door creaks open and my mother saunters in, her face hidden behind her hair.

"Wanna watch *Titanic*?" I ask.

"I'm tired," she mumbles. She tosses a plastic Walgreens bag at me. "Happy Valentine's Day."

I sift through the random assortment of heart-shaped chocolate inside the plastic bag while my mother shuffles past the couch and toward her bedroom, her wool socks leaving parallel tracks on the dusty floor.

After Leonardo DiCaprio and Kate Winslet have hot and steamy sex, I turn the movie off; it's all downhill for the flushed-faced couple from here on out. I'm on my way to my bedroom when something makes me stop outside my mother's closed door.

I never say good night to my mother, but she seems especially despondent tonight, so I will.

I knock against the wood paneling and wait.

No answer.

I can hear the muffled sound of a man's voice on the other side of the door—my mother has a major crush on Kevin Costner; she must be watching *Dances with Wolves* again.

I knock harder; Kevin Costner responds with a battle call.

I knock again.

Silence.

Typical. I'm trying to commit a random act of kindness and my mother won't even open the door.

As I start up the staircase toward my room, my stomach stirs and churns. Indigestion? Or instinct?

I turn back and push on my mother's door with my palm; it opens just an inch. Lamplight leaks through the sliver of space between the door and the jamb and a blue glow flashes from the television screen. The door doesn't have a lock, but it's latched from the inside.

"Mom?" I say, my voice warbling. "Are you all right?"

No response.

Panic surges up from my stomach to my chest; I grab my dirty dinner fork from the kitchen counter and shove it beneath the latch. The hook flips up and the door swings open.

My mother is in bed, her head flopped to one side, eyes closed.

My body heaves a sigh of relief. *Not even Kevin Costner in a loincloth could keep you awake!* I imagine teasing her the next morning.

I'm walking toward the television to turn the movie off when an envelope propped on the dresser catches my eye.

It is addressed to me—in my mother's handwriting.

In an instant, I understand. I lunge at the bed and a confetti-like pile of pills bounces off the bedspread. I grab my mother's bony shoulders and shake her. Drool dribbles from the corner of her mouth.

"Mom!" I scream. Her eyes pop open and roll around in her head like hard-boiled eggs. She mumbles a few unintelligible words.

Now that I know she's alive, I sprint to the phone; the first person I call is Cesar.

"My mom," I say, barely able to breathe the words into the receiver. "My mom . . . took some pills."

"Call the paramedics!" he says. "I'm on my way."

Moments later, the house fills with the wail of sirens, revolving red and blue lights, the footfalls of heavy leather boots, and booming voices. My mother, wedged between the burly bodies of two firefighters, stumbles out the door in a stupor.

Someone pats my back and says, "You saved her life."

Maybe I did, but a part of me dies that night, too.

* * *

At the hospital a few hours later, the ER doctor ushers me back to see my mother. She is sleeping after a thorough stomach pumping. Tubes spiral like vines from her bed. When I pat her hand, she rolls away from me.

"I'm too scared to sleep alone," I say to Cesar in the car. He holds my hand tenderly and doesn't let go for the entire drive back to his apartment.

A few days later, when my mother is released from the hospital, I receive a delivery from Bachman's. When I unwrap the two-foot-tall purple package, I expect a floral arrangement from Cesar.

It's a pot of dirt. From my mother.

I'm a garden! reads the tag protruding from the moist soil. *Watch me grow!*

I'm not sticking around to watch *anything* with my mother; she's abandoned me enough for one lifetime. There was the divorce, breast cancer, remarriage, and now this. Her suicide attempt solidifies the deal.

Cesar and I marry in March, a week before his visa expires.

At first, marriage suits me. I like the stability. I feel safe. Cesar provides for me financially, emotionally, sexually; he is sensible, steady, and rational. He comes home every evening from his growing chiropractic clinic when he says he will, we have pizza and rent a movie every Wednesday night and we attend church every weekend. Our social network is small, but intimate, consisting mostly of Cesar's chiropractic contacts, his parents, his brother, and his sister-in-law.

Over time, however, the stability turns stale. What was once reassuring is now too routine and I'm restless. After completing my bachelor's degree in record time—two and a half years—I yearn for a new challenge: motherhood.

At age twenty, I discover the secret to effortless weight loss: first trimester pregnancy hormones! As soon as the embryo of our firstborn burrows in my belly, an incessant morning sickness overtakes me.

One odd side effect of pregnancy is a heightened sense of smell. Suddenly, I can detect scents at an animalistic level, as though my nose had been activated after a lifetime of stuffiness. I can smell every musty fiber of the carpet in Cesar's chiropractic clinic, the slightest suggestion of mold from the bottom of a garbage can, a single drop of sweat from Cesar's underarm.

The first day that nausea attacks, I'm in the dark room at Cesar's chiropractic clinic. The rotten-egg odor of developing chemicals shoots up through my nostrils and sends my stomach spinning. My throat tightens, sweat beads sprout on the back of my neck, and my feet propel me to the bathroom.

I careen to the toilet, executing a baseball-worthy slide up to the bowl, and lurch splinters of noodles in red, brown, and gray hues. My stomach contracts hard, over and over, until I gag up air. Exhausted, I flip down the lid of the toilet, flush, and rest my forehead on the cool porcelain.

I rinse my mouth out with water, undecided between shame for the mess of it all and pride that my body is producing the appropriate hormonal cocktail to sustain a pregnancy.

The end of my first trimester coincides with my twenty-first birthday.

It's a low-key shindig, a kill-two-birthdays-with-one-cake party, as my mother-in-law's birthday is the day before mine. Cesar's father, brother, and sister-in-law also join in the celebration. We order in my favorite Veggie Lover's pizza from Pizza Hut, which is really an appetizer for the main event—a thickly frosted birthday cake from the bakery at Babb's, my favorite grocery store.

After the fifth slice of deep-dish pizza slides past my lips, my stomach begins a chortling protest. I burp up a few bubbles of onion-scented air and the sweating starts. A slam of nausea hits me like a soccer ball to the gut. A rush of half-digested vegetables tickles the back of my throat, and the familiar, unwelcome acidity shoots up into my mouth. I dash to the bathroom, slamming the door behind me as I retch over and over into the toilet.

I've never liked throwing up—my typical response is a torrent of tears—but this time the slightest sensation of relief from the nausea is welcomed. Vomiting has never felt so good. Now that my system is emptied of pizza, I'm ready to eat again.

I return to the dining room table; the women sigh sympathetically and the men make raunchy jokes.

"Now," I say, rubbing my palms together. "How about that cake?"

"Would you like to eat your slice in the bathroom?" my father-in-law asks. "Save yourself a trip?"

Like most twenty-first birthday parties, this one will be memorable because I barfed.

Food has never been so toxic to me before. The list of aversive items grows, including items as mundane as chicken and cherries. There are only a handful of foods that go down without trouble—macaroni, grilled cheese sandwiches, mashed potatoes, Cheetos, and stacks and stacks of saltines.

I'd been so excited to eat for two, but this is no fun. The one time in my life I'm expected to gain weight, I can't. By my four-month checkup, I weigh two pounds *less* than I did pre-pregnancy.

My obstetrician, Dr. Torgerson, is a hefty woman with short brown hair, thick glasses, and a face as expressive as a stone.

"We need to schedule an ultrasound," she informs me. "To make sure the baby's growing, even if your belly isn't."

As excited as I am to see my baby on the small screen, I'm also worried about my inability to fatten up. In the two weeks leading up to the ultrasound, I make eating my mission. I stuff myself with full-fat dairy products, peanut butter sandwiches, Quarter Pounders with cheese, and super-size French fries.

I gain one measly pound.

"What is your due date?" the ultrasound technician asks. A grainy gray and white picture flashes before me.

"January fourth," I say.

The tech switches to a black screen filled with numbers, types in the date, and the computer spits out a calculation.

"These measurements are moving your due date up to December twenty-ninth."

"You mean . . . the baby is bigger than expected?"

"Much bigger."

By the second trimester, the nausea is gone and my weight is increasing steadily. By fall, both Cesar and I are sporting substantial bellies.

"Which one of you is pregnant?" Cesar's brother teases. I'm so excited to be a mother, I don't mind the gargantuan breasts and the obtrusive stomach. If having a healthy baby means I have to fatten up, so be it.

The contractions begin on December 29 at 11:00 A.M. as I skim the local news section of the *Star Tribune*.

My stomach clenches as tight as a fist. I pat my beach ball belly, trying to contain the hardening between my palms. After a few seconds, my stomach softens.

"That was weird," I say.

Twenty minutes later, it happens again.

I waddle across the room for a pen and paper.

"What are you doing?" Cesar asks.

"They're starting!" I say.

I jot down the times of the contractions. Every twenty minutes my stomach steels and releases.

"It sounds like early labor, but these things take a while," the nurse says when I call the clinic. "There's no hurry to come in."

No hurry? *No hurry?* I've waited long enough to meet my baby!

Cesar ushers me to our SUV, and we take off for the hospital.

"Need a wheelchair?" the emergency room attendant asks upon our arrival.

"Nah," I scoff, head held high. I hoof it through the maze of underground halls to the maternity ward. Within minutes, I've changed into a gown and the attending OB is sliding his latexed fingers inside me.

"Am I close?" I ask, lifting my head as though I could take a peek at my own uterus.

The doctor stands up and shakes his head.

"Only two centimeters dilated," he says. "It's going to be a while. This stage could last for weeks."

"Weeks?!"

I sink back down into the hospital bed and a frown forms on my face. I won't be meeting my offspring tonight.

"If you'd like," the doctor says. "You can walk for half an hour and I'll check you one more time."

Walk? That's for sissies. I'll climb stairs instead!

I huff and puff up and down the service stairway as Cesar and my mother wait below.

"I'm going to go get a sandwich," my mother's voice echoes up the stairwell. "Be careful, Erica!"

By the time I return to the bed for my check, my calves are burning and butterfly-like patterns of sweat have formed on the underarms of my gown.

"No change," the doctor says.

All that pain and no gain. Apparently the rules of exercise don't apply to giving birth.

"Go home, have a nice dinner, get a good night's sleep," the doctor says. He turns to Cesar and winks. "It might be your last night alone as a couple."

I change back into street clothes and gather up my overnight bag.

"Have sex," a nurse whispers into my ear as I pass by. "Orgasms can jump-start labor."

"You've got to be kidding," I say with a raised eyebrow. My gargantuan breasts are leaking colostrum and there's a hemorrhoid the size of a small water balloon up my butt. I *have* worked up an appetite, though not for sex.

"What got the baby in is also what gets it out," the nurse says with a sly smile.

The contractions kick in again at Noodles and Company an hour later. I've barely had a bite of my lemon garlic chicken when the pressure in my pelvis forces me back to the comfort of home.

"I'm having this baby tonight," I insist from my fetal position on the couch.

"Let's hope so," Cesar says with a sarcastic smile. "If only for the tax return."

The contractions don't come fast enough, so I decide to give my body a little help. I hop on the treadmill, crank up the incline, and walk as fast as my belly will let me. My heart thumps along at rabbit speed, but the contractions, while more intense, are sporadic at best.

Three miles into my walk toward motherhood, I give up and go to bed.

At 4:00 A.M., someone stabs me in the crotch.

At least, that's what it feels like.

I stumble out of bed, gripping my lower abdomen as though I could keep the baby from spilling out of me in a sudden rip tide. I hobble into the bathroom with the intent to shower, but the pain is so intense, I can't get my nightgown over my head.

"I can't move!" I yell, dropping to my knees on the bathroom floor.

Cesar rushes in, fumbles for his cell phone, and calls Dr. Torgerson.

"I don't know, I don't know," Cesar repeats over and over into the phone. "She's on the floor and . . ."

"Waaaah!"

The screams explode from a primal pit inside me. Each contraction is a vise literally squeezing the life out of my womb.

Cesar's eyes appear to pop out of his head.

"Sounds like you're having a baby!" I hear Dr. Torgerson exclaim through the receiver. "See you at the hospital!"

I am only four centimeters dilated when I arrive at the hospital, so I try to coax my body along by soaking in the shower and trying out the birthing chair. My goal is to avoid an epidural and give birth naturally like my mother did.

Then comes the point—the mildly named "transition" stage of labor—when pain completely subsumes me. All I can see is a white light flashing before my eyes, a light so bright it obliterates all other stimulation.

A nurse shoots me up with Nubain, a drug that gives me sailor's legs—and the mouth to boot. Soon, I'm confined to bed and cursing every well-meaning pair of hands that comes near me. The immobility makes me paranoid, frantic, all sobs and screams.

No baby could possibly be worth this much pain.

"I'm going to die!" I blurt out when the nurses prop up my legs in stirrups. "I can't do it!"

The nurses are not in the friendliest of moods this Monday morning.

"You *have* to do it!" one snaps back as she secures an oxygen mask over my mouth.

Well, then.

After what seems like an eternity of violent contractions and gasping breaths, it's time to push. My mother holds back one knee, Cesar another, and the nurses count to ten.

I should have practiced my Lamaze. Each time I bear down, I run out of breath around number seven. After asthmatic-like inhales, I emit moans so fierce my whole body vibrates.

"Be quiet!" the nasty nurse says. "You're wasting your breath!"

Dr. Torgerson disappears between my legs with a syringe and I feel . . . nothing. After twenty-five hours of effacing and dilating, squatting and shitting, pulsing and pushing, Dr. Torgerson snips her scissors and slashes my perineum. A cry—not my own this time—echoes around the room.

Through my drug-induced haze, I hear Dr. Torgerson calmly proclaim, "It's a girl."

I hold my breath, and hold out hope, that Dr. Torgerson is wrong, that the nurse hasn't spread the baby's legs far enough apart to see the little willy hiding between the folds of baby fat.

A voice in my head chants *No no no no no no no no. Not a girl, please, not a girl.*

I always thought I would be one of those mothers who burst into tears upon the sight of her chubby-cheeked cherubs. I used to cry while watching the birth of strangers' babies on Lifetime, for Christ's sake.

On this, the birthday of my first baby, I do not cry.

Amid the bustle of medical personnel and a stream of family members, all I want to do is scream at everyone to get the fuck out of the room and leave me alone. The only thing I want to bond with is an ice pack between my thighs.

The nurse passes my daughter, Julia, to me.

She is big: eight pounds, four ounces.

I feel awkward and clueless, as though I'd just been handed a swaddled squash. What am I supposed to do with *this*?

I stare at the squirmy stranger in my arms, amazed at how unattractive she is. Her face is mottled and inflamed, as though she had taken a few knocks from Muhammed Ali just before bursting from the womb. A crescent of zits dots her forehead, and her long, unruly hair sticks up in all the wrong places.

Cesar turns to the nurse. "She doesn't have Down syndrome, does she?" he asks.

The nurse giggles. "No, of course not."

Cesar peers over at Julia's face again. "Are you sure?" he asks.

"She's perfectly normal and healthy."

Cesar breathes a sigh of relief.

I don't.

I imagine the avalanche of My Little Ponies, Barbies, and Disney princesses. I imagine being forced to buy tutus and ballet shoes, endure tea parties and potty training. I imagine the hoarding of hair products, the mess of maxi pads, the agony of prom dresses and pantyhose.

Worst of all: the diets.

If only I could inoculate her against eating disorders along with measles, mumps, and rubella.

If I had a son, there would be no restrictions. I'd allow him spoons of peanut butter for breakfast, nachos for lunch, cupcakes at bedtime. It wouldn't matter if I took him into public with bed hair and mismatched clothes.

But a daughter . . . a daughter is different.

If I'm her role model, I'm afraid I'll pass on the adolescent body hatred like an undesirable family heirloom.

My hospital stay is a fiery blur of pain, breast-feeding foibles, and uncontrollable crying outbursts. The baby's fine, but my body is another (gruesome, horrific) story. To avoid the brutal reality of my postpartum figure, I stay in hospital gowns and robes until moments before my discharge. As I change into clothes to go home, I see my mommy body in the mirror for the first time.

It is beyond frightening.

My stomach hangs like a half-deflated balloon from my torso.

The skin surrounding my newly deformed bellybutton is loose and wrinkled; my breasts are as hard and misshapen as footballs. A road-map of broken blood vessels covers my face, and my cheeks are in-flamed as though I've had my molars removed.

I've never hated my reflection so much.

The going-home outfit I packed—a stretchy pair of maternity pants and lace-trimmed V-neck blouse—fit until I was six months pregnant. I hadn't expected my body to bounce back instantaneously like a mommy-to-be Barbie, but when the pants, despite the stretchy waistband, won't rise above my knees, I crumple into a teary ball on the bathroom floor.

Once I compose myself, I put on the outfit I was wearing when I arrived at the maternity ward forty-eight hours earlier. The one consolation is that public attention won't be on me, it will be on my new baby. Of the two of us, she has the better body.

The first few months postpartum are a roller-coaster ride of ex-haustion, elation, irritation, frustration, hopelessness, and sporadic happiness. My diet is a disaster. I subsist on turkey sandwiches, granola bars, and trail mix—foods I can gobble down with one hand while I nurse or change diapers with the other. Of the thirty-five pounds I gained while pregnant, twenty-five are still stuck to my waistline.

I'm sleep deprived and depressed. As soon as Julia nods off fol-lowing the 3:00 A.M. feeding, I medicate myself with trays of Oreos dunked in milk while watching *Will & Grace* reruns. I drop the cookies one at a time into the plastic cup to marinate in the milk. In thirty-five seconds, the chocolate wafers reach the ideal squishy state—not so saturated that they crumble when I fish them out with a spoon, but soft enough for the wafers to separate seamlessly from the cream in my mouth.

I don't worry about losing weight yet; Cesar and I have already decided to have our children as close together in age as possible. This is a practical decision, not a passionate one. If I'm going to stay at home with one baby, I might as well pop out the next one right away while I'm accustomed to the sleep deprivation, the diapering, and the bottle washing.

While waiting for the go-ahead to get pregnant again, I delve into a culinary compulsion. I buy several Pillsbury cookbooks and spend the early morning hours ogling the bright, crisp photographs that accompany the recipes. Each enticing recipe is flagged with a sticky note color-coded to the day of the week I will prepare them. My grocery lists occupy entire notebook pages, every item organized according to aisle.

This spring, I'm a slave to appetites: cooking and procreating consume my life. My obsession with food helps pass the time between menstrual periods as I await a positive pregnancy test.

By July, I have another bun in the oven, and a dream informs me a daughter is on the way. In the dream, I'm in the hospital bed when a nurse wheels my baby in. A pink knit cap pokes out from the rolls of blankets. Oh, no. Another girl. As I unwrap layer after layer of teddy bear–decorated blanket, my calm detachment transforms into the irksome feeling that the baby is too small. When I finally reach skin, I snap my head back in shock—the baby's legs are as thin as chopsticks.

Baby number two's birth is fast and furious. On the morning of April 1, two weeks before my due date, a series of cramps awaken me at 3:00 A.M. The sensation isn't excruciating, but I can't sleep, so I douse myself beneath the hot rays of the shower. After the water relaxes my body and reignites my sleepiness, I crawl back into bed.

The next time the cramps kick in, around 6:30 A.M., I know they mean business.

Not that I'd let something like labor alter my morning routine;

the stay-at-home mommy show must go on. Cesar readies for work while I bathe and dress fifteen-month-old Julia between contractions. It isn't until I'm scrambling eggs at the stove that a hard contraction knocks me to the ground. I'm crawling to Julia's high chair, determined to serve my daughter breakfast, when Cesar intervenes.

"I think we should call your mom," he says.

I'd been giggling the night before about playing an April Fool's Day joke on my mother by calling to say I was in labor.

This is no joke.

By the time my mother arrives I'm writhing on the linoleum, wailing.

"I'm going to split in two!" I say.

Cesar lugs me to the car and speeds south on the highway at a hundred miles an hour. I grip the door handle, his thigh, anything I can reach every two minutes when the contractions overtake me. The pressure is about to pop between my legs.

Cesar screeches to a halt outside the emergency room, but he can't get me out of the car. The pain has forced me into a ball, my body curled like a snail under attack.

This time, when I'm offered a wheelchair, I take it.

This is beyond agony; the sensations radiating through my pelvis sear and scorch me at the cellular level. My body feels like one big open wound being prodded with hot metal pokers.

Fuck natural birth.

"Give me drugs!" I wail at the first nurse I see.

"We have to check you first," she says, helping me assume the position on the hospital bed.

"Re-*lax*," she says as she slips her lubricated finger inside me.

"Drugs!" I scream.

"No wonder you're in pain." When she removes her hand, my legs clamp back together like a clamshell. "You're nine-and-a-half centimeters dilated!"

"Give me something, please."

"Too late—this baby is ready to be born. *Now*."

The comfortingly dorky Dr. Torgerson rushes into the room with a curled hook in her hand.

"I'm going to break your waters," she says.

"No!"

"I have to."

"But then it will *really* hurt!"

"Well, yes," she says in her unemotional monotone. "But that's the only way to get the baby out."

I feel a prick, hear a pop, and a gush of fluid spills from between my thighs. Then a lightning bolt of pain splits my body in half and a ring of fire forms around my overstretched labia.

"The baby's crowning!" a nurse yells from the end of the bed. "Push!"

Three hard pushes later, a slimy, bony body slips out of me.

"A girl!" a nurse announces. "Seven pounds, thirteen ounces!"

I've been at the hospital for only twenty minutes; a few red lights and Lola would have been born in the car.

After Lola's birth, my desire to diet comes back with a vengeance.

Weight loss is a skill you never forget; all the dietary knowledge I amassed as a teen tattooed itself on the wrinkles of my brain. The skinny synapses have been waiting to fire.

Sun shimmers through the windows of St. Francis Hospital and falls onto the burrito-like bundle sleeping beside me. Lola's rosebud lips still pulse, pucker, and search for my nipple even though her feeding is long over.

A knock sounds on the door and a pint-size woman wearing a hair net enters.

"Food service," she whispers.

She rolls her cart toward me and passes me a covered plate. I wait until she leaves to lift the top; before me is a cheeseburger on a heavily buttered bun, a pile of oily potato chips, and a bumpy pickle spear.

A familiar voice slips into my ear.

You're not pregnant anymore. Don't you dare eat all of that.

Though I've always longed for three children, Cesar has made it clear that there will be no more babies. Two daughters, fifteen months apart, is enough parenthood for him. There's no point in arguing; in Cesar's macho Mexican mentality, what he says, goes, whether we're talking children, checking accounts, division of household labor, or diversion.

The only area of my life that I control is my body—except, apparently, my womb. If I'm being reproductively retired, I want my slim figure back as soon as possible.

I know what I have to do.

I scrape the melted cheese off the hamburger patty. I limit myself to half the meat, a slice of tomato, and a leaf of lettuce. The bun and potato chips remain on the plate; the crinkly paper beneath them soaks up the grease.

And so it begins.

The rules and restrictions fall into place with domino effect. Doughnut ban, cereal strike, sugar boycott. My postpartum diet consists of Lean Cuisine microwave meals and sugar-free Jell-O in a rainbow of flavors. When hunger strikes, I attack the next item on my to-do list. There is always a diaper to be changed, a toddler to chase, a surface to be wiped down, dusted, swept, vacuumed, reorganized, sanitized.

I'm not supposed to exercise for six weeks, but the stirrings to shed the baby weight are too strong. My new exercise obsession is steps. Before my housewife feet hit the floor each morning, I clip on a pedometer and watch the numbers click away. The average Jane is supposed to walk ten thousand steps a day; I vow to do at least twice that, plus an hour on the elliptical.

But it isn't enough. I want to run.

Idling in my SUV at a red light one afternoon, I watch runners trot by in neon spandex pants and sporty sunglasses. My soul feels as though it could leap from my chest and sprint down Diffley Road alongside them. Restlessness rattles beneath my ribs. I have to run.

Lola is barely two weeks old when I load the girls into the SUV and shuttle off to the Mall of America. I wind the double stroller, daughters squirming, through aisle after aisle of athletic footwear. Running shoes have undergone major makeovers in the three years since I last ran. What are stabilization sneakers? Do I need cushion support? Will racing flats make me faster?

As I lace up a pair of yellow-and-black Nikes, my heart pumps louder and faster than the pop music beating through the store's speakers. They fit. I feel like Sporty Cinderella who's just found her slipper.

The next morning, I take off down Johnny Cake Ridge Road. My legs clunk beneath me; my breath borders on wheezing. I barely make it half an hour, but when I burst through the door, deliciously exhausted, my face radiates pure joy.

I vow then to reform my body, to become fitter than ever.

Losing weight as a stay-at-home mom is like peeling the ruddy outer layer off an orange. Running shaves the top layer of flab from my figure, revealing a streamlined form beneath. Exercise is my only opportunity for quiet contemplation. The realization I return to again and again is this: Despite the dream house, the four-person family, the homemaking gig, and Cesar's successful clinic, I am miserable. In fact, "I" have faded into the background of my life.

At breakfast, Cesar peels his banana meticulously; sometimes he likes to trick me by placing the banana peel, seam-side down, on the table. I'll reach hungrily for the banana, only to find the peel empty inside. This is how I feel as Cesar's wife and as a stay-at-home mom in Midwestern suburbia: Despite the bright, wholesome image I project on the outside, I am completely hollow and devoid of sweetness on the inside. I am the husk of who I used to be.

My time as a stay-at-home mother must be accounted for; in addition to caring for the girls, Cesar leaves me to-do lists every day.

When he comes home, he hurries to see the checkmarks proving I've completed the tasks.

My leisure time is secret, stolen, limited to reading a chapter a day of a historical novel. When I make the mistake of mentioning the book to Cesar, he snaps, "You had time to *read* today?"

"I was pumping at the same time, jeez," I say, indicating the breast pump that I still use to extract breast milk for Lola's bottles.

"Well," he snickers, "the garage could use a good sweeping. Remember that next time you want to read."

My existence is devoted to putting a picture-perfect family on display. Yet we are far from perfect. Cesar's macho Mexican roots are starting to emerge, threatening to strangle me. If I even mention another male's name, Cesar's possessiveness rears its ugly head.

"Jared stopped by today," I say one evening during dinner.

Cesar's fork freezes halfway to his mouth.

"Who's that?" he asks. "Your boyfriend?"

I know he's only mocking me, but his voice has an edge to it.

"No," I say. "He's one of the landscapers doing a bid for the plants out front. I think we should hire him. He's nice."

"Do you think he's sexy or something?"

"No way! He's got a lazy eye."

"And if he didn't? Would you want to fuck him then?"

Cesar ruins more than one dinner with this kind of talk.

Soon not even female friends are safe from interrogation.

"Isn't Janine a lesbian?" he asks once when I float the idea of having coffee with a friend. "She might try to convert you."

I've given him no reason to be so suspicious, so I choose to believe it's simply in his Latin blood and ignore his jealousy as best I can.

There are moments in the day—when the girls' naps overlap, when I walk to the mailbox, when I'm allowed a rare moment alone on the toilet—that the house is completely silent. In those moments,

I glimpse the next seventy years as a parade of dish-washing, dog-walking, ass-wiping, floor-scrubbing mundanity.

The endless uneventfulness terrifies me. Life is *too* stable.

I want to get to the bottom of my disillusionment. An attack of the maybes overtakes me.

"Maybe we need a vacation," I suggest to my husband.

We take three trips in as many months. I still feel stressed out.

"Maybe I need a new look," I say.

I wax my eyebrows and highlight my hair and cut it into a perky bob. I still feel like a frumpy suburban mom.

"Maybe I need to go to church," I say.

I up my attendance at Mass. I still feel alienated from the rest of the world.

My mood disintegrates as winter descends. Marital disagreements become more frequent and more ferocious; Cesar and I spit insults at one another in front our children. When we disagree in the car, I purposely swerve and jerk the steering wheel to get Cesar's attention. One evening, in a fit of rage, Cesar hurls his cell phone at me. Lola, less than a year old, is in my arms. Luckily, he misses us.

"No matter what you get in life, you're always going to be unhappy!" Cesar shouts.

"Of course I'll be happy," I say. "As soon as . . ."

As soon as I get back to school, as soon as the girls are in daycare, as soon as we buy a new car. . . .

I am always one step away from satisfaction; constantly on the verge, but never crossing over, to bliss.

When I run out of things to improve, I come to the only remaining conclusion: Maybe this marriage is the problem.

My husband appears to be Mr. Reliable, but beneath the glossy exterior lurks my greatest fear: that this is the calm before the storm. Steadiness like this can't possibly last. It certainly didn't in the case of my parents. Why would it be any different for Cesar and me?

The only option, as far as I can see, is to launch a preemptive attack. Though I'm twenty-four years old, I'm not adult enough to take *responsibility* for my chronic dissatisfaction. I have to get caught doing something unforgivable. I have to piss Cesar off.

It's time for the big guns—in the form of my ex-boyfriend, Jeremy.

I've been curious about him lately; though we had sporadic contact after *Fiddler* closed, I swore off contact with him when I wed. Now, thanks to Google, I track him down in California. Frantic e-mailing ensues. So much has happened since that summer I was sixteen; it's a thrill to fill Jeremy in on my accomplishments: marriage, my completed bachelor's degree, and the births of my daughters. The witty repartee between us reminds me of the bubbly, spontaneous girl I used to be. Though Jeremy and I have no intention to ever reunite in person, our messages grow from mutual ego strokes to randy fantasies.

I'm reading one such e-mail on a Friday morning in February, seven years to the day of my first cup of coffee with Cesar. My hubby and I don't have anything special planned to celebrate our first-date anniversary, though Cesar has given me permission to take myself out to Chipotle for lunch. I've been cutting discretionary calories all week in preparation for the splurge.

Cesar is in the basement working out, the girls are thoroughly engrossed in tossing their books from the bookshelf onto the floor, and I am on the computer.

I'm smiling and shaking my head at Jeremy's deft double entendres when I hear heavy breathing behind me. At first I think it's just our cocker spaniel, Bella.

It's not.

Cesar is reading the screen over my shoulder.

I click the screen shut.

"What was that?" Cesar asks as he wipes the sweat from his brow.

"Just an e-mail from Katrina," I say.

"Put it back on the screen. I want to see it."

I have half-prepared for this moment by setting up two e-mail accounts with almost identical screen names—one with my middle initial; one without. With all that adrenaline pumping through him, I'm sure Cesar won't notice the slight difference in spelling. I log onto the clean account and open an empty mailbox.

"Whoops," I say with a shrug. "I must have deleted it."

Cesar pushes me out of the chair and sits down at the computer. He frantically clicks and types, growing more frustrated and flustered by the moment. He can't find the phantom message.

"Wait a minute," he says. "This isn't the same e-mail account."

He spins around in the chair and grabs my wrist hard. He looks livid.

"Show. Me. The. Message."

I don't put up much of a fight. I open up the dirty account and produce the message. Cesar reads it stonily, then stands up. With one fierce tug, he pulls the power cord from the wall and wraps it around his arm.

"I'm taking this with me," he says.

On his way out the front door, Cesar pauses, rifles through my purse, and takes my wallet.

"And you can forget about your burrito!" he yells up the stairs.

The weekend that follows is a blur of broken promises, brutal accusations, and plea bargains. I tell lies to cover up lies. Cesar comes to the brink of forgive and forget, then free falls into an abyss of distrust.

I try to take and bake my way to forgiveness. For Valentine's Day, I buy a pepperoni pizza in the shape of a heart. As tomato sauce bubbles audibly and the oven floods the kitchen with mozzarella-scented heat, I set the dining room table down to the last detail. Heavy sage plates—the ones we only use on special occasions—grace a checkered tablecloth. I roll cloth napkins and slide them through matching rings like delicately wrapped scrolls. Wax drips down the crystal candlesticks we received as a wedding present almost six years before.

Cesar sits down at the head of the table. He doesn't speak, much less look at me.

The static from the baby monitors buzzes on the countertop behind us; tonight, Lola's gentle breaths sound like thunderclaps.

It's been like this for days.

Neither of us prays before picking at our soggy pizza, the crust
undercooked from my hurry to start our makeup meal. Despite my
efforts, the dinner is a disaster.

We make one final attempt to salvage our relationship in couples'
therapy.

"Cesar, what would it take to repair this marriage?" the counselor, a bearded man who resembles my father, asks.

"I'd need complete control," Cesar says. "No phone or Internet
access. No checking account. It's the only way to stop her from
cheating on me."

"If Erica is going to cheat, she'll find a way to do it," the counselor says. "What we need to do here is rebuild *trust*."

"What Erica needs," Cesar says, "is to be punished."

I don't need to be married to suffer; I can do that all on my own.
So I begin the best way I know how: by embarking on a diet. My
first goal is to lose 180 pounds—in the form of my husband.

chapter six

Injustice System

As soon as I hire an attorney and file for divorce, the fighting begins—me for full custody of the girls, and Cesar for the money. The only thing we don't disagree on is the furniture.

"Take anything you want," I say when we sit down with paper and pens to write out our wish lists. "As long as I get the elliptical machine."

My priorities, clearly, are in order.

The early stages of the separation, though emotionally exhausting, reawaken my passion for life. I reenroll in my master's in counseling program, land a stimulating part-time job, and rent a town house. For the time being, my child support and spousal maintenance payments provide me with a plush financial cushion and our child-share schedule leaves me with Tuesdays, Thursdays, and every other weekend kid-free. In my wired state of starting over, I feel like Wonder Woman reclaiming her missing cape. I'm free! I can fly! I'm so busy rebuilding my life, I forget to grieve.

"Would you believe," I say to my mother, "that I haven't cried once over this divorce?"

"Don't worry," she responds with a pat on the shoulder. "You will."

My family does not comment on the end of my marriage, save for Jay's "I never understood how you two ended up as a couple" remark. They stoically help me move, provide babysitting, and occasionally share a pizza with me. They support me, sans judgment.

The legal process is not so compassionate or easy to navigate. Previously, I believed that women were awarded whatever they asked for when it came to the kids; custody was guaranteed to the mother along with a hefty alimony package.

Neither belief turns out to be true.

Minnesota is becoming ever more mindful of the importance of dual-parent involvement, so when Cesar demands joint custody, I have two choices: accept his request or submit to an evaluation by a neutral party selected by the court.

I'm unsure I even *want* our daughters with me full-time; after being holed up for years with two noncommunicative kids, I'm enjoying the newfound freedom that shared parenting allows. I'm tired of fighting, but I need money, and sole custody is the best way to ensure a substantial child support payment.

I fight.

I drive myself insane in preparation for the evaluation with Ms. Sanchez. While the girls are at Cesar's, I scour, polish, wax, vacuum, and launder every visible surface in my home. The girls' room is pristine: comforters pressed, bilingual board books stacked on the shelf, photos of my smiling daughters and single-mom me staggered across the dresser.

In the kitchen, I construct a bouquet of muffins—blueberry for Ms. Sanchez and low-fat bran for me—and brew the strongest, most expensive coffee I could find at Starbucks. Jovial salsa music wafts through the living room as I straighten the Diego Rivera murals on the wall. I look as culturally competent as a Midwestern white woman can in the hopes of racking up some brownie points with the evaluator. I fill out my slender 125-pound frame with a billowy, embroidered blouse and disguise my battered runner's toenails with ruby red polish.

There's just one glitch—the girls haven't arrived yet. The 9:30 A.M. drop-off time has come and gone, and Cesar hasn't called. I dial and redial his cell phone but the calls click directly into voicemail.

Conditions for a blood-sugar crash are stirring: I'm exhausted after my ten-mile morning run, I've burned through my minuscule excuse for breakfast (fat-free yogurt and strawberries), my children are missing, their father is unreachable, and Ms. Sanchez is set to arrive any minute.

"Aaarrrggg!" I scream as I shake my fists at the sky.

Then the doorbell rings.

Thank God, I still have ten minutes to change the girls into their matching gingham dresses.

I run to the door and fling it open.

Cesar is not on the other side—Ms. Sanchez, the evaluator, is.

Ms. Sanchez reminds me of a peacock with her impeccable posture, dangling turquoise earrings, and inky black hair.

"Good morning," she says as she steps over the threshold.

I lead her to the kitchen and try to wipe my weepy eyes inconspicuously.

"Can I get you some coffee?" I ask.

"No, thank you," she says.

I turn toward the coffeepot anyway and gulp down a few deep breaths.

"Muffin?" I trill as I twirl around on one heel. I offer up the plate like a possessed Stepford Wife.

"No," she says, rocking back and forth on her heels expectantly. "So . . . where are the girls?"

I crack.

"I . . . uh . . . Cesar . . . hasn't . . . brought . . . them . . . back!" My lips begin to quiver and before I can stop myself I am crying uncontrollably.

Ms. Sanchez glances uncomfortably from side to side, unsure of what to make of this pale-faced woman weeping in the middle of a spotless home, trying to force muffins down her throat.

"Calm down," she says. "He's probably just running late."

Starvation makes a person very suspicious, if not paranoid, about the world around her. Since shedding the fatty sheath from my body, I'm hypersensitive to every slight.

"What if he's taken them?" I rant. "He's doing this to punish me, I know it. He's trying to make me look bad!"

"How does this make you look bad?" she asks. "He's the one who's late."

I try to stifle my sniffles as we sit down across from one another on the living room sofas.

"Why don't we start with some questions," Ms. Sanchez suggests.

"Sure," I say, my voice finally steadying.

Ms. Sanchez removes a yellow legal pad and pen from her briefcase.

"What reason do you have for sole custody?" she asks.

My fear shifts to infuriation; why should I have to make a case to keep my children?

"I have two girls under the age of two," I say between gritted teeth. "They need to be with their mother."

"But with joint custody, they will be with you, just not all the time."

"That's unacceptable," I say.

Ms. Sanchez frowns and notes something on her paper.

"How will you contribute to the cultural development of the children?" she asks.

"I speak Spanish fluently; it was my major in college. I've also worked at a battered women's shelter for Latinas and at Cesar's clinic, where the majority of clients are Hispanic."

"Hmm," she says, her earrings jangling as she nods. "But you do not have Latino family members? No connections to the community?"

"Not except Cesar and his family—"

"What happened there?" Ms. Sanchez asks, indicating two large bandages across the tops of my feet. Due to my high running mileage, my tennis shoes have worn away the skin. I thought covering the wounds looked less ridiculous than donning socks with a skirt.

"I run a lot," I say. "My shoes give me blisters."

"Uh-huh," she replies without an ounce of conviction. "How do you find time to run with such young children?"

"When my mom babysits," I say.

Before I have to ad lib any more lies, the doorbell rings.

"How dare you!" I hiss at Cesar when I open the door.

I usher the girls inside, coddling and kissing them so hard they wiggle away as though afraid of being smothered. When I stand back to examine them, I see that Lola is still in her pajamas and Julia's hair is unbrushed.

"Look how he brings them to me!" I say. "They were going to look so pretty! Everything was going to be perfect . . ."

When Ms. Sanchez submits her report to the court a few weeks later, she unequivocally recommends joint custody.

To buoy any oncoming sadness from losing sole custody, I e-mail Dave, a former high school teacher whom I always had a crush on. Over the years, my brother, who took one of Dave's classes, has answered many "How's Erica?" inquiries from Dave. As a lifelong bachelor old enough to be my father, Dave is the ideal rebound relationship material.

I send an innocent "Remember me?" message to Dave's faculty e-mail account; when he replies "Of course, I do! I'm your biggest fan!" I drop a dinner invite. For our first meal as equals, we agree on a charming pizzeria a few miles from the high school. Though neither of us has said the word *date*, I've dressed for one in a lacy undershirt and tight sweater.

"Do I shake your hand or hug you?" I ask the six-foot-something blondie when he walks through the restaurant door.

In response, Dave pulls my body up against his worn leather jacket and squeezes me hard.

Dave sits across from me at our corner table, nervously smoothing the butcher paper tablecloth with his hands. His smile hasn't sunk an inch since our hello.

"It's so good to see you," he gushes as I flash doe eyes over the top of my menu.

"So what're we having?" a young waiter with ash black skin and dreadlocks asks.

"I'm up for anything," I say.

"I like to eat pizza a certain way," Dave says as he fiddles with the parmesan cheese and red pepper shakers. "But sometimes waiters don't understand it."

"Try me," Dreadlocked Dude says.

"It's simple, really. I want a four-topping pizza with two criss-crossed, overlapping halves."

Dreadlock Dude cocks his head. "Huh?"

Dave swings into instructor mode. "One half is black olive; one half green olive," he says, raising his hands in front of him and visually mapping out the perfect pie. "Then you rotate the pizza one quarter to the side—at a ninety-degree angle—and top it with half-pepperoni, half-sausage."

"I think I get it," Dreadlock Dude says.

"Visualize the pizza divided into four hemispheres," Dave says, employing the geographical route. "One black olive and pepperoni, one black olive and sausage, one green olive and pepperoni, one green olive and sausage."

"Got it," Dreadlock Dude says and snatches up the menus.

I rest back against the chair and shake my head.

"I'm glad he got it, 'cause I didn't," I say.

"Should I draw a schematic on a napkin?" Dave asks.

"It might help."

Rather than be annoyed, Dave is eager to teach me a lesson. He plucks four worn crayons from their holder at the edge of the table and goes to work on the butcher paper. He's barely finished the grid when the bubbling pizza arrives.

"Solid!" Dave exclaims when he sees his dream pizza manifested.

If Dave is particular about the production of his pie, I'm even pickier about eating it.

"What are you doing?" Dave asks as I dab my saw-size slice of pizza with napkins.

"Taking off the grease," I say. I crumple the saturated orange napkins next to my plate. "It eliminates a lot of calories."

I stuff the grease-free slice into my mouth, barely keeping the toppings from avalanching off the crust.

"But the fattening cheese and high-carb dough are all right?" Dave asks.

I force my sausage-and-olive-packed mouth into a smile.

"Man, you look good," Dave says when he pushes away a plate of crusts. "We'll have to do this again sometime."

That's it? No PDA attempts? No overnight invites?

"I'd like to see where you live," I say.

Dave removes his gold-rimmed glasses and rubs the bridge of his nose.

"Err, um, I don't know . . ."

"Come on!" I say. My smile drops into an exaggerated frown. "Is it because I'm your student?"

Dave replaces his glasses and his eyes widen as though seeing me through different lenses.

"*Former* student," he says.

I lean across the table to maximize my peekaboo cleavage. *"So?"* I say. "What's it going to be?"

"My apartment is really messy," he says.

"As long as there's no porn, I promise it won't scare me off."

Dave considers my condition and swipes his car keys off the table. "Don't say I didn't warn you."

Dave takes me back to his place—very messy, no porn—and by midnight I charm the pants right off him.

"Breakfast?" Dave asks when I emerge in a swirl of steam from the bathroom.

It's our first Sunday morning together—less than a week after our first date—and Dave is at the stove, bare-chested.

I smile and shake my head in disbelief. Dave's body is a sight for my sex-starved eyes. Though he's pushing fifty, he has the musculature of a college track star. My gaze traces the edge of his six-pack abs and follows the trail of hair that drops from his belly-button to his pelvis.

"I'm starving," I say.

Dave spins a spoon around the rim of the pot and pours a thick river of oats, apple chunks, and walnuts into a bowl.

"Cinnamon?" he asks.

"Sure."

"I love spices," he says as he shakes a powdery storm over the oatmeal. "They give so much but cost so little calorically."

Dave dribbles vanilla soy milk atop both bowls while I scout out spoons.

"What's up with your silverware?" I ask. "Nothing matches."

"Ah . . ." Dave steps up behind me and rests his chin on my shoulder. "There's a secret to the spoons."

I half-turn my head and raise my eyebrows.

"I collect them," he says, smoothing down my wet hair. "As souvenirs." Dave picks up the shiniest spoon in the drawer. "This one, for example, is from our dinner the other night."

"So you *steal* spoons," I say.

Dave spins me around and clasps his hands behind my hips. I

rest my head on his bare chest and breathe in the scents of sweat and sex.

"Only memorable ones."

Kleptomania isn't Dave's only flaw; when it comes to eating, he has a slew of oddball behaviors.

His hot sauce collection is so large it takes up the entire kitchen countertop, he insists on Grey Poupon at every meal, and he dedicates Sunday evenings to an elaborate preparation of turkey roll-ups meant to last for a week's worth of lunches.

"Don't put that there," Dave says one evening as I replace a packet of cold cuts in the fridge. "There's a system."

Dave is a devotee of The Zone diet, which advocates eating minimeals every three hours. The diet requires a specific ratio of protein to complex carbs and healthy fats in order to balance blood sugar and promote even-keeled emotions.

"Protein on top," he explains, moving the turkey slices to their proper place. "Carbs in the middle, and healthy fats in the crisper."

"So *that's* how you stay so thin," I say.

"Eat to live," he says. "Not the other way around."

Though Dave doesn't eat for enjoyment, his appetite for sex is excessive—and overenthusiastic. After a few broken condoms, I decide to get back on birth control.

The patch is all the rage, but once I'm on it, the body that had been slimming down—thanks to an excess of stress and sex—starts to fill out again. Within two cycles, I gain fifteen pounds. I'm hungry all the time, assaulted by odd carbohydrate cravings—for sugary cereals, for bread, even dried fruit.

My latest obsession is coffee ice cream—topped with slivered almonds, chunks of Heath bar, and caramel drizzle—from Cold

Stone Creamery. As long as I share sweets with my sweetie, I figure the calories don't count.

"You're going to love this!" I say as I scoop up two bowls of ice cream.

Dave smirks and pushes his bowl away. "You didn't bring this for me," he says. "You just wanted an excuse to eat ice cream."

Damn Dave. He's right, but couldn't he pretend to have a sweet tooth?

"Besides," he says, pulling a rainbow-colored container from the freezer. "I'm a sherbet man."

"Why eat something that tastes like fruit?" I ask. "Just eat the fruit."

"Why eat something that tastes like coffee?" he shoots back. "Just drink the coffee."

We glare at one another in a sugary standstill.

I transfer Dave's rejected ice cream into my bowl.

"I can't believe you're going to eat all that," he says as I shove a gooey spoonful into my mouth.

"Love me, love my ice cream," I say. "You can keep your sorry excuse for dessert."

Dave serves himself a plum-size scoop of fruity fluorescent goo.

"That's it?" I ask.

"If you eat when you're not hungry," he says. "How do you know when you're full?"

That evening, Dave's gaze sears through me in a way it never has before. I react in a novel way, too, and furiously stuff my face though my stomach aches for me to stop. Each spoonful of softening ice cream, each toffee-infused crunch of Heath bar between my teeth, each swirl of melted caramel is a silent fuck-you to the man who wants to deny me pleasure.

Yet as much as Dave criticizes my sweet tooth, he supports it. I often unpack my gym bag at the Y and find a Snickers bar nestled inside my running shoes. I don't particularly like candy bars but if I have them, I eat them, often on the drive home from my workout.

"Please don't put chocolate in my bag anymore," I beg Dave. "It undoes all my hard work at the gym."

He substitutes Nature Valley granola bars instead.

"These have just as many calories as a Snickers bar," I whine.

He moves on to walnuts.

"No more nuts," I say.

"Why not?" Dave asks.

I can't explain my urge to eat unsalted nuts—they're flavorless, after all—yet I toss them by the handful down my throat like fat-free popcorn.

"Because I eat them all in one sitting," I say.

"The key is moderation."

"The one thing I am incapable of."

When it comes to portion control, Dave trumps me every time.

"Enough is as good as a feast," he often reminds me.

For me, there's never enough. I'm increasingly preoccupied with how often I eat, what I eat, when I will eat again.

My appetite isn't the only thing out of whack. The patch is messing with my menstrual cycle, too. A red-tinged discharge leaks from between my legs all day, every day. When I tell Dave I want off the patch, he agrees that the incessant bleeding is annoying.

"Not only that," I say, spooning a big glop of peanut butter onto a graham cracker. "The patch is making me fat."

Dave raises an eyebrow; on such a thin man, every expression is chisel-sharp. His eyebrows could talk.

"Yeah," he says, biting into a Golden Delicious. "I'm sure it's the patch."

My healthcare provider doesn't believe my fattening birth control theory, either.

"Some women think that being on birth control is an excuse to overeat," Nurse McCormack, a sixty-something woman with mousy facial features, says. "When they pay attention to their caloric intake, however, they see that it's not the hormones causing the weight gain."

"Well, I want off it."

Nurse McCormack shrugs. "It's your body."

As soon as she leaves the room, I reprimand myself for my carelessness.

Last chance, I tell my body. *If you don't slim down on a hormone-free existence, you're going back on the diet track.*

When Dave and I celebrate my twenty-fourth birthday, he surprises me—though not with a cake.

"Is this a joke?" I ask Dave as I hold up the present I've just unwrapped.

"I thought it would be funny," Dave says.

"Ha ha."

Dave's smile fades. "You like reading pop culture."

"French Women Don't Get Fat?"

"The author was on NPR," he says as though this might redeem the purchase.

"Well, in that case . . ." I say and roll my eyes.

Dave is practically a diet expert himself. He's especially talented at restricting affection.

"How 'bout I come over?" I ask over the phone one Tuesday.

"It's a school night," Dave says.

"So?"

"So I have to get things ready for class."

"Five out of seven nights of the week are school nights," I say. "Am I only going to see you on the weekends now?"

"I'm just tired," Dave says. "I want to catch up on my sleep."

"Me, too," I say. "That's the point. We can sleep *together.*"

"I'd rather not," he says.

I hang up the phone flabbergasted. How could Dave choose sleep over sex with me?

That night, as I prepare for bed alone, I examine my naked body in the mirror. Being off birth control has quelled the carb cravings and I've dropped down to 135 pounds, but my body is still voluptuous. Too big. Too round. Too *much*.

I slap my stomach hard, as though spanking a misbehaving child.

It's obvious what's happening: I'm getting fat, so Dave's pulling back.

I can't control Dave's neediness—or lack thereof—but I can control my body's. I can rein in my appetite, be it for commitment or coffee ice cream.

The Body Project is back on active status.

chapter seven

Help Wanted

My official title at Teen Transformation (TT), where I'm employed part-time, is residential care counselor—aka glorified babysitter—for mentally ill adolescents.

Teenagers are tough enough when they're sane; the ones I work with are off the wall. Some even experience hallucinations and homicidal urges. I like the anorexics and bulimics the best because I can relate to their struggles.

"It's freezing!" Maggie moans from the backseat of the van. At five feet, eight inches and 115 pounds, Maggie is always cold. At least she heeded my advice to be proactive and bundled up today. Maggie zips her puffy parka closed and flips the fur-lined hood over her head. She looks like an emaciated walrus.

I steer the twelve-seater van that screams *lunatics on board!* into a space at the end of the Super Target parking lot. Friday afternoons at the treatment center are so laid back that ho-hum errands become field trips.

"What do you want to look at?" I ask as Maggie and a half dozen other adolescents head toward the entrance.

"Foooood," the teenage Morticia Addams says. Maggie doesn't speak so much as whispers, albeit in the raspy tone of an emphysemic grandmother. All that regurgitation must have damaged her larynx.

Maggie exhibits other trademark signs of self-torture: weakened from the extended loss of electrolytes—the result of puking on cue one too many times—she shuffles around like a robot whose batteries are about to run out. Her long black hair hangs like limp noodles from her scalp, her alabaster skin reveals a river of blue veins beneath, and eyeliner exaggerates her vacant glare.

"Food?" I ask, whipping my head her way. I've never seen Maggie eat more than a fruit roll-up or a handful of Skittles.

"Yeah, food."

The gust of air from the automatic doors whips Maggie's unkempt hair across her face. She brushes the curtain of bangs from her eyes.

I sigh as I take in the newly renovated supermarket Mecca. Slushies in unnatural colors churn in plastic cases, nacho cheese bubbles in a metal vat, and the bitter scent of Starbucks Sumatra wafts over me from the food court.

"I didn't think Target could get any better," I say. "And then they added groceries."

Though I'm just as fucked up about food as Maggie is, at work I pretend to be completely free of psychological defects. On my off days, however, I troll the aisles of Super Target for fun; a few hours of staring and salivating at the food I no longer eat is like pornography for my deprived palate.

This unusual shopping addiction is subsuming my life. I grocery shop every day, sometimes twice a day; when I'm not buying food, I plan and prepare my meals. At any given time, I can enumerate how many bags of prewashed lettuce, how many cucumber slices, how many pounds of grilled chicken, are in my fridge. I keep tally on my food supply with the eye of a Wall Street stockbroker. Like the Dow Jones, when the numbers dip too low, I panic. My bank statements attest to this obsession: all my checking card purchases are groceries—or gas to drive to the grocery store. In other words, I spend all my money on fuel.

Maggie and I start in the packaged snacks aisle.

"Arg," Maggie huffs after a few minutes of shelf-scanning. "I can't find what I want."

"What are you looking for?" I ask in my perkiest tone. "I'll help you."

Maggie's eyes fixate on the space just above my shoulder; her sunken stare has a ghostly quality to it. She looks like she is about to drop from low blood sugar.

"I can't describe it," she says, slowly turning from one side of the aisle to the other. She staggers around the corner. I gaze at the plethora of granola bars, fascinated by the concept of food engineered to taste like other food, as though the goal were to confuse one's taste buds.

Someone's hot, sour breath spreads across the back of my neck. I spin around to find Maggie clutching a bag of pizza-flavored Goldfish crackers.

"One dollar," the zombie wannabe says with as much enthusiasm as a newly widowed woman.

"What a deal!" I say.

Maggie adds a can of SpaghettiO's and a stick of Starbursts to her plastic basket. "Can we go now?" she asks.

We round up the rest of the kids and return to the van. Maggie's barely munched a school of fluorescent orange fish when she exclaims, "Blech!"

"Don't you like them?" I ask.

"I'm lactose intolerant," she says.

"So?" I ask.

"So the bag says these are made with cheese and cheese is milk."

"I don't think it's real cheese," I say.

"It still counts," Maggie says. She drops the crackers back in her Target bag as though they were fish food.

I've never heard that excuse before. Most of the anorexics at TT claim to be vegetarians so they don't have to eat the greasy institutional meat. I file the lactose intolerance cop-out in my brain for future use.

"Can you open the snack cupboard?" Maggie asks later. The three celery stalks and thumbprint of peanut butter she dubbed dinner didn't fill her up. I'd like to call her on her ridiculous diet, but as my supervisor, Stefan, always says, "We don't power struggle with clients over food. Leave that up to their therapists."

Snacks are stored behind locked doors, to which only staff have access. Because many of TT's clients come from abusive homes, where food was withheld as punishment, they use food to self-soothe. Keeping snacks under lock and key is meant to teach moderation.

That is the theory.

In practice, TT is a psychotic fat farm. The overabundance of food, combined with boundless adolescent appetites, means that someone is always eating. Meals are brought in from a cafeteria at the agency's headquarters. Twice a day, The Food Lady, a rotating roster of women with coolers, arrives and restocks the center. Though they are supposed to meet nutritional guidelines, most meals are carb-heavy. Even the vegetable selection—sweet creamed corn, baby carrots, peas, mashed potatoes—is pure starch. The meat is always breaded, fried, or drowning in gravy.

Even the building's architecture encourages overindulgence: the kitchen is smack in the middle of the house, a thoroughfare between the boys' and girls' wings. Within weeks of arriving at the treatment center, the average client gains twenty pounds, suffers excruciating acne breakouts, and unpredictable mood swings.

"Can you pass me the Tootsie Rolls?" Maggie asks as we lean against the open cupboard doors.

Clients are allowed to buy junk food, though they don't amass much booty with the measly allowances they earn doing chores around TT. What goodies they do get they protect like the newest iPod incarnation in individual plastic buckets stored in the snack cupboard.

I hand Maggie her five-pound bag of Tootsie Rolls. She cradles the bag to her chest like a beloved stuffed animal and plops down on a living room couch. While we watch the latest teen comedy, Maggie unwraps the candies one by one, chewing as sloppily as an old lady with dentures.

"Holy moly, Maggie!" another client exclaims from across the room. "That's a lot of candy!"

Maggie drops her chin to her chest.

"It makes me feel better . . ." she whimpers.

I understand. Though I despise Tootsie Rolls—in my mind, they're akin to eating hard hamster turds—their one redeeming quality is portion control. Each mini Tootsie Roll has twelve calories. When I indulge, I usually stop at five, total—not five pounds. These teens have no self-restraint.

But Maggie has a trick up her oversize sweatshirt sleeves.

"Can I go to the bathroom?" she asks, passing the bag of baby chocolates back to me for safekeeping.

This is the latest counselor responsibility—potty patrol. The higher-ups have installed locks on the bathroom doors to prevent the bulimics from using the restrooms unaccompanied. Clients with a history of on-demand ralphing have to wait forty-five minutes after eating to use the bathroom. With a staff member outside the door, most are too embarrassed to barf up their binges.

I look at the clock, then back at Maggie. We both know what I'm thinking, but I also know how quickly the guilt sinks in after a sugar overdose.

"Can I?" Maggie asks, gasping as though this were her last breath.

One of TT's former clients was so determined to purge, she vomited in her dresser drawers; her creative technique worked for a few days, until the stench wafted across the living room and into the staff office. If Maggie's going to upchuck anyway, she might as well do so in the toilet.

"Sure," I say.

Later that night, after I sign off on Maggie's "awesome afternoon!" in her daily log, I notice a new inspirational sign on the filing cabinet door:

> *A Native American grandfather was talking to his grandson:*
> *"Sometimes I feel as though there are two wolves fighting in my heart. One wolf is the mean, rude, and violent one. The other is the kind, polite, and passionate one."*
> *"Which wolf will win?" the grandson asked.*
> *The grandfather replied, "The one I feed."*

And if I starve them both, I wonder, who will win then?

Exercise is a multitasking coping mechanism: It inoculates me from appetite, boosts my body image, and floods me with endorphins. But like any addiction, I have to continually increase my exertion to experience the same mellow high. Every time I run, I add another lap around the lake.

"We can walk!" is my new mantra.

"Wanna go to Dairy Queen?" Dave asks one evening after we finish our dinner salads.

I do, but I'm not allowed to eat ice cream—unless I exercise beforehand.

"We can walk!" I say, disappearing into my closet to change out of my flirty skirt and into loose pants and tennis shoes.

The DQ is a mile away, but Dave doesn't balk. On the evenings we get together, he skips his three-mile runs, so he's just as eager as I am to get in extra exercise.

"Slow down," Dave says as I take off down Cliff Road, arms pumping with the drive of an Olympic speed-walker. Doesn't he get it? I'm preemptively burning off the 230 calories in my chocolate-mint dilly bar.

"Dinner at El Loro?" Dave suggests another night.

"We can walk!"

"It's going to rain, Erica," he moans as he peers out the window.

"Those meteorologists are full of shit," I say, selectively ignoring the big black clouds in the sky.

There isn't even a path to walk *on* to get to our favorite Mexican restaurant, but that won't deter me. Dave and I play chicken with the rush-hour traffic for the entire two miles.

"I guess we won't do that again," Dave says when we collapse into a booth at the back of the restaurant.

Maybe *he* won't.

"Still up for a movie later?" Dave asks.

"We can walk!"

"Erica," Dave sighs. "It'll be past ten when the movie gets out. I don't think we'll want to walk then."

"Cold weather's coming soon; we'll be housed up long enough. We should walk while we still can."

My daughters' lives are as restricted by my diet as I am. As my weight drops to 125 pounds, my motivation to bond with them wanes. Though I can haul my ass to the Y up to three times a day, I don't have the energy to schlep two toddlers to the wading pool.

Necessity is the mother of invention and the girls are very clever; sometimes, they put on their swimsuits and belly-flop from the couch to the carpet, pretending to be swimming.

One morning, blessed with an inexplicable burst of energy, I hurriedly bathe my daughters, eager to embark on a day of unscheduled emptiness. When I pull Julia's duck towel over her head, she scowls at me.

"You need to be a better mommy," she says.

Julia is not even three years old. She hardly speaks and when she does, she guilt trips me. I feel like the lowest form of life on the planet.

The only care-taking activity I'm good at is grocery shopping. In the name of easy indoor activities, we take field trips to Super Target. After all, nothing quiets a preschooler's cry like a wild ride in a squeaky cart and a free frosted cookie.

Julia, with her razor-sharp memory, recites the list: "Toothpaste, Kleenex, Pampers, and . . . cookie!"

"Cookie?" I ask, feigning forgetfulness.

Julia squeals.

"What do you like more: being with me or getting treats?" I ask.

Julia considers my question with a furrowed brow; I want to believe that my query is too complicated for her pint-size brain.

"Treats!" Julia finally says. "Yes! Treats!"

That's what I thought.

Lola bops along to easy listening music as we swerve our cart through the store. We stop at the bakery and peruse the cake-decorating book. Julia fantasizes about which character will top her next birthday cake, unable to decide between Barbie and Strawberry Shortcake.

A baker hands the girls sugar cookies with fluorescent frosting. Julia and Lola devour every last bite; they don't even have the decency to drop a chunk on the floor so I can pick it up and eat it when they're not looking.

Now that I'm not even rewarded with a cookie crumb for my maternal efforts, the outings stop all together.

Thank goodness for Cesar. Every other day, I rest assured knowing the girls are getting quality parenting at his house. The visitation schedule has its upside for me, too: kid-free days mean playtime for Mommy and her man.

"Look at this!" I say to Dave one evening. I open a kitchen cupboard and point out a wrapped Reese's peanut butter cup. "I've had this chocolate for three weeks and I'm not even tempted to eat it!"

"Good for you!" he exclaims, as though I've just been awarded my doctorate in dieting. He wraps his arms around my waist and kisses me. My theory has proven true: The slimmer my body, the hornier my boyfriend.

Dave couldn't be more pleased about my diet—now neither of us is eating. More important, we aren't eating *out*. To ensure we stay in The Zone, Dave cooks most of our meals.

"It's so pretty!" I say when Dave slides a card-deck slab of seafood on my plate. I've never eaten salmon before, but I adore its pastel pink hue. I wolf down the filet as daintily as possible. "Delicious!" I exclaim.

The next morning, my stomach starts to gurgle; for the next twenty-four hours, I remain chained to the toilet bowl.

When the deluge subsides, I look in the mirror, aghast. For the first time in my life, my stomach is completely flat! Apparently, diarrhea is the secret weight-loss wonder. A viral nudge was all I needed to obtain the torso of a *Sports Illustrated* cover girl.

A few days later, I browse the incontinence aisle of Walgreens. Laxatives are tucked among the at-home enemas, the detox supplements, and organic cleanse shakes. If I can buy the pills over the counter, how bad can they be? "It doesn't *make* you go; it makes it easier to go"—isn't that what they say in the commercials? Nothing wrong with making my life easier.

Correctol is my drug of choice. Is it the feminine hue I adore? Do I identify with the picture of a serene blond woman on the package? Or is it the promise embedded in the brand name? *Correct-All.*

My heart quickens as I free the pretty pink pills from their foil wrapper. I pop each pill in my mouth and the crispy coating dissolves into a sweet sludge on my tongue, clunks down my throat, and lands with a thud in my gut.

At the eight-hour mark, the pharmaceutical activation is evident in my mood. I become explosively irritable and, not unlike my toddler daughters in the throes of toilet training, I scuttle off bashfully to shit my guts out.

Like bulimics who barf, I can look into the toilet when I am done and identify what I've purged from my body. Cashews? Check. Raisins? Check. Spinach? Check. I determine my weight-loss progress by the streaks and Jackson Pollock patterns on the pot. The dirtier the bowl, the cleaner my bowels.

The threat of another Minnesota winter looms and I'm terrified about maintaining my current level of fitness.

"I want this one," I say to the Arnold Schwarzenegger look-alike manning the fitness store counter. I hold up a print-out picture of my dream treadmill.

"I don't think so," he says with a pity-packed smile. "That's professional grade. The other models are good enough for recreational runners."

Arnold motions to a wall of flimsy-looking treadmills from no-name companies. They look so unstable that a child's trot could topple them.

"I want the best," I say.

Arnold leads me to the LifeFitness T-9i and rattles off a script about the cushioned deck, the extra-wide belt, the high-speed motor. It is a monster of a machine; sturdier, sleeker, bigger than it looks at the YMCA.

The price is also higher than I expect: $6,500.

"Wow," I say. "My first two cars *combined* didn't cost that much!"

"I told you," he says. "They're pricey."

But I have my mind set on *this* treadmill. I've already cleared the entire corner of my bedroom for it. How much is a great run worth?

"Think of it this way," Arnold says. "You're not wasting your money; you're *investing* in your body."

I hesitate for a moment—max.

"If you can get me this on credit," I say. "I'll take it."

Arnold shakes my hand and arranges a delivery date forty-eight hours away. I'm so psyched about my purchase that I celebrate with a run. The sun is at its noontime peak when I pull up to Blackhawk Lake. Gravel crunches beneath my feet, mild September air wicks the sweat from my skin, crinkly copper leaves flutter down around me. As I bound down the last hill, endorphins flood my nervous system and overwhelm me with a sense of unity with the universe.

It is ecstasy. It is almost orgasmic.

Yes. I will pay anything to feel this good every day.

Anything.

Up to this point, the exercise feels empowering. Proactive. Healthy. As if I really were doing it in preparation for cabin fever. Then the mini-binges begin, and exercise becomes my form of punishment for lack of willpower.

One afternoon, half an hour shy of the end of my shift at TT, I get ants in my pants. Is it my impending date with Dave that unnerves me so? Lately I've been fantasizing about breaking up, not making love, with Dave.

Whatever ambiguity that has bubbled up must be stuffed down. Thanks to the Food Lady, I have medication at hand. Along with her afternoon drop-off of frozen waffles and Malt-o-Meal cereal, she's left the staff an extra-extra-large bag of peanut M&M's.

"Tear and share," the label reads.

So I do.

Each handful of nutty chocolate soothes me with sweetness.

I cannot stop.

I'm so focused on chomping, I barely hear the heavy footsteps ascending the stairs.

Instead of embarrassment, I'm relieved; the universe has intervened on my behalf.

I fold the top of the bag down, shove it back into the cupboard, and plop down at my desk.

"How's it going, Erica?" my supervisor, Stefan, asks as he settles into a chair beside me.

"Good," I reply, nonchalantly running a finger around my lips as though applying ChapStick. I pray there are no brown smears on my face or slivers of peanut between my teeth.

"Do you like my shoes?" he asks, lifting up one foot and showing off a plain white tennis shoe.

"Are they new?"

"They're magnetic," he says as he slips one off. When he hands it to me, I almost drop it—the shoe weighs at least five pounds. "They're supposed to rebalance my energy."

I try, unsuccessfully, to suppress a giggle.

"Who knows?" he muses. "They might work."

I have my own method to rebalance energy.

All those peanut M&M's are rolling around like rocks in my gut, so as soon as my shift ends, I rush home and jump on the treadmill. I run as though a flame nips at my heels, as though pursued by a rabid dog.

Exercise eclipses everything. I wake daily before dawn, run ten miles, do dozens of ab exercises. The world receives the leftovers of my energy. The tongue of the treadmill belt swallows my soul.

chapter eight

Higher Education

As my body fat drops, my brain atrophies.

I struggle through my courses at school, but because I'm on the fast track to finish my master's, I double up on classes on the weekends the girls are with Cesar. This is a feat so rare my classmates gawk in amazement.

"How do you do it?" they ask.

"I'm Super Woman," I reply.

But Super Woman is slowly being brainwashed by her diet. The margins of my notebooks are filled with caloric calculations and motivational scribblings like *Nothing tastes as good as being thin feels!*

For my final paper in the diversity course, I have to write about a personal prejudice that might interfere with my ability to be a compassionate counselor. Most of my classmates write their papers on race, nationality, religion, or sexual preference.

I write my paper on how much I hate fat people.

For five double-spaced pages I rant about how there is no excuse for *anyone* to be overweight. People have a choice about what to put in their mouths, I argue, and being fit is simply a matter of self-discipline and willpower. My conclusion: Obesity is a coverup for uncomfortable issues. People hide behind their blubber, plain and simple.

"Of course," I concede at the end of the essay, "if I had a fat client, I would put my judgments aside and focus on his or her psychological healing."

My professor returns my paper with the comment, "It doesn't sound like you have fully dealt with your prejudice yet."

What do I care? I still earn an A.

In anticipation of the last weekend of classes this term, the professors organize a potluck and ask each student to bring a food item representative of their cultural background. Being Swedish and Norwegian—and completely disconnected from my culture, not to mention food—I opt for the easy way out.

The only Scandinavian bakery in the city is oddly empty for a Friday morning, but the shelves are packed with fresh, sweet-smelling pastries. I gape at the daintily decorated doughnuts, the towers of Swedish wedding cake, and the doughy shortbread cookies.

I choose the blandest, most boring offering: a loaf of bread. I wouldn't want to be tempted to *eat* at the potluck after all.

My stomach starts rumbling as soon as I sit down in class that evening. The party room next door is rife with scents of home-cooked dishes: cheesy tuna casserole, lamb kebabs, fried chicken, buttery mashed potatoes and gravy.

These are just the entrées.

The desserts—deep-dish apple pie, fudge brownies, frosted cake—smell even better.

I unwrap my loaf of bread, drop it on the table like a concrete block, and slap a plastic knife beside it. Eyes averted, I shoot out of the party room; one more whiff of food and I might attack the banquet table.

In the adjacent classroom, I try to ignore the stream of students returning with heaping platefuls of food. My envy gives way to anger, and I seethe silently at everyone else's ability to eat.

"You're skipping the potluck?" a professor, Jack, gawks as he passes by me with a few fried chicken wings.

"I already ate with my family," I lie.

My dinner that night was a handful of pistachios and a string cheese.

"There's always dessert!" he says with a wide smile. "Go grab a plate before the lecture starts."

I want to eat, God I want to; my mouth salivates, my nose sucks down the scents, but I can't. Something bad is bound to happen if I indulge. Just one pleasurable bite and I'd never be able to stop. I'd binge until I burst.

"I'll go check out the selection," I say.

I bolt for the bathroom.

The graduate school's restrooms are an egomaniac's haven with their wall-length mirrors. Tonight, I don't scrutinize my body as usual; I give myself a pep talk instead.

"Sure, you can eat that potluck food," I say to my reflection. "But you won't be able to keep this body."

I smooth my hands over my loose size 2 pants.

"All those people in that classroom, stuffing their faces, are over-weight. You are the thinnest person in that room and the reason why is because you know how to say no."

I return to my seat just as my classmates toss their empty paper plates into the trash can. The eating portion of the evening now over, I'm safe.

The potluck continues to haunt me on Saturday; all the nonper-ishable items are still spread out on the banquet table, meant to sustain us through Sunday evening. I restrict myself to the food in my lunch bag, but as the late afternoon slump sneaks in, I can't concentrate on the class discussion. All I can think about is the potluck.

I squirm and shift in my seat, cross and uncross my legs, chanting *Focus, focus, focus!* but the food woos me with a siren song that only I can hear.

During the next break, I linger over the half-eaten treats in aluminum pans.

"I know you want some cake, Erica," Professor Jack says, waving a knife over the pastry.

I gaze at the squiggles of icing and admire the rainbow sprinkles around the edge.

"Ok," I say. "One little piece."

He slides a corner of the cake onto a plate for me. I eat it with anal precision, crumb by crumb, one ridged arc of buttercream at a time.

You're going to pay for this, a voice whispers as I toss my empty plate into the garbage.

As soon as class adjourns, I retreat to the park across the street, and walk lap after lap around the pond until my legs turn to rubber.

"I see you're not registered for winter semester," another professor, Sam, says before we all disperse on Sunday.

"Nope," I reply. "I need some R and R."

"I really think you should reconsider," he says. "One semester often snowballs into a leave of absence."

"Don't worry," I say, remembering all the bureaucratic hoops I had to jump through to be readmitted to the program. I wouldn't dare jeopardize my career, especially with young children to support. "I'll be back."

"What are you going to do for two whole months?" a classmate queries.

I cock my head in consideration. I don't have plans, per se. All I know is I'm exhausted. With the girls, my part-time position at TT, and the divorce, I'm beyond overwhelmed and completely worn out.

"I'm going to read," I say. "For pleasure!"

Bullshit.

The books I read over the next eight weeks are not for pleasure;

they are as instructional as any textbook I've tackled in my master's program. I work my way through *The Thin Commandments*, *Thin for Life*, *The Runner's Diet*, *The Maker's Diet*, *The South Beach Diet*, and *The Sports Nutrition Handbook*, scrounging for the secret that will transform my body.

I read until I'm cross-eyed; when I tire of books, I go to the Internet instead. Websites offer lengthy lists of alternatives to eating: chewing gum, brushing and bleaching teeth, making collages of fashion models, and, of course, exercise. I read up on how many laxatives one can ingest without killing herself—up to forty a day!— what foods are the best diuretics—grapes, asparagus, coffee—and how to burn 100 extra calories per day simply through fidgeting.

All that reading exhausts my brain, so I schedule a stay at a secluded spa in southern Minnesota while the girls spend the weekend with Cesar. My plan is to massage, exfoliate, and manicure my stress away, to make friends with my body, to purge internal pain through healing touch. An emotional enema.

The trip begins with a bang. Fumbling my way through unmarked turnoffs and pitch-black bypasses, I get lost twice. When I reach my destination, I'm disappointed to see the spa is not the state-of-the-art facility I expected; instead, it is an old house with an apartment-style two-story building on the side.

The living room in the main house is dimly lit by Tiffany lamps, and a fireplace crackles in the corner. A woman in a ratty armchair looks up from her book as I close the door behind me. I smile and steel myself for forced sociality. I'm grateful when she returns to her reading without uttering a word. I didn't come all this way to *interact* with anyone; I want to be completely, totally alone.

A short woman with unnaturally orange curls and a freckled face saunters in.

"Welcome," she says. "You must be Erica. I've been expecting you."

"How many other people are here?" I ask.

"There's a bridal party here this weekend," she says cheerily.

A bridal party? Great.

"Come," she says. "I'll give you a tour."

The innkeeper leads me down a set of stairs and into a waiting room, where a large white board covers one wall.

"This is the schedule," she says, indicating the hand-written chart of names spaced in forty-five-minute intervals. Each woman, it appears, has been assigned a suffocatingly tight itinerary of beauty procedures.

"You mean I don't get to choose my own appointment times?" I ask.

"No." She smiles weakly at me. "Our aestheticians like to have back-to-back appointments."

I prefer my facials in the morning and massages at night, ideally with a nap in between. When I trace my name across the board, I discover my schedule is the exact opposite of what I want.

The innkeeper turns to another board.

"And this is the daily menu," she says.

The words blur before my eyes; I can barely make out *oatmeal*, *pasta*, and *casserole*.

The innkeeper reads the shock on my face.

"The meals are very hearty," she reassures me with pride.

"I thought I could order what I want," I say through clenched teeth. I can't relax unless I'm in control of what goes into my mouth.

"No, dear," she says, shaking her head. "We only have one cook, and she makes one meal for everyone."

"Can I eat in my room?"

"Our meals are family-style. We eat together at the dining room table."

I never eat in front of strangers; hell, I rarely eat in front of my family. I cringe at the thought of an hour with a perky bridal party surrounded by stacks of pancakes and mounds of hash browns.

"What time is breakfast?" I ask as my shoulders tighten and rise up to my earlobes.

"Eight A.M."

Eight A.M. on vacation? What happened to sleeping in?

"If you miss a meal, there's always fruit," she says, pointing to a bowl packed with a questionable collection of Red Delicious apples, thick-skinned oranges, and bruised bananas.

"Is there a grocery store nearby?" I ask.

The innkeeper looks at me as though I were mentally ill. "There's one in town, but there's no refrigerator in your room, dear."

If I want to run before breakfast—and I *have* to run beforehand, because I can't eat until I create a caloric deficit—I'll have to get up at 5:00 A.M.

"And the gym is . . . where?"

"We don't have a gym, dear. We do group hikes when the weather's nice."

Where will I run if it rains? I bet there isn't a single treadmill in the entire hick town. Why didn't I check this out earlier?

My heart picks up its pace. This haven is a runner's hell. This isn't a spa—it's a fatty farm.

"You're tired," she says. "Let me take you to your room."

I slog along as the innkeeper leads me outside, across the lawn and up to the second floor of the apartment-style building. She opens a rickety screen door and I almost double over with disappointment. The room is lovely—if you're into geriatric-style decor. The twin bed is covered with a frumpy quilt and bookmarked on each end by a metal frame. There are doilies everywhere.

"I'll let you settle in."

After the innkeeper leaves, I pace the room. It's quiet, yes, but not in a meditative way. It's an eerie, haunted-house kind of silence. The windows creak when the wind blows, the bedside lamp buzzes with electricity, and the furnace clangs before heat exits the vents.

In an instant, I sprint back to the main house.

"Is there a problem?" the innkeeper asks.

"Yes," I say, breathless. "This isn't what I thought it would be."

"What did you think it would be?" she asks, crossing her arms.

"Not this," I say. "I'm sorry, I can't stay."

"Can I ask why?"

Do I even know why? Because I'm afraid to sleep alone in a strange place. Because I'm terrified of the bridal party interaction. Because I might miss a run, or breakfast, or both.

The innkeeper wouldn't understand. No one would.

I shrug in response and shoot back out the door. My car tires spit gravel as I blaze down the driveway, fumbling for my cell phone.

"Up for an overnight?" I say as soon as Dave answers.

"How soon can you get here?" he asks.

I speed all the way back to the Twin Cities and burst through Dave's door. He's fresh out of the shower and we fall into a horny heap on the bed. I fuck like my life depends on it, but my heart isn't in it. I use my body—no, abuse my body—and lose myself in the sex. Each orgasm erases an unwelcome emotion—anxiety, fear, insecurity. I fuck not to feel better, but to feel nothing at all.

"Do you think I'm getting too thin?" I ask Dave one night as we spoon dispassionately in bed.

"Is this a trick question?" he asks.

"No, I'm serious."

"I think you look hot," he says, taking one of my butt cheeks in his hand. "You're not thin, you're *slim*. There's a difference."

"Which is?"

"Slim is sexy. It means you take care of yourself. Anyone can be thin, but you're taut and tight."

I consider his distinctions.

"Do *you* think you're too thin?" he asks.

"No," I say. "Though I've been really tired lately and all I think about is food."

"You're a smart girl," he says. "You'd know if something was wrong, right?"

"I guess so . . ."

"I think," Dave says, pulling me closer, my skin stretching translucent across my hip bones. "That *you* feel better when you're slim."

But I don't feel better.

I am constantly covered with goose bumps. My gums recede and bleed. The ladder of bones on my chest cracks when I stretch. My knee clicks like a car turn signal. My stomach composes impromptu symphonies that provoke stares from strangers. My bowels belch and hiss and gurgle at random. A mild rotting scent seeps from my pores; even freshly showered, I never feel clean. My brain spins thoughts so scattered I run around like a crazed squirrel.

I treat my daughters like hairy beanbags, plopping them in front of the TV for entire days while I read diet books and try not to think about eating. The food I do eat is all low-calorie, often followed by a handful of laxatives.

I am beyond exhausted.

"What's wrong with you?" Dave asks as he rolls over in bed one morning.

"I can't decide what to do," I say, craning my neck to check the time on the clock radio. "There are too many choices."

Dave cocks an eyebrow at me. "What are you talking about? It's Sunday. Stay in bed with me."

"But Sunday is the day I go to church with my mom," I explain. "And I can't go to church until I work out."

"Why not?"

"Because if I wait too long, my workout won't be any good."

"I doubt that."

"If I leave right now, I'll have just enough time to run, shower, and get to Mass."

"Yeah," Dave says, slithering toward me. "But you'd miss out on sex with me."

I want to slap him. Is he nuts? If anything, accompanying my mother to church is on top of the priority list because it comes around only once a week at a certain time. Next on the list is running. Or is running first? The longer I take to make up my mind, the higher my anxiety climbs. Indecision spreads like a flame inside my stomach and up through my throat; I might puke from sheer vacillation. My nervous system is on overdrive; I am going to have a full-on freak-out, an epileptic-like fit.

Dave's hands begin their well-practiced choreography over my thighs.

"Dave!" I scold, pushing him away. "We can have sex anytime; running and church can't wait until later."

My boyfriend's face looks as though I just slapped him. I swear his entire self-worth is stored in his dick.

"I have to go," I say, leaping from the bed.

"Where to?"

"I don't know," I say. "I just have to go."

I end up at Lake Harriet, which is packed with weekend warriors squeezing in one last run before cold weather arrives. I'm jumping out of my skin because running, like sex, is better in the dark when my brain hovers between the asleep and awake states. Now it's light out and the path seems longer. The sun roasts me through my track suit; every single step reverberates up my legs and through my spine.

Weaving around the mediocre runners and bikers, I can't shake the feeling that an ominous presence, in Grim Reaper form, is sidling up beside me. When I try to speed up, my legs resist; they feel as heavy as concrete.

At the end of my route I collapse on a patch of brown grass to stretch. Clouds slither across the robin's-egg-blue sky; leaves with Swiss cheese holes flutter down and scratch my skin. For a moment, I touch a twinge of calm.

But just for a moment.

Then a creepy-crawly feeling infects my entire body. I don't need to run, I need to run *away*.

And I'm racing again: to the gym to shower, to Starbucks for a frappuccino, to church to meet my mother and receive a communion wafer on my tongue (which I spit out immediately in the bathroom—who knows how many calories those things have?). Seeking relief, I speed along Interstate 94 toward the outlet mall for an afternoon of retail therapy.

Pair after pair of almost-identical jeans slide on and off my legs, followed by sweat suits not truly meant for sweating in every color of the rainbow, then turtlenecks that are still too toasty to wear. I buy them all, sliding my Gap credit card across the counter with a single plea.

"Please," I say to the cashier. "Don't tell me the damage."

She doesn't. I sign the slip with my eyes half-closed, blurring the triple digit total.

I'm on the freeway again when I spot a Dairy Queen on the side of the road. It's been so long since I had ice cream, the red-and-white emblem registers like a stop sign in my brain. I swerve onto the exit ramp, run a red light, and pull into the drive-through. In an instant I'm shoveling hefty spoonfuls of a chocolate extreme Blizzard into my mouth. Brain freeze be damned, I eat so fast I barely register the moist lumps of brownie and hard shards of chocolate scraping the back of my throat as I swallow.

Back on the freeway, a voice chimes in.

How dare you ruin your run with ice cream. Do you know how many calories are in one of those things? Try 1,200. That's way more than you burned off this morning. Payback time.

I gun it to Lake Nokomis and rummage around in the trunk for my emergency stash of exercise clothes. I change in a putrid Porta Potti and take off, not even bothering with a Walkman.

It's after 7:00 P.M.; the picnic area and beach are deserted. The rain starts to fall like little wet needles on my face. I can't see the path before me. I don't care. There's no stopping now; I *must* burn off that ice cream.

Stupid, stupid, stupid, the voice chants with each slap of my foot on the blacktop. *You'd better run like hell, Bitch.*

One lap, two, three at breakneck speed. I finish soaked. I drive home shivering.

After my run—the second of the day—I shower and stand before the mirror, groping my stomach for evidence of the ice cream taking hold. Dave is on his way for an overnight. I consider drying and styling my hair. I debate about doing my makeup. I think about putting on tight jeans and a low-cut top.

But it's almost bedtime and Dave isn't worth the effort.

"Already in pj's?" he gawks when he walks through my front door.

"I'm exhausted," I say, slumping against the wall.

Running twenty-one miles in one day really takes the wind out of a girl.

Dave unloads his overnight bag from his shoulder with a scowl.

"Well, let's go to bed, then," he says.

Dave is only pretending to be compassionate. I know that as soon as we step into the boudoir, he'll do his ceremonial strut toward me, pelvis at the ready. I have to stall. I linger over a cup of cocoa, attempt to instigate an argument but fail. When I can't delay any longer, we head to my room.

I practically lunge onto the bed, bury myself between the sheets, and pull the comforter up around my chin like a cocoon.

"What's going on with you?" he asks as he slides into bed next to me.

"I'm just tired."

"Then why were you talking so much upstairs?"

I roll over and try my damnedest to look offended.

"What do you mean?"

"You're stalling," he says. "You're trying to make the time pass until it's too late to have sex."

"That's absurd," I say. "But now that you mention it, it *is* too late to have sex. I have to get up early tomorrow."

"For what?"

"To run."

Dave and I simultaneously turn our backs to one another, saturated in silence until we fall asleep.

"Don't take your coat off," Dave says the next time we get together. "We're going out."

"Where to?" I ask as he ushers me to the car.

"It's a surprise."

My heart flutters inside my chest. *This is it! He's going to pop the question!*

Two minutes later, Dave pulls to a stop in front of Dairy Queen. He turns to me, beaming with pride.

"This is it?" I ask.

Dave pulls the key from the ignition and grips the steering wheel hard.

"I'm *trying* to be spontaneous," he says through gritted teeth.

I've been putting the pressure on Dave to pop the question. What I want is a rock, not rocky road.

"I'm on a diet," I remind him. "I don't eat ice cream anymore."

"Get a MooLatte then."

"I don't drink my calories."

Dave throws up his hands.

"Well, we're here," he says. "I'm going to get a cone."

Dave stalks off and orders a boring vanilla cone. I follow and order a chocolate extreme Blizzard. If I'm going to jump off the skinny bandwagon, I'm doing so with gusto. We sit outside at a concrete picnic table, eating in silence and perfecting our eye-contact-avoidance dance. The autumn wind is so chilly, I weld my biceps to my torso as I spoon the creamy treat into my mouth.

On the outside, I'm rigid with cold; on the inside, a fiery tantrum rages.

This is an ache even ice cream can't assuage.

"You know, Erica," Dave says as we lie with our backs to one another in bed that night. "Sometimes I think this relationship isn't about you and me at all. Sometimes I think you just want to fill the husband void and I'm the most convenient man at the moment."

chapter nine

Dangling the Carat

Dave's right; I *am* looking for a husband and it's clear he's not ready for that role. If Dave avoids carrots because of their high carb content, he's even more cautious about the *other* kind of carats. There's only one thing holding me back from breaking up with him; it's called the Thirty-Degree Rule.

Each morning as I eat my prerun snack and drink my coffee, I watch the weather report on TV. If the temperature is over thirty degrees, I have to run outside. No exceptions. This is why I need Dave around. When I have the girls overnight, I depend on him to hold down the fort while I'm hoofing it outside. Though they all sleep through my run, it's comforting to know that *someone* is home in case of an emergency, not to mention the fact that leaving young children unattended is illegal.

I'm ready to cut my losses and break up with Dave, but how can I do so without bending the Thirty-Degree Rule? I consider what a Dave-free morning would be like. As long as I run before the girls wake up, no one will be the wiser. After all, in almost a year of single motherhood, no calamities have occurred. What are the chances that something would happen to my sleeping daughters during a measly ninety minutes unattended?

The first time I leave my daughters home alone at 4:30 A.M. to run outdoors, I'm so nervous I'm shaking. Though I make sure to leave a light on, I can't help but wonder: Will they stay asleep? What if Julia crawls atop a dresser and the furniture topples over? What if Lola tries to scale the staircase and falls?

Around my third mile, a fire engine with a wailing siren and flashing lights speeds by me. I stop. And watch. Is it headed toward my house? When the big red engine turns the corner—away from my street—I sigh. Then I realize that if something does happen— an impromptu inferno, for instance—I'd know by the wail of fire engines and could sprint back in no time.

I am omnipotent, after all. I can run faster than a fire engine! Knowing my daughters are waiting for me back home, I run harder than ever.

By the time I trot back toward my house, I'm free of any anxiety. In fact, I finish all the more energized from the extra adrenaline pumping through me. Who could've guessed child abandonment would be good for weight loss?

Just as my cravings waned when I stopped eating sugar, I acclimate to keeping Dave at a distance, too. I stop returning his calls, go to the movies alone, and buy single tickets for concerts we would have enjoyed together.

"I feel left out of your life," Dave complains one evening.

"I'm not leaving you out," I explain. "I'm setting up boundaries. No more overnights until we're engaged."

"You can't just change the rules like that, Erica," Dave protests.

"If you want to play house with me, you'll have to marry me," I say.

Our new routine consists of dinner salads, sex, and an episode of *Seinfeld*. Around 2:00 A.M., after the last punch line, I make Dave punch out.

"It feels wrong to leave after we have sex," Dave complains with puppy dog eyes.

"It feels wrong to share a bed with an uncommitted man," I say.

"I *am* committed."

I raise an eyebrow and open the door.

"Come on," he says, smoothing my hair back. "This is ridiculous."

"See you on Friday," I say. "Drive safe."

chapter ten

Better Than Chocolate

Both Dave and I are fed up with the feuding, so we decide to take a break. To distract myself from heartache, I throw myself headfirst into dating.

In the company of men, I convert into a giggly chatterbox who subsists off oxygen. The hormonal cocktail of infatuation knocks out my nutritional needs and the prospect of getting naked motivates me to shape up. Sex, with the right partner, doubles as a workout, so I do the wild thing as enthusiastically as any other form of exercise. There are so many ways to hook up now—online, speed dating, blind dates, professional matchmakers—I try them all. Singledom is fun—in the way auditioning contestants for a freak show would be fun—for a while.

I'm sitting on the quaint but uncomfortable bench of one of the Twin Cities' most popular lunch spots. Paul—the third Paul in as many weeks—sits across from me, nibbling on flatbread. He chatters about skiing, riding snowmobiles, and other outdoor activities I don't enjoy and don't have the funds to participate in.

"So," he says, taking a sip of his wine spritzer and erecting an eyebrow. "How is it that such a beautiful woman is still single?"

My heart sinks. Confession time.

"I'm divorced," I say, starting with the smallest of bombs about to be dropped.

He shrugs. "No biggie."

"...And I have two kids."

There's a slight dissolution of interest on his face that he replaces with a forced smile.

"Boys or girls?"

I slouch in defeat. If I had boys, at least there'd be the illusion of male bonding before the inevitable break-up.

"Girls," I say.

Paul's forehead crumples as he mentally calculates the effects of PMS to the third power.

"Hmm," he says, tossing back the rest of his drink. "How old?"

"Julia is almost three and Lola will be two in April."

"They're practically babies!"

"For the time being, yeah," I say. The certainty that the date is over incites my sassiness. "But the funny thing about kids is that they grow!"

The waiter appears and elegantly presents our plates—shepherd's pie for Paul, grilled salmon and asparagus for me.

"Anything else for you two?" the waiter asks.

"A to-go box and the bill," Paul says, taking an exaggerated glance at his Rolex. "I have to get to a meeting..."

As if my single-mother status isn't deterrent enough, soon the men I'm seeing see through *me* and uncover my wacky eating habits.

"Aren't you going to eat that?" my date asks. A man twice my age and half my height strokes his beard opposite me. As a Johnny

Cash look-alike, he's spot-on; as flavor-of-the-week, he's as bland as white bread.

I look down at my chicken pasta something or other. I already picked out and ate every chunk of grilled chicken; only cream-coated pasta tubes remain on the platter.

"I don't like carbs," I say as I squirm in the red banquette.

"Aren't you a runner?" he asks.

"Yeah."

"Runners need carbs," he says. "Eat your penne."

I feel like a child being forced to finish her Brussels sprouts. The creepy feeling that I'm on a date with my dad—no, my *step*dad—crawls up my spine.

"I told you I'm more of a salad girl."

"No, no, no," Mr. Wrong protests. "If I'm treating, you can't have salad."

My date stares me down like he's about to draw a pistol from his belt, so I steer the conversation back to his ex-wife. As he drones on about his astronomical alimony expenses, I silently pray that he won't push the dinner rolls on me. The doughy mounds lurk beneath a burgundy cloth napkin in the basket between us. Mr. Wrong pauses his diatribe on the ex and reaches for the bread.

Oh God. Oh God. Oh God.

Saved by the cell phone—Mr. Wrong's honky-tonk ring tone sends him scurrying from the table.

When the waitress appears at my side, I whisper, "We're in a hurry. Please bring the check ASAP." She smiles at me knowingly; no discussion necessary. The rotten aura of a Very Bad Date hangs in the air.

By the time Mr. Wrong returns, our dinner plates have been cleared and the check is standing at attention in its black leather folder on the table.

"That was fast," Mr. Wrong marvels. "They must be busy tonight."

*   *   *

The thinner I get, the harder it is to garner male attention.

"Do you have a body fat problem?" an exotic-looking hottie asks me in the middle of our flirtatious conversation.

"No," I want to say. "I have a *boyfriend* problem."

"I'm a little low," I say, examining the wiry veins on my arms. "But I'm working on it."

"What's happening with those biceps?" he asks, miming a squeezing motion with his fist. "Are you a bodybuilder?"

"I lift weights, yeah," I say. "But mostly I run."

Exotic Hottie looks me over with a furrowed brow. I can't tell if he's impressed or disgusted; either way, I don't land a date.

Scraping the bottom of the dating barrel, I return to my old faithful—Jeremy—who eagerly responds to my booty call. Though we haven't seen one another in ages, the first thing out of his mouth is, "You're so thin!"

"Hello to you, too," I say.

Jeremy slides a finger beneath the slack waistband of my size 2 jeans.

"You've lost a lot of weight," he says.

"I *know*," I say with an annoyed eye-roll as though we were discussing a herpes flare-up. "I bought these pants two weeks ago and they're too big already!"

I usher Jeremy through my front door. "But enough about me—want a tour?"

We head straight for the bedroom. The multiple orgasms that result from our romp are a relief—not just because they feel good, but because I thought I'd lost my mojo. The last few times I had sex, I'd been reduced to Oscar-worthy performances of pleasure. But with Jeremy, I'm on fire. I feel like a sexual Sleeping Beauty roused from slumber.

After we consummate our friendship-with-benefits, Jeremy embraces me, strokes my hair, and caresses my bony body like an adored pet. The tenderness feels foreign, almost uncomfortable, on my skin.

"Do you mind if I do something totally disgusting?" I ask.

"What do you have in mind?" Jeremy says with a glint in his eye.

"Nothing like *that*," I say, jumping out of bed and into my nightie. "I really want a scrambled egg."

"By all means."

While my egg sizzles on the stove, Jeremy leans against the counter in his boxers and bites into a Honey Crisp apple.

"Don't be surprised in the morning," I say. "I'll probably be at the gym when you wake up."

"You're okay, aren't you?" Jeremy asks, his face softening.

"What do you mean?" I ask as I scrape my egg onto a plate.

"With all the exercise, you are eating enough, right?"

"What a silly question," I say, spearing a few yellow lumps with my fork. "I eat all the time." I exaggerate my egg chewing with an open mouth.

"I've had experience with this sort of thing," he says, reminding me of his ex-wife's multiple hospitalizations for anorexia.

"Don't get all parental on me now."

"I'm not just your fuck buddy," he says. "I want to make sure you're taking care of yourself."

"I could gain a few pounds," I say as I rinse my plate. "But that's what you're here for!"

"What?"

"To stuff my turkey."

Which is exactly what we spend the entire weekend doing.

"Has anyone ever suggested to you that you might have an eating disorder?" my new dietician, Mandy, asks timidly. She is stunning with her smooth peaches-'n'-cream skin and red hair that grazes her shoulders. Her body is sturdy and strong, a perfect balance between athletic and voluptuous.

Mandy is a semi-celebrity in the dietetic world, appearing regularly on local newscasts and radio programs promoting the power of healthy eating. After hearing her "Better Foods for Better Moods" presentation, I scheduled a consultation, hoping a dietary tune-up would rid me of depression.

"An eating disorder?" I say. "No way. I had one when I was fifteen, and believe me, this is not it."

"Would you mind stepping on the scale and doing a body fat assessment just to make sure?" Mandy asks.

"Sure."

I step on the scale and Mandy slides the first block to one hundred. She nudges the smaller one past ten, then twenty, pounds.

"You've still got a ways to go," I say smugly.

The metal pendulum balances at 123 pounds. Taking into account that I've had two meals today and I'm still dressed in winter clothes, the numbers are impressive.

"Wow," I say. "That's less than I imagined."

"Let's check your body fat now." She passes me what looks like a handheld video game. "Stand with your arms apart, straight in front of you."

I do.

"This sends an electrical impulse down one side of your body and up the other, and it will tell us how much of your body is fat."

I stand very still but don't feel anything. After a moment the machine beeps, and she takes the apparatus into her hands.

"Hmm . . ." she says, jotting the numbers down and referring to a chart in her folder. "Erica, let me show you something."

Mandy uncaps a yellow highlighter and marks a few boxes on the sheet.

"Here's your height, almost five feet, eight inches, and your current weight. As you can see, you're at least five pounds under the lower limit."

I feel a bubble of pride inside me. Underweight? That's good, right?

"As for your body fat, that's where I'm really concerned. The average woman is 20 to 25 percent body fat. Fit women are around 18 percent. Professionals athletes, like figure skaters and body-builders, are around 14 percent. The minimum amount necessary for vital organ functioning and survival is 12 percent."

I nod.

She takes a deep breath and passes the chart to me. "You're twelve point four percent body fat."

I stare at the paper in disbelief. I don't think I'm that thin—I still have a postpartum kangaroo pouch hanging around my belly button.

"What does that mean?" I ask.

"You absolutely can't lose any more weight. And you need to be assessed for anorexia."

When I step onto St. Clair Avenue at dusk, Punch, a hip Italian restaurant next door to Mandy's office, is enjoying its evening flush of customers. Cars line the streets and pack the parking lot. An end-less stream of people enters and exits through its doors, carrying sleek cardboard boxes of the award-winning pizza pies.

The aroma of melted gourmet cheeses, tart tomatoes, and olive oil on fresh baked pizza crust overwhelms me. I imagine the menu: the pasta slick with pesto sauce, the snap of crispy breadsticks, and the crunch of spinach salad. For a moment, I almost invite myself to din-ner, but an increasingly menacing force inside me won't allow it.

It's Thanksgiving tomorrow, the voice reminds me. *You'll indulge then.*

Cesar gets the girls on Thanksgiving this year, so I pick up a shift at TT for the double-time pay. There are only two clients at TT today; Rodney and Ronda are talkative, polite wards of the state who don't have relatives with whom to celebrate the holiday. My coworker, Katherine, suggests we surprise them with a trip to Old Country Buffet for lunch.

"We can eat, too," Katherine says. "On the house."

As soon as we arrive at OCB, as the kids call it, we take a lap around the deep aluminum trays of steaming holiday offerings. The food doesn't look particularly appetizing, but I am—quite literally— starving. I linger over the huge squares of cornbread, the hand-carved slices of ham, the mounds of mashed potatoes, the buttery heaps of broccoli.

Armed with Mandy's insistence that I not lose any more weight, and inspired by my enthusiastic coworker and two teenagers with insanely high metabolisms, I eat with abandon.

My first three plates of meat and potatoes are only appetizers for what I really want: dessert. I stuff my face with two chocolate cookies, a slice of cheesecake, a serving of pumpkin pie, and a brownie. I eat, but don't taste, any of it.

"I won first place!" Rodney exclaims when we all lean back against the booth, uncomfortably stuffed. "I ate five plates and five desserts!"

Rodney rubs his chin inquisitively and looks around the table. "And second place goes to . . . Erica!"

I high-five him, pretending to be proud of my ability to throw back a week's worth of food in thirty minutes.

At home that evening, I stare at my bloated belly in the mirror. The self-loathing rises up in my throat faster than the gravy-laden burps.

Now you've done it, you fat pig, the voice in my head hisses. *Permission to gain weight doesn't mean you can stuff yourself with sugar.*

I open the medicine cabinet and finger the Correctol box. This is a major cleansing mission. Four pills down the hatch. *Plunk, plunk, plunk, plunk.*

I curl up on the couch and await the intestinal tsunami. Between tears—and trips to the bathroom—Mandy's words return to me: "You need to be assessed . . ."

The next day, I call the eating disorders ward at Mendota Hospital. The next available appointment isn't until mid-December, two long weeks away.

This is the moment every woman dreams of.

My heart thumps in time to the techno beat pumping through unseen speakers. Bright lights create a halo over my head and blaze down my body.

I'm not on a stage; I'm shopping. And I've just put on a pair of Express pants in a size 0 for the first time. This is no small feat; sure, I've been able to slip into the 0's at the Gap for a few months now, but Express has stricter standards for their models. Express pants are the tightest, most slim-waisted slacks in existence. And today, they not only zip up, they're too loose.

A salesgirl knocks on the dressing room door.

"How are you doing in there?" she asks.

I fling the baggy pants over the door.

"Do you have these in a smaller size?" I ask.

I know the answer already, but I want to hear her say it out loud. I want the other shoppers to hear my declaration of emaciation.

I listen as the salesgirl digs for the tag in the folds of cotton.

She pauses.

"Um," she says, the warble in her voice suggesting she can't believe it, either. "These are zeros."

"Yeah," I say.

And?

"We don't sell anything smaller than a zero."

"Oh," I say with feigned disappointment.

The salesgirl flips the pants back over the door; the printed tag hangs before me.

0.

The word echoes in my head in a singsong voice: *Zero, zero, zero. Zero rhymes with hero.*

That clothes tag is worth more than a winning lottery ticket. That big black oval—like an open, empty mouth; like a mouth stretched wide in ecstasy—is the ultimate ego boost.

I'm not just skinny—I'm skinnier than all those other women who wear sizes 1 to 16. I'm in that select 2 percent of the population with an impossible figure, corporeally on par with Heidi Klum.

This is better than any diploma. This is better than an engagement ring. This is better than a baby. This state of skinny is achievable only through willpower, discipline, persistence. I did this all on my own; it may be my greatest achievement ever.

I must be special.

"Do you still want them?" the exasperated salesgirl asks.

"No," I say. "They're too big."

I'm not even a number anymore. I've transcended clothing sizes.

There is one pair of pants that fits, another size 0. These pants are skintight, bloodred velvet, and ride low on my hip bones. They hug the few curves I have left and flutter into flares at the bottom.

I twirl before the full-length mirror and admire my body. I look like sex on a stick. Fantasies of me, in these pants, flash like a slide show in my mind: me on tiptoe, kissing a mystery hunk beneath the mistletoe; me, the impossibly trim single mother at her daughter's birthday party; me, ringing in the New Year in Times Square with a drunken group of girlfriends. These pants, like Aladdin's magic carpet, could transport me anywhere.

They are the softest, most sensuous pants I have ever worn.

They are also priced in the triple digits.

I have to have them.

Happy holidays to me, I think as the cashier swipes my credit card. She folds the pants delicately into a black bag.

I make a vow to save the red pants, tags still on, until I have an occasion worthy of wearing them. In the meantime, they will be my fashion yardstick, the pants I'll use to determine whether or not my thighs have expanded.

And if I never make a date that warrants their debut?

I'll save them as an artifact of the thinnest adult I've ever been.

The holiday season incites nostalgia in Dave. He calls and asks to reunite to discuss our relationship.

Dave doesn't propose as much as he acquiesces to my ultimatum. At the end of an argument in the predawn hours in December, he pulls a black box from his coat pocket and kneels on the carpet.

"Will you marry me?" he asks with trembling hands and tears in his eyes.

"Yes!" I say and leap into his arms. I'm ecstatic—not because of the proposal, per se, but because I've won the marriage argument. I've finally snagged Dave.

See? I say silently to myself. *I always get what I want.*

Dave slides the ring on my finger. The rock is beautiful and brilliant in a white-gold setting, but the band is several sizes too big.

"Don't worry," Dave says, tucking the bauble back into its leather case. "We'll have it refitted."

On the morning the ring will be ready, I awake to the sound of giggles from my daughters' bedroom. Dave is still asleep in my bed, the hood of his high school mascot sweatshirt pulled up over his ears. I kiss him on the forehead, my cheek rubbing up against his scruffy stubble.

"Good morning, fiancé," I say, the title still awkward in my mouth.

Dave rubs his eyes open and yawns.

"The troops are getting restless," I say as something thumps on the other side of the wall. "Mind if I set them loose?"

Moments later, the girls tumble onto the bed between Dave and me. Lola curls up beside him and he strokes her feet in a special way that calms her instantly.

For a moment, I'm in heaven: the early winter sunshine, my daughters' smiles, my soon-to-be-hubby cuddled up against me. All my worries dissolve like snowflakes landing on warm concrete. I turn to Dave, searching for words with which to describe this lightness, this elusive emotion called happiness.

Then I see his face. Dave's eyes are wet. My heart plunks into my gut and my breath evaporates in my throat.

"What's wrong, sweetie?" I ask.

"I'm sorry, I can't, I thought I could, but . . ."

Dave's words muddle before they reach my ears, but I know that any familial fantasy forming in my brain is pure illusion. I sweep my children from the bed as though confronted by an intruder in my home.

"We're going to church," I say. "I want you gone by the time we come back."

"I'm so sorry, Erica, I just . . ."

The girls, sensing my unspoken urgency, are already running down the hall.

Before I slam the door on what was supposed to be my future, I spin around and a foreign voice springs from my mouth. "I hope you regret this for the rest of your life."

chapter eleven

My So-Called Recovery

december 2005

Shortly after my assessment, anorexia diagnosis, and in-patient recommendation from Mendota Hospital, I schedule another therapy
session with Garrison.

"I got a call from Mendota Hospital," Garrison says as soon as I
sit down in his office.

"Oh, *that*," I say with an exaggerated wave of my hand.

Garrison scratches his eye—no, he wipes away a tear. I've seen a
lot of shrinks in my twenty-four years, but I've never seen one
weep.

"Why didn't you tell me?" he asks.

"I didn't think I was that thin."

Garrison tugs uncomfortably at his therapist-issue turtleneck.
The ridged cotton fabric is the same cobalt shade as his eyes.

"So where do we go from here?" he asks. "What are your thoughts
on treatment for the eating disorder?"

"I think I can handle it on my own."

Garrison tilts his head. The pity posture.

"Don't you trust me?" I ask.

"I trust *you*," he says, pointing a trembling finger at me. "I don't trust *it*."

Is there a difference? Anorexia and I are one and the same.

It's time to give this life-sucking force a name.

Some women call their eating disorders "Ed," but that's my latest ex-boyfriend's name, and I don't want to get the mind-fuckers confused. A girl only needs one asshole, after all. Besides, my anorexic ego isn't masculine.

The initials for eating disorder are also out; thanks to Bob Dole, we now know the male equivalent of ED is slightly more embarrassing than the female version.

The ED Demon is a possibility, though if my eating disorder were a demon, it would be of the *There's a Nightmare in my Closet* variety—ugly, but irresistibly friendly.

The Anorexic Rabbit might fit, as I eat a lot of lettuce, like a lot of sex, and exercise like I have an Energizer up my ass. But if I'm going to be a rabbit, I want to be Jessica Rabbit, the fiery-haired vixen with water-balloon boobs. Anorexics may be a lot of things, but well-endowed in the breast department is not one of them.

So I'll settle for Ana, like the die-hard anorexics do.

Ana and I are attached at the rapidly deteriorating hip bone. If my best friend were made incarnate, Ana would look like the most popular girl from the high school yearbook. She'd be a natural knock-out, the girl with the impossibly clear complexion and shiny hair that rolls in thick waves down her back. She'd be the girl who mysteriously smells of freesia and lavender, as though a flower dripped its dew directly onto her body.

And of course she'd be thin.

"Do you think I'm too skinny?" I ask my brother as he steers his beater-of-the-week onto the freeway.

"Um . . . yeah, you could use some body fat," he says, his eyes fixed on the road ahead.

It's less than a week after my Mendota Hospital assessment and I'm ready to craft a recovery plan.

"What do I do to gain ten pounds?" I ask.

"How much do you eat now?"

"A ton."

Shane raises a bushy eyebrow at me. "Seriously."

"Eighteen hundred calories a day."

"You need at least a thousand more, and even then you'll barely maintain."

"A thousand calories more?!" My mind spits out an itemized statement of caloric possibilities: ten apples, twenty bags of lettuce, three hundred grapes. "That's a shitload of food!"

"Then run less."

"No way." The calculations continue: a thousand extra calories per day for seven days equals two pounds of weight gain. "This could take . . . months!"

"Don't think about it so much," Shane says. "Just eat more."

On my first shopping trip as an official eater, I dawdle through the aisles, studying the packages of crackers, cookies, pasta, and granola. The grocery store is a foreign country and I am an emigrant from the land of anorexia, desperate to assimilate. I stare in wide-eyed amazement at the shoppers around me, all of them extraterrestrials.

Even the food is alien. Everything comes in a zillion flavor combinations, in whole-wheat, low-carb, and sugar-free varieties. I fill my cart with bricks of Muenster cheese, plastic totes of rotisserie chicken, trans-fat-filled snacks, and robust loaves of rye bread.

Food, food, glorious food! I want to bear-hug the colorful bags and boxes. I want to kiss the apathetic cashiers. When the automatic doors spread and blast me with heat, I want to throw my arms up and toss my baseball cap in the air like an anorexic Mary Tyler Moore.

Come 10:00 P.M., the food turns into my personal boogeyman.

Night falls, and the kitchen becomes a haunted house where green-faced ghouls hide behind boxes of spaghetti noodles. The cupboards emit an invisible stimulant that makes my stomach growl nonstop. So much variety. So much temptation. A line from *The Thin Commandments* echoes in my head: "The more foods in your fridge, the fewer clothes in your closet."

I have to get rid of the groceries.

Like a rape victim who must look behind every coat in the closet, who must double- and triple-check each window to ensure it is locked before bedtime, I must seek out my packaged predators and destroy them.

I fill one big garbage bag. Good-bye cinnamon raisin bread, sayonara sun-dried tomato Triscuits, so long Kraft shredded cheddar, farewell Fig Newtons. I'm almost to the Dumpster, hauling the Hefty on my back like an emaciated Santa Claus, when a force inside me drops the food to the floor.

I can't throw away perfectly good, unopened packages of food. It seems wrong somehow, even sinful. Before I toss it, I have to taste it.

I tear open the Hefty, shove my whole arm in, and grasp whatever I can. I stuff a crust of bread, a nugget of Fig Newton, and a few slivers of cheese into my mouth. Entranced, my hand scoops food into my mouth over and over. I feel like Veruca Salt, the girl from *Charlie and the Chocolate Factory*, who blows up like a blueberry after overeating. Only I am not inflating like a sweet piece of fruit; I am bursting with noxious gasses, burping up putrid flavor combinations. It is disgusting enough to make me puke. If only I could.

* * *

Everything is better in the morning. I am in control again. I can handle carbs. I can handle anything! The food from the previous night hasn't even rotted in the Dumpster yet when I load my daughters into the SUV for a sugar safari.

The Cheesecake Factory is empty this early in the morning and, two days away from Christmas, is gaudily decorated in red, green, and gold. The three of us press our faces to the glass display case and make goo-goo eyes at the desserts. I feel frisky; a sexy vibration radiates through my whole body. Which flavor will be my lover tonight? There are at least twenty to choose from, including chocolate cherry, Heath bar, cookies and cream, turtle. I am determined to try them all.

"One slice of peanut butter cookie dough cheesecake, please," I say to the counter girl. She squirts two mounds of whipped cream into a transparent box and slips my 1,200-calorie bomb inside. I ogle the sweet pebbles of peanut butter buried between thick wedges of chocolate cream cheese, balanced on a chocolate graham cracker crust. Chocolate, peanut butter, and cookie dough all rolled together. What could be better?

"Mommy," Julia says when we return to the car. "Don't forget to leave cookies for Santa, okay?"

When and where did she learn that? Certainly not from me. I barely speak to my children anymore, much less instruct them in holiday traditions.

"Okay," I say, nestling the take-out container onto the front seat like a newborn baby.

"Treat, treat!" Lola cheers when she hears the crinkle of the plastic bag.

"I want some!" Julia whines.

"Here you go!" I say, tossing them tiny bags of Care Bear fruit snacks from the glove compartment.

"No," Julia huffs. "I want *that*."

Her stiff, outstretched arm is pointing directly at my treasured cheesecake.

"That's . . . uh . . . that's a special treat for . . . Santa! Yeah, Santa. We have to save it for him."

Julia's chubby face considers this for a moment. Surely for Santa she will make a sacrifice.

"Okay," she sighs.

Jesus Christ almighty—I'm taking St. Nick's name in vain so I can stuff my face after the girls have gone to bed. I am going straight to hell.

My first Christmas as a single mother is aesthetically pathetic. I have no tree, no decorations, and only one small gift for each daughter.

At least I do the food up right.

The line at the Honey Baked Ham Company is out the door and down the block. The Christmas Eve crowd reassures me that I, too, can pretend to be normal, just another stay-at-home mom taking care of holiday errands with her kids.

I am nowhere near normal.

Other customers grab frozen packages at random, doubling up on side dishes in case Uncle Harry insists on seconds of sweet potatoes. They demand the heartiest ham slathered in the signature sugary glaze. They buy white rolls by the dozen. They pick out pies in three fruity flavors.

I check the calorie count on every box. I purchase less than necessary to avoid leftovers from taking up residence in my fridge. I buy the lean roasted turkey loaf and three flavors of mustard. I do not buy bread. There will be no dessert.

My father, mother, Jay, and Shane come over for the feast on Christmas Eve. After we eat, they shower my daughters with presents, though I don't join in the gift opening. I'm too busy in the kitchen, getting rid of the dinner leftovers. The only boxes I open this Christmas are Tupperware as I frantically pack away green bean casserole and au gratin potatoes. I label the containers "Mom" and "Dad" and set them by the door so they won't be forgotten. Out of sight, out of mind, off my thighs.

A few days later, the family reconvenes for Julia's birthday.

"Blow out the candles!" my mother trills. Julia kneels on her chair, eyes wide with amazement at her custom-made cake. Barbie is on tiptoe, surrounded by a mound of vanilla cake. Ribbons of buttercream icing adorn the edible dress. There is enough cake for a preschool class—or for one starving woman.

"Do you want a slice?" my mother asks.

Stupid question. Hell, yes, I want a slice. I ran ten miles, walked two, lifted weights, and overworked my abs just to carve out a caloric niche in my diet for a splurge today.

Like mother, like daughter, both Julia and I scrape globs of pink and blue frosting from the cake and shovel it into our mouths simultaneously. When my family has had their fill of cake, they retire to the living room to open presents.

My pulse quickens as I clear the table. I want more cake. No— just more frosting. No—fuck it, I want to eat Barbie's entire outfit. The term *skirt chaser* suddenly has a whole new meaning.

Back turned to my family, I sink my fork into the creamy folds of the cake over and over, shaving the top layer of Barbie's gown clean. My tongue twirls around each tine of the fork, every lick of icing inciting a rush of ecstasy. In an instant, the rest of the world drops away, until it is just me, my mouth, and my stomach. I hear the commotion—the *ooh*s and *aah*s, the cheers and applause, the happy birthday song—as though the celebration were taking place in the apartment above me. As I shove forkful after forkful of frosting into my mouth, my daughter opens every last gift without me.

JOURNAL ENTRY

MY NEW YEAR'S RESOLUTIONS

1. No eating in front of TV.

2. Run 10-mile race in Twin Cities Marathon.

3. Maintain weight at 120 pounds.

4. Get treatment for eating disorder.

5. Take better care of myself.

The rest of the winter, I live my life shuffling between the bedroom, the bathroom, the kitchen, and the couch. I do not go out, except to go to therapy, the grocery store, and the gym. My two-month break from school turns into a leave of absence.

"School is where you kick butt," Garrison says when I announce I'm not going back to my master's program.

"I'm burned out," I say, rocking in the brown recliner opposite him. "I have too much going on right now. I need some me time."

Saturday morning, as my former classmates endure yet another lecture at grad school, I'm on the treadmill at the Y. Not only am I fast, I last longer than anyone else. As I charge ahead—five, seven, nine, miles—a slew of men exhaust themselves on the machine beside me. Every man's hand slam on the stop button reassures me of my superiority.

It's exhilarating the way my breath, hot and heavy, fills every inch of my limbs, cleansing me from the inside out. Sweat sprouts on the nape of my neck and rolls down my back. I watch the odometer on the console click into the double digits. Do I have one more mile in me? Why not? I have time. My entire weekend is devoted to Ana.

The eleven-mile mark flashes in red digits. I've never run this far before. Twelve miles sounds like a good goal. That's practically a half-marathon. I'm running my own race today: me versus me.

I don't make it to twelve. Around eleven and a half, I lose it. The treadmills on either side of me ascend and the other exercisers tip crookedly at the edge of my eyesight. It feels like Novocain shoots through my veins. I'm dizzy and drained. I'm flying.

Whoa, Nelly.

I have been on the treadmill for two hours.

To refuel, I stop at Babb's. As I wander the aisles aimlessly, I feel like my feet levitate, and I float in a delirious daze. Mind disconnects from body, and I see myself from the ceiling, a ridiculous stick insect pretending to be a woman who actually eats.

The steady thump of my heart switches rhythm and skips a beat as I round the meat section. This is it. Poetic irony: I will kick the can from starvation surrounded by food.

I imagine a heart attack here, among the frozen turkeys. Yes, my dead body would fit in quite nicely with the decapitated creatures and their mangled limbs, taut beige skin, protruding bones. The only question is: Am I limber enough to get into that wacky poultry pose?

To my disappointment, I don't faint. I don't black out. My stubborn body keeps chugging along.

"If your heart ever feels like that again," Garrison pleads at our next session, "promise me you'll go to the hospital."

"I promise," I say too quickly to be believed. "Don't worry; nothing will happen."

"How can you be so sure?" he asks, his eyes moistening.

"If I was going to drop dead, it would have happened already."

"What's it going to take for you to make some changes?" Garrison asks.

"Something big would have to happen."

"Like what?"

"Fainting, falling down."

"You just said you almost did on Saturday."

"Almost."

chapter twelve

Ana's Worst Enemy

In a half-assed attempt to avoid hospitalization, I make an appointment with the Center for Eating Disorders to inquire about treatment options.

Garrison preps me for the initial interview; this one conversation will determine my eligibility for the highly regarded Intensive Outpatient Program (IOP). The Center for Eating Disorders is rumored to be pickier about their patients than an Ivy League university, and I am competing for one of five coveted openings.

"Nice to meet you, Erica," the program director, Daniel, coos when he meets me in the waiting room.

Daniel's appearance is surprising to me. His effeminate body language clashes with his Wild West wardrobe. Even in high-heeled cowboy boots, Daniel barely reaches five feet. What could this Howdy Doody know about women's skinny obsession?

I follow Daniel's exaggerated gait down the hall to his massive office. There's so much furniture, I can't decide where to sit. Daniel indicates a spot on a couch across from his desk. He walk-wheels his chair closer to me.

"Tell me what's going on," Daniel says.

"My life is on hold," I say robotically. "All I think about is food and exercise."

"How do you feel about your weight now?"

I shrug.

"Do you want to lose weight?"

"God, *no*," I lie. "I just want to maintain. And not feel so crazy."

Daniel rattles off the components of the program: treatment four days a week, four hours a day, consisting of communal meals wedged between support groups.

"Is there a cafeteria in the building?" I ask.

"No," Daniel says. "Even better. We order in or go out."

"You mean . . . to *restaurants*?"

"Yes. Green Mill, Pizza Hut, China Buffet."

My limbs twitch. Big drops of sweat dribble from my armpits. Restaurant food four times a week? I only allow myself such extravagant meals if I work out an extra half hour beforehand.

"Can you handle that?" Daniel asks, delicately crossing his legs.

"As long as I don't have to eat junk food."

"Such as?"

"Well, I wouldn't eat French fries, for example."

"Part of the program requires you to experiment with forbidden food. Our setup is incredibly effective; you eat in front of your peers and process your feelings afterward. The other clients in the program are very supportive."

Of course they are. There's no greater joy than watching a fellow anorexic beef up unwillingly.

"You have time to think about it," Daniel reassures me. "Even if you are awarded a place, it will be another four weeks before a slot opens up."

"And in the meantime?"

"I'll set you up with a nutritionist and therapist."

* * *

My nutritionist, Lily, is the original Skinny Bitch.

"How do you feel about your eating, Erica?"

Lily is as thin as me and her hair is stylishly disheveled, as though I had caught her napping between clients. She lifts and reviews pink page after pink page in her lap; my food log, a line-by-line account of everything I put in my mouth last week.

"Isn't it obvious?" I say. "I'm eating junk food."

I indicate the half-cup serving of honey-roasted cashews from Saturday's entry, the tablespoon of peanut butter licked off the surface of my daughters' PB&J's, the dozen mini dark chocolates I pilfered from my father's candy jar.

"There is no junk food," Lily says. She sets the log aside and crosses her arms. "Just junky *relationships* with food."

"You're telling me that honey-roasted cashews are not junk food?"

"Nuts are healthy fats. And protein."

"And the chocolate?"

"That's a dessert, but there's nothing wrong with that."

I scowl.

"Any body image issues?" she asks.

"I hate my body so much I can hardly look in the mirror."

"Then cover up the mirrors."

What am I, the Elephant Anorexic?

"Lots of clients cover up their mirrors in the early stages of recovery."

"Isn't that denial?"

"It makes the transition easier until your brain catches up with your body."

These so-called recovery experts are crazy.

"What else is on your mind?" she asks.

"I'm totally bloated." My belly is on par with a second-trimester pregnancy.

"You don't look bloated."

"I *am*. It feels like the button is going to pop off my jeans."

Lily sighs. "Perhaps your perception is overblown."

"No pun intended," I say with a sarcastic giggle.

Lily doesn't laugh.

"Your exercise hasn't decreased since your initial interview," she says as she reviews the exercise section of my log.

"Yes it has! I'm down to nine-mile runs."

"But you added two miles of walking. You didn't do that before."

"Walking hardly burns calories anyway."

Now it's Lily's turn to scowl.

"Besides," I say, "I cut back on my ab exercises. Three times last week instead of four."

Lily shuffles the papers into a neat pile. "You know what I'm going to say about goals for next week. Less exercise."

"Not gonna happen."

"Then more grains."

"How many servings?" I ask.

"Five a day."

"Five?!"

"Your body needs carbs for energy."

I imagine globs of wheat mixing with my digestive juices, creating a thick sludge inside my stomach.

"When I eat carbs, I crave sugar like mad all day long," I say.

"You crave sugar because it is the most concentrated form of carbs."

"I will never make it to five servings of grains."

"That's your choice."

"It certainly is."

Despite my anorexic efforts, the numbers on the scale creep up, and my mood plummets.

"The depression looks heavy today," Garrison says during our next session.

"As predicted," I say. "I'm not only unhappy, I'm also fat."

"Is that the eating disorder talking?"

"It could be, but jeans don't lie."

"Your clothes feel tighter."

I roll my eyes. "Don't tell me you haven't noticed."

I look down at my legs, which look like they could burst the seams of my size 1 jeans.

"My experience is that men do not prefer women as thin as women prefer one another," Garrison says.

"But you're not fucking me."

"Excuse me?"

"Your job is to make sure I don't kick the bucket from a heart attack tomorrow. Other than covering your ass legally, you have no claim to my body. If you were fucking me, you might feel differently."

"I feel protective over your body," Garrison says. "Is it all right that I feel that?"

"Feel whatever you want."

"I'm concerned about your health, Erica, not your appearance. And the best indicator of whether or not you're at a healthy weight is your period."

"What do I need a period for anyway? It's not like I'm going to have babies anytime soon."

"There are other factors to missing periods, like bone loss."

"That's for old ladies."

We sit in stony silence and stare at one another, the therapeutic equivalent of chicken.

Garrison shifts in his chair. "Is there something you haven't grieved that we need to talk about?"

"What?"

"Sometimes, when people don't grieve, their pain comes out sideways, through the body."

I consider Garrison's theory; it makes sense, the urge to exorcise something from within, be it through starvation or sweat or laxatives. It even accounts for the two tattoos and multiple ear piercings I've acquired since my divorce.

"You can lose all the weight you want in here."

I raise my eyebrows. "You're kidding."

"What I mean is, you can unload whatever baggage you need to."

"I'm on to you," I say with a wave of my finger.

"Say more about that."

"You want me to cry. You want me to spill my guts and have a breakdown."

"You think I want to make you cry?"

"I know you do. It's the sadistic wish of all therapists."

"My wish is for you not to be in battle with your body."

"Wish away."

I rock forward and back; Garrison swivels.

"How is the new food plan working?" he finally asks.

"It's not," I say. "I can't do the whole-grain thing."

"Remember that food is your medication. Even if you don't *like* it, you take it at a certain time every day to manage your mood. If you don't take enough—restriction—or you take too much—bingeing—you won't feel your best."

"So that's my prescription? To eat?"

"In healthy moderation, yes."

Moderation. Perhaps the only exercise I am incompetent at.

I leave Garrison's office in a daze. I don't feel sad; hell, I don't feel *anything*. I wind onto the freeway, and before I realize it, I'm pulling into the parking lot of the Asian Buffet where Cesar and I had our wedding reception.

I am welded to the steering wheel with indecision. What's so scary about a buffet anyway? It's just eating. I'm following doctor's orders. Taking my medication.

The plan is not to stuff myself, but as soon as the scent of sweet-and-sour sauce, stir-fried vegetables, and egg rolls hits my nostrils, an uncontrollable force possesses me. I don't have a name for this alter ego yet, the one who wants to devour and destroy every morsel of food in sight, but in time I will name her the Binge Bitch, or BB for short.

And on this boringly normal Tuesday afternoon, she takes control of my mouth.

I pile a plate with mounds of glistening Chinese food. The first round is experimental; I only take a bite of each item, paying close attention to which substance provides the most satisfaction. I plot which items I want to overeat in advance and return to the buffet line for another serving of the flavor finalists: spongy tofu lo mein, broccoli florets in full bloom, kung pao shrimp studded with peanuts and chili peppers. The fried wontons are so adorable, like little gift bags bursting with cream cheese; I serve myself six.

But the food is pure texture, no flavor. Each cube of tofu tumbles onto my tongue, the crunch of broccoli echoes through my ears, the shrimp snap between my teeth. My stomach is stuffed after the second plate, but feeding myself isn't the point anymore—the sensation of food slithering down my throat is.

Though I am on the brink of bursting, I can't resist dessert, so I grab a fortune cookie.

My fortune? "You are in control of your destiny."

Today, my destiny is to cleanse myself, which is why I walk straight out of the Asian Buffet and next door to Snyder's drugstore. It's going to take a Correctol wrecking ball to demolish the Great Wall of China in my gut. I err on the side of overdose; *plunk, plunk, plunk,* laxatives down the hatch.

The cocktail of MSG, soy sauce, and Correctol turns toxic in my stomach. The sensation starts as a tightening around the waist and pressure drops into my pelvis. Am I going to throw up? Or poop in my pants? Sometimes I can't tell the difference. All I know is that everything that just went in needs to come out—*right now.*

Home. Must get home.

My head is so heavy I can hardly hold it up; I slog along the freeway like a bobble-head doll on her first driving lesson.

By the time I pull into my driveway, my stomach feels exposed and raw, as though someone were kneading it like bread dough, braiding my intestines into pretzel form. Each breath feels as though it will burst the water balloon that is my stomach.

I stumble like a drunkard into my den. I lie down. I stand up. No matter what position I assume, everything aches inside. The only logical response to pain this searing is to call my mother.

"Mom," I whine like a preschooler into the phone. "My stomach hurts."

My mother is a nurse; she should know what to do, right? Wrong. All she offers are a few exaggerated theories and some well-spun worries.

"Maybe you aren't eating enough," she says.

If I had the strength, I'd slam the phone down, over and over, on the edge of the sink.

"That's not the problem," I say. And it's not—at least, not the immediate problem.

I hear my mother's muffled chatter with someone else. It's impossible to talk to her on the phone.

"Mom!"

"I don't know what you want me to do." She sighs.

"Take me to urgent care."

"I'm at work. Can't this wait?"

My stomach lurches.

"Never mind," I wheeze. "I'll figure it out on my own."

Maybe I just need to warm up. Bony knees to bonier chest, I curl up in the tub while hot water rushes over my legs. When my body is submerged, I turn on the shower; the stream pitter-patters over my head.

The heat makes me sleepy, so I crawl out and bury myself in the folds of my fluffy blue bathrobe and collapse on the unmade bed.

When I wake an hour later, the pain has subsided. There's just enough time to dress in clean sweats and slap a baseball cap over my scraggly hair. En route to pick up my daughters from Cesar's house, I guzzle a diet Mountain Dew.

Ha! I think. *I have a stomach of steel.*

My invincibility is short lived. As soon as I ring Cesar's doorbell, a phantom prizefighter socks a fist into my gut. Tremors of pain reverberate through my core and swirl around my rib cage.

"Here's Mommy!" Cesar cheers as he swings open the door. Two overbundled girls in pink and purple parkas toddle out. Cesar's smile flattens. "Are you all right?"

"I'm having . . . this . . . weird . . . pain," I gasp, pointing to my pelvis. "Like contractions."

"It's probably just your period," Cesar says as he loads the girls into their car seats.

"Yeah, I'm sure that's all it is."

"Where are we going, Mommy?" Julia asks.

"Mommy needs to go see the doctor," I say.

By the time we arrive at urgent care, the pain is so intense I would happily perform my own abdominal surgery if I had sharp instruments handy.

From the looks of the waiting room, the entire population of the south metro suburbs has decided that today is the day to get checked out for sinus infections, sore throats, and sprained ankles. The clinic reeks of unbathed bodies and boots sopping with day-old snow. Children sneeze in an uneven chorus and adults assault them with Kleenex. On the corner television, *Oprah* is airing a feature story on what not to wear. Worse than the pain in my stomach is the one in my ears. Shut up! Shut up! Every sound feels like a needle piercing my eardrum.

The girls muscle their way to the color table and wrestle crayons away from other red-nosed rug rats. They whine and cry and shed their coats with body shimmies. I am useless to them, curled up against the wall on two plastic chairs.

"Erica?" a nurse calls.

I grab the girls by their sleeves and half-walk, half-drag them back to the examination room.

"What is problem?" the doctor asks in a thick Middle Eastern accent.

"My stomach hurts."

"PMS?"

"No."

"Why so sure?" she asks.

"Because I don't have periods."

"Pregnant?"

"No."

The girls are antsy now; they climb up and down my legs, toss magazines on the floor with triumphant cheers, and giggle mischievously.

"How do you know?" the doc asks.

"I don't have a boyfriend," I say. "Besides, I don't have periods."

"But you might still ovulate."

"It's not *that*," I say.

"Urine sample first, just in case."

"Fine."

The door opens unexpectedly; my mother enters like an angelic escort and ushers the girls off. The doctor sends me to the vending machines for apple juice. The only reason I drink the sugar-laden beverage today is the hunch that something *big* is happening to me. Death? Probably not. But will I finally be caught in bed with anorexia? Very possibly.

I pee in my assigned cup and send the fluorescent yellow fluid spinning in a metal turnstile. Back in the exam room, the fructose hits my stomach and I feel worse than ever. Gurgles and growls rise up from a digestive bog inside me; the skin around my belly-button tightens. Cool sweat blossoms on the back of my neck. My head spins and my stomach twitches. Instinctually, I take a big gulp of air, lean over the table, and spew an amber fountain into the garbage can. Hurl. Breathe. Breathe. Hurl. Breathe. Breathe.

Knees to chest, I roll back onto the treatment table and fall asleep.

The doctor's shrill voice shocks me back to consciousness.

"Good news! Not pregnant!" she trills. "How do you feel?"

I push myself up to sitting. I feel, surprisingly, fine.

"Come back if you feel bad later," she says.

"Okay," I say and hop down from the table.

I trot back to the waiting room where an entourage awaits me: mother, father, brother, daughters. My mother is passing books from a canvas bag to my father, who glances at them indifferently.

"Oh, please, Mom," I say, indicating the titles, all of which feature *bulimia* in big, bold letters. The insult is not that she is reading up on eating disorders, but that she's pegged me as a bulimic. Am I fat enough to warrant such a diagnosis?

"I'm just learning," she says.

Before our bickering begins in earnest, my father asks, "What did the doctor say?"

"Nothing," I say, slinging the diaper bag onto my shoulder. "Stupid doctors. They don't know anything."

"Nothing?" my father says. "What were you doing back there?"

"Throwing up."

My mother cocks an eyebrow and nods toward the stack of books.

"Not *on purpose*," I say. "Jeez."

My parents maintain their concerned expressions.

"I took a nap," I say. "I feel much better now."

As peppy as a Tupperware party hostess, I wave good-bye to my family members.

"Thanks for coming!"

I shuffle off, my daughters' hands gripped in mine, leaving my family stunned, immobile, in the waiting room.

*   *   *

That weekend, I awake from a nap to a blindingly sunny afternoon. I am alone in my Cupid Loves Me pajama set that dangles limply from my shoulders and hips. My grip tightens on the fuzzy fuchsia blanket, creating a fleece shell around me.

What happened to me? I used to be Wonder Woman. I used to set ridiculously lofty goals—and surpass them. Now I'm the kind of woman I despise: the drama-queen single mom, endlessly irresponsible and down on her luck.

Traffic hums on the street outside, frigid breezes shake bare tree branches, and yelps echo across the field as someone searches for a lost dog.

There's life out there. I can hear it.

Yet I cannot get off the couch.

chapter thirteen

Shrink Wars

While the decision regarding the intensive outpatient program is still in limbo, the Center for Eating Disorders arranges for me to meet with one of their therapists. Dr. Peterson and I sit across from one another on cushy suede chairs. She is tiny, with facial features so pinched and puckered it looks like she just sucked on a lemon. Dr. Peterson flips open a manila file folder; my entire anorexic history reduced to a one-inch-thick stack of papers.

"Was there ever a time in your life when you didn't worry about your weight or how much you exercised?" she asks in a nasal-tinged tone.

"When I was married."

"And what did you weigh then?"

"Somewhere between one hundred thirty-five and one hundred forty-five."

"About ten pounds more than now?"

Am I that fat already?

"Well, I—"

"You run seventy miles a week?" Dr. Peterson interrupts; clearly, she plotted her interrogation beforehand.

"Yup."

"And how much did you run when you were married?"

"Twenty miles, maybe?"

Dr. Peterson smiles as though I had just fallen into her psychological booby trap.

"Now, Erica, I see you're a very intelligent woman. Does this make *sense*? For ten little pounds you run more than three times as much? For ten little pounds. Is that rational?"

I bite my lip. It *is* rational: If I want to be thinner, I have to put in my time on the treadmill.

"I have something I'd like you to read for next time." She passes me a copy of the infamous Keys study, a psychological experiment that made anorectics and bulimics out of previously healthy men simply by restricting their caloric intake. I've read the Keys study before—any anorexic who's picked up a self-help book knows the study backward and forward.

"I hope this isn't too challenging for you," Dr. Peterson says.

Thanks for the vote of confidence, Ana says as I tuck the article beneath my arm.

"Have you been in therapy before?" Dr. Peterson asks.

"I'm in therapy now. I have a great therapist."

"Then why are you here?"

"Because he works with me on other issues."

As physicians specialize in an area of the body, shrinks are experts on different aspects of the psyche. My plan is to work with the Center for Eating Disorders on anorexia and focus on relationship issues with Garrison.

"I've already signed a release of information," I say. "So you two can coordinate my treatment."

"I treat patients exclusively."

"You don't *have* to talk to him," I say, feeling like a go-between of quarreling parents. "I just thought you'd want your techniques to mesh."

"You need to make a choice," Dr. Peterson says. "Either you take on the program here or you stick with your current therapist."

This is a no-brainer.

"Let's schedule for two weeks from now so you can have some time to think about it," she says.

I scribble down the appointment in my date book, making sure to note Dr. Peterson's phone number so I can call and cancel the night before.

I'm convinced I can overcome Ana solely through therapy with Garrison, so I leave a message on Daniel's voicemail asking him to remove my name from the waiting list for the Intensive Outpatient Program.

By my next session with Garrison, I'm ready to reveal Ana.

"There's a voice in my head," I say.

I'm waiting for Garrison to laugh. He doesn't.

"What does the voice say?" he asks.

Fucking fat bitch. Disgusting pig. Poser. Sorry excuse for a human being.

"I can't tell you. It's horrible. It says things I wouldn't say to my own worst enemy."

"How much play time does this voice get?"

"Eighty-five percent."

"And the rational voice in your head?"

"Ten percent."

Garrison doesn't ask about the other 5 percent—the voice I won't admit to anyone. The suicidal voice.

"Humor me," Garrison says as he flips open his laptop. "Let's get the voice up on the screen."

Garrison likes mapping; whether this is a managed care habit or a male hobby, I play along. The projector hums to life on the table between us. Garrison types *What if I gave the ED up?* with his pointer fingers. The words appear in a big black bubble on the screen. He nods in my direction.

"I would have to stop running," I say.

Garrison drags a line from the first bubble and types my statement on the screen.

"Then what?" he asks.

"I'd be giving up the one thing I'm good at."

"And then?"

"I'd have to find a new talent."

"And then?"

"I might find out that I'm not good at anything else."

"And then?"

"The depression would take over."

"And?"

"I wouldn't have a reason to get up in the morning."

Garrison looks up from the computer screen.

"What about your daughters?" he asks.

"I'm so incompetent at parenting. Being with them only makes me feel worse about myself. They'd be better off without me."

"That sounds like the voice again," he says, drawing another bubble on the screen.

"I'm not exaggerating when I say that running is the highlight of my day. I set that ten-mile goal and I reach it. It's an achievement. Instant gratification. My body is the evidence of that."

"So while you can't necessarily control the world around you, you can make those little red digits on the treadmill go as high as you want?"

"Exactly."

"And if you couldn't run every morning, how would the voice respond?" Garrison asks, returning his attention to the screen.

"Giving up running . . . would kill me faster than the eating disorder would."

Garrison's lips tremble as he sketches one last bubble.

"Is that its plan for you? To die?" he asks.

I never thought of the eating disorder as a form of suicide, but maybe that *is* what I'm doing. Killing me softly à la starvation. What a drawn-out, masochistic way to die! So passive-aggressive.

"Is that the plan, Erica?"

I meet Garrison's hypnotizing eyes.

"Yes."

I never do anything half-assed, and mental illness is no exception. At first my unraveling manifests itself in random waves of weepiness. Many mornings, I awake crying.

How can I be upset before the day even begins? The tears increase as the days drag on. A pastel sunset? A pair of watery eyes. A cocker spaniel pulling her owner down the parkway? A few fat tears. A couple with twin coffee cups? A short crying session. A doughy baby in a baseball cap? Complete breakdown.

"Crying is not a sign of sadness," Garrison reassures me. "It's a sign of being alive. You're finally feeling."

Don't fear the tears, I tell myself.

"Are you crying, Mommy?" Julia asks one evening from the bathtub. I'm seated on the toilet with a fistful of Kleenex.

"Yes," I say as I kneel down beside the basin. "Mommy's sad."

"Why?" she asks. She takes my face in both her hands and pulls it uncomfortably close to hers. She bats her big emerald eyes.

"Mommy doesn't feel well."

She tugs on the skin just under my eyes as though searching for the cause of my malaise.

"Then you need to go to the doctor," she says with a definite nod.

"Yes," I agree. "Yes, I do."

"When I'm big, I'm going to be a doctor," Julia says.

I shut the shower curtain and bury my face in my hands. Not only am I messing up my life, I'm traumatizing my children, too.

* * *

My emotional incontinence doesn't last for long—soon apathy takes over, encasing me in full-body bubble wrap. I can't feel *anything*, good or bad. I'm a walking corpse.

My heart pleads with my mind to cry again. I do all I can to lift the waterworks restriction to no avail. One evening, after singing the last good-night song to the girls, I light my lilac candles and soak in a luxurious bubble bath. I give myself permission to let the emotions out, signaling safety with a closed bathroom door. I wait, watching the intense little flames fighting to climb higher and higher into the air.

Nothing. Numb. Deaf. Dumb.

The depression rises up like a black poison behind my eyes, clouding my vision, preventing me from seeing beyond this moment in which I am alone and as miserable as I've ever been.

JOURNAL ENTRY

This is beyond isolation. This is abandonment by God.

I feel like I'm in a wave pool of grief. There I was, coasting along on an inner tube, the rush of water propelling me forward, intoxicated by speed. Suddenly, a wave sucked me under and won't let me go. Every time my head emerges and I think I've finally escaped, another wave comes crashing down and tugs me farther underwater.

I try to describe what's happening, but no one grasps quite how deep I've sunk. They can't see that beneath the gentle ripples of the water's surface, my body is flailing, struggling to stay afloat.

"Your thoughts are what's disordered, Erica," my mother says. "Stop being so pessimistic."

Is it all in my head? Do I just need an attitude adjustment? While the chemical imbalances characteristic of depression do muck up cognitive functioning, they also provide a raw, realistic filter through which to see reality. I analyze my life without the hazy pink happiness that clouds everyone else's view. My blinders have been stripped away, and I'm struck with the sublime knowledge that no, life is not a balance sheet of pleasure and pain—it really is just one disappointment after another, an unending marathon of suffering.

"Pick a card, any card," I say as I spread out a fan of business cards on Garrison's desk. "How many experts will it take to put Humpty Dumpty back together again?"

My recovery squad consists of a social worker, a Reiki body worker, an astrologer, a nutritionist, a masseuse, a tattoo artist, and two aestheticians; together, they provide a Band-Aid level of treatment.

"I feel some tension here," Dorothy, my Reiki bodywork specialist, says as her hands hover above my naked abdomen. "Tell me what hurts."

What a quack. For her amusement, I recount an episode from my childhood about being locked accidentally in the basement.

"You're worried you'll be forgotten in the darkness again," she says. Maybe she's right, but at $140 per hour, I want something slightly more profound for my money.

Sunflower, my astrologer, flips through a dictionary-thick book and looks up my Gemini sign. Her diagnonsense? I'm in the midst of "The dark night of the soul."

"This is the greatest upheaval of your life," she informs me with a disconcertingly cheerful tone. "Once you reach thirty, life will turn, and it will never be this hard again!"

I'm twenty-four. Six years more years of this seems like an eternity.

"By the way," Sunflower adds with a smirk. "No love commitments on the horizon until 2010."

"Cut out the edamame and veggie burgers," Nutritionist Mandy advises when she reviews my food log at a follow-up appointment. "Soy can cause mood swings."

My primary-care physician sends me through round after round of antidepressants. Zoloft knocks out my sex drive. Wellbutrin makes me manic.

"Is it always going to be this way?" I ask as she scribbles out an order for Effexor.

"Oh, no," she says, passing me the prescription. "There are lots of other meds you can try."

I nod in silence. She's completely missed the point. I don't want a new med. I want a new frame of mind.

When traditional techniques fail, I develop my own treatment plan. Dubbed "The Pleasure Principle," it involves the guilt-free participation in anything that produces even a pinprick of joy. I indulge in unlimited facials, massages, and shopping sprees. I discover the joy of decorating my home.

My strategy works . . . for a while. Then, subtle signs that I'm dipping into the cookie jar of despair resurface. Too exhausted to primp, I wear my wet hair in ponytails, hide my eyes under baseball caps, and swap sexy sandals for tattered tennis shoes. I skip eye shadow and skimp on lipstick.

My face is as swollen as a puffer fish; my complexion, studded with acne. My shoulders slump forward, unable to support the heft of my upper body. My feet slog along like flippers. The bitterness in my soul seems to overflow and seep out in my sweat. I can't look people in the eyes anymore; if someone really *sees* me, I'll shatter. I keep my head down.

I look so disheveled, so often, that I cancel multiple appointments last minute, unwilling to explain to one more well-meaning but nosy person what's wrong with me. It's not as if I could say, "Please excuse me, I'm on the brink of a breakdown." Society isn't set up that way. I alienate my friends and stand up lovers, silently encouraging everyone to abandon me. Entire days pass without adult interaction.

Everyday life suddenly seems silly—why waste time on non-essential tasks? I give up bed making and keep my bedroom blinds drawn. Food, long past its expiration date, takes up residence in my fridge; the dishes assemble themselves in a rank, crusty tower in the sink. My car is a mobile garbage can, an explosion of abandoned books, half-devoured suckers, snot-soaked tissues, and green Starbucks straws poking like blades of grass from the cup-holders. A sticky, nondescript film coats the dashboard; the windows are smudged with a collage of fingerprints.

I no longer frequent Gap for fashion splurges; I have more than enough clothes to last the rest of my life. I rotate a few favorite outfits; one pair of black cotton capris even earns the title of The Depression Pants. The clothes I do wear never make it into the closet; on the rare occasion I do the laundry, I don't separate the colors from the whites. If anything shrinks on the default dryer setting, I'm unaware of it; my weight and wardrobe dissolve in unison into oblivion.

I cease highlighting my books and toss the Sunday paper in the recycling bin without unfolding a page. Why fill my brain with useless knowledge? I've permanently put down roots in the land of "later," the nation of "not now," the world of "whatever."

By 8:00 A.M. every morning, I'm already worn out and overwhelmed. I curl up like a shrimp under my covers, stewing in the cocktail sauce of my displeasure.

Then I realize: The problem isn't my circumstances. The problem is me. Knowing that, what other solution is there but to destroy myself?

I spin the idea of suicide every time I cross the Minnesota River Bridge on my way home. I contemplate how much force it will take to send my car careening over the edge, but given my track record for achieving goals, I'd probably fail. What if I don't drive fast enough? What if the car doesn't make it over the guard railing?

Surviving a wreck injured or dismembered—and unable to exercise—
would be far worse than being dead.

Mortality and I play a precarious game of chicken, waiting to see
who will give up first. Will I slam on the accelerator or swerve out
of the way to safety?

JOURNAL ENTRY

I'm not dead yet, but no one in their right mind would call this
living.

While depression initially feels like a slow drowning, the decision
to commit suicide is a jackknife dive into shallow water. All of a
sudden, I know I'm going to do it.

Suicide is a major endeavor; it takes a lot of preparation for a perfectionist like me. I agonize over the details: should I vacuum before
I go? Alphabetize my CD collection? Pay off those pesky credit card
bills? I have to prioritize—everything must be left just so.

Infused with a refreshing spurt of mania, I embark on the project
of my existential exit. I compile lists of my e-mail account pass-
words, unpaid credit card balances, and cash card PINs. On expensive rainbow-bordered paper from Kinko's, I print out a list of
friends, family, and coworkers to be contacted in order of importance. I compose a letter titled "The Reasons Why" in which I wax
poetic about my undoing. I stack three red leather journals in
chronological order by my bedside in the hopes that I'll be published posthumously.

Once I decide that death is the only way out of my personal hell,
I experience a luscious new lightness in life. The immense joy in the
midst of my darkest depression is such an odd juxtaposition. I suddenly sense the height of pleasures as though my body recognized
the despair and is sounding the internal sirens. Every sensory organ
pumps into overdrive: food flavors explode on my taste buds, and I

notice temperatures more acutely. Money becomes a ridiculous appendage, random numbers without consequence. Time opens up, as there's no reason to get to bed early, no need to rest. I skip the breathy Denise Austin exercise tapes, as no man will ever see my naked two-pack again. I smile at strangers, even the ugly ones, because I hold the secret to great living: certain death.

After much debate, and some online research, the plan is set: I'll attend my regular session on Valentine's Day with Garrison and give him a card expressing my appreciation for his help. I'll have a facial at Cole's Salon and attend the Duncan Sheik concert downtown. Afterward, I'll fill up the gas tank, drive into my garage, and leave the motor running.

On the big day, a series of unexpected events occurs. I forget Garrison's card at home; we have a ho-hum session that leaves me wanting more. Then a funny thing happens at my facial. After my pores have been professionally picked and my skin exfoliated, after my shoulders have been kneaded and my limbs slathered in cherry-chocolate scented lotion, I'm deliciously exhausted.

I *do* want to sleep, but not forever.

I leave the salon, skin glowing, body emanating softness and warmth from the inside out. I skip the concert and drive home in silence. When I pull into the garage, I cut the engine right away. I hold the key, heavy as an anchor in my hand, and examine the slight curve in its teeth where I once slammed it in a door.

I can't die tonight. I'm not sufficiently pissed off to kill myself. Not yet.

The divorce settlement check finally arrives, and it's burning a hole in the pocket of my skinny jeans. A starving brain, coupled with anorexia-induced omnipotence, makes bad decisions.

I know I'll buy the house before I even see it. When Kathy, my

Realtor, maneuvers her Jeep toward Hamilton Drive, I gasp. The sidewalks are lined on both sides with crabapple trees. Their branches drip over the road, forming a botanical tunnel. The split-level is situated on a nature reserve, and a dirt trail serpentines along the edge of the big backyard.

This would be an amazing place to run, Ana says.

"Sold," I say to Kathy.

"Maybe you should talk to someone before you do this," my mother says as she looks over the MLS stat sheet later. "And come up with a budget."

Hardwired to ignore every comment that comes out of her mouth, I wave off the motherly advice.

Because my family barely talks about anything—least of all money—this is as far as the financial conversations go. My parents stand idly by as I drop a $70,000 down payment on a crumbling house I can't afford.

Life is looking up—until my body breaks down.

When I arise for my 4:00 A.M. runs, my legs ache and my knees creak like old cellar steps. Instead of relishing the ten-mile trek ahead of me, I dread it. But even with the corporeal warnings, I am unprepared for the day I wake up and can't walk a step. My left leg, hard as steel, won't bear weight. Every step feels like a butcher knife slashing its way deep down inside the muscle and scraping up against the bone.

The Athletic Institute is the first sports medicine clinic that pops up on my Google search. I pick Dr. Ken based on his credentials— athletic, not educational—as a marathon runner.

The clinic is located next to the hospital where the wealthy CEOs of Minnesota go to have their heart attacks. The reception area reveals a streamlined operation; multiple receptionists with big hair and overdone makeup, bowls of candy at the appointment desk, a slew of fitness magazines on dustless coffee tables.

Each treatment room has a theme, gaudily decorated by someone who had too much fun on e-Bay. I await Dr. Ken in the Nordic Room, where red paper horses line the window ledge, an old sweater hangs in the corner, and pairs of skis, snowshoes, and a sled are nailed at crooked angles on the wall. A plaque above the sink reads, *You Can Always Tell a Norwegian, but You Can't Tell Him Much.*

I smile to myself. Yes, I think Dr. Ken and I will get along just fine. A knock sounds on the door and the doctor strides into the office. Dr. Ken is even dreamier in person than his Internet picture, a spitting image of Tom Cruise in his *Top Gun* days. His feathery brown hair rises in a wave across his forehead, and his build is so defined I can trace the line of his pecs through the thin fabric of his dress shirt.

"Calf pain, huh?" he asks, flipping up the screen on his laptop. "How many miles do you run a week?"

"Seventy," I say.

"Seven-*teen?*"

"Seventy."

Dr. Ken whips his head up, and wrinkles form on his forehead.

"Are you . . . training for something?"

"No. I just like to run."

"Riiight," Dr. Ken says, setting the laptop aside and referring to my paper file instead. "I see you checked 'anorexia' on your health history form."

"Yeah," I say with a shrug, as though I'd just admitted to something minor, like my tonsillectomy.

A subtle squirm spreads from Dr. Ken's waist to his shoulders.

"And . . . uh . . . how is that going?" he asks.

"So-so."

"You know your weight is low."

"It's higher than in the past."

"Hmm."

Dr. Ken leads me through a series of resistance tests: I push my foot into his palm, my knee presses against his hand, I flex and rotate my ankle.

"You have really strong legs," he marvels, eyeing my gams up and down like a man on the make.

I smile; apparently, I've passed the test. I'm not injured. A little RICE (rest, ice, compression, elevation) and I'll be back to normal in no time.

Then the other—running—shoe drops.

"Hop on one foot," he says.

I hop on the right. Hop, hop, no problem.

"Now the left," he says.

I squat. I'm stuck.

"Ha ha ha," I giggle, flinging my hair back.

Dr. Ken's gaze fixes on my left calf as though he could see straight through the skin. He frowns.

"Hop," he says.

I bend my knees, tighten my glutes, and squat again. Nothing happens. It feels as though an invisible anchor is holding down my lower half.

I cannot hop to save my life.

"I can't," I say.

"But you can run ten miles a day on it, huh?"

My lower lip trembles and my eyes fill with tears.

"Apparently not," I say.

Dr. Ken taps furiously on his keyboard.

"This sounds like a stress fracture. Six weeks, no running," he says with a definitive slap shut of the laptop.

Six weeks without endorphins? I'll die. Even worse, I'll die fat and flabby.

"No way," I say.

"If you keep running on that leg, you will end up with a broken bone, and then you'll be off your feet for months. Even professional marathoners don't run as hard as you do without recovery time."

"What am I supposed to do until then?"

"Pool running."

"Excuse me?"

"Pool running. You put on a flotation device and do laps upright in the water. It's great resistance training."

I raise my eyebrows. "Can you tell I don't believe you?"

"Your other option is spinning."

"I don't bike."

"It's an excellent workout."

"Not like running."

Dr. Ken stands with an aggravated sigh. "Well, nothing's like running, but in the meantime . . ."

"The elliptical!" I say, as though he were an exercise auctioneer with whom I can bargain.

"That's still weight-bearing exercise."

I cross my arms and scowl.

"Okay, the elliptical," he relents. "But only if it doesn't hurt."

And even if it does, Ana snaps.

Dr. Ken taps my file with his pen.

"We should draw some blood—check for anemia and thyroid problems—and I'm ordering a bone scan as well."

A few moments later, a sassy nurse with mocha skin leads me to the radiology room. A sleek machine glides over my bare legs, clicking like a camera shutter.

I return to the treatment room where Dr. Ken meets me with a handful of films. He holds the first one up to the fluorescent light. There, staring back at me is my pale ass, the outline of my lace thong clearly visible between the cheeks.

Dr. Ken blushes. "That . . . err . . . that's just there because I like to check the hips, too."

I nod, feigning a bashfulness I don't feel. I work hard for that impressive backside and I'm not ashamed to show it off to my hunky doc.

"Erica," he says, setting the films down. "You have osteopenia."

"Huh?"

"You have the bones of an old woman."

"Impossible. I'm twenty-four."

"You're on your way to osteoporosis."

"So what am I supposed to do?" I ask, thinking there must be a medication, an herb, a supplement—something I can swallow to reverse the damage.

"Nutrition is the only way," Dr. Ken says. "More calcium."

"I eat cottage cheese."

Fat-free and a quarter cup per serving, but that still counts, doesn't it?

"Not enough," Dr. Ken says. "Try milk instead."

"I don't drink my calories."

"Yogurt, then."

"I don't like yogurt. It's not filling."

Dr. Ken shakes his head and runs his fingers through his impeccable coif.

"Here," he says, reaching behind me. He pulls a giant dispenser of Caltrate calcium chewables from the window ledge. He hands me a few trial packets. "Take these."

I do.

"On second thought," he says. "Take them all."

Dr. Ken shoves the box toward me.

"Gee, uh, thanks," I say.

"Follow-up in six weeks."

I walk out on my old-maid bones with enough calcium to rebuild an elephant's skeleton.

"It happened," I tell Garrison at our next session. "The Something Big."

"What do you mean?"

"I have a stress fracture. I can't run."

"It was only a matter of time," Garrison says softly with a shake of his head. "So how are you coping?"

"I'm not," I say. "It's called denial."

"Have you discussed this with Dr. Peterson?" Garrison asks.

"No," I say. "Because I told the Center for Eating Disorders I no longer needed their services."

Garrison sighs like a father disappointed with his daughter's irresponsible decision making.

"Any particular reason why?"

"Dr. Peterson wanted me to choose between you and her," I say. "So of course I said I'd rather work with you."

Garrison's eyes fill with tears; his in-session weeping has become a regular occurrence since Ana appeared on the scene.

"Erica, if it were a choice between me and them, I would have wanted you to do their program. IOP offers more support than I can give you. I don't want you to become dependent on me."

"It's a little late for that," I say. Garrison is the only one who knows about the daily ins and outs of my emotional life; he's the only one I've exposed Ana to. If my family and friends are aware of my deteriorating state, they haven't said much to me. Garrison is my sole sounding board and, on some days, the only adult I converse with.

"Besides," I say. "I don't do well in groups. Instead of getting better, I'd learn the other patients' tricks. So much focus on the eating disorder would only encourage me to get thinner."

"I want you to call the Center for Eating Disorders," Garrison insists, "and mend fences."

"You want me to go back and *grovel*?"

"I'm sure they'll understand. If you want, I'll let them know how important this is—"

"They're fucking food Nazis! Every practitioner I've worked with there has been insufferable. The nutritionist wants to fatten me up, and the psychologist thinks I'm stupid."

Garrison takes a big belly breath.

"I have something to tell you," he says. "I'm leaving the clinic."

"My insurance is awesome," I say. "I'm sure I can switch to your new office."

"No, Erica," Garrison says with a shake of his head. His gaze stays fixed on the ground. "I'm leaving the field of psychology altogether."

It feels as though God himself just flattened my heart with a hammer. I try to breathe, but the best I manage is a wheeze.

"What's going through your mind right now?" Garrison asks.

"That this sucks."

My mouth shuts down, followed by my ears. In a tin-can audio stream, Garrison mumbles on about seeing two sides to every experience; this isn't a tragedy, it's an opportunity to immerse myself in the Center for Eating Disorders.

One sentence finally tumbles through the filter. "Do you think I'm leaving because I don't care about you?" Garrison asks.

"Yes," I say, silently cursing myself for forgetting that card for him on Valentine's Day.

"You didn't cause this, Erica. You couldn't have prevented it, and you can't change it."

"But if I mattered enough, you'd find some way to stay."

Garrison shakes his head. "This isn't about you."

He's right. It's about Ana; one by one, she's eliminating people from my life.

chapter fourteen

Death Becomes Her

It seems like a good day to die.

It is a Monday, shortly after Garrison's good-bye. The wind wheezes and howls at my bedroom windows; the sky outside is a hazy shade of gray, like the underbelly of a newborn kitten.

I spend the morning as one should if death is on the docket; I take my daughters to the Minnesota Zoo for a final family outing. I pay extra attention to my preschoolers as they draw farm animals with bright Crayolas, as they point out the sun bear sleeping on a log, as they imitate monkey calls. We watch the turtles: one big, three small, swimming in an aquarium with green-tinted water. The mother turtle keeps trying to scuttle away, but her babies pursue her relentlessly. Poor Mama Turtle. She needs a break. Just like me.

After their nap later that afternoon, I chauffeur the girls to my mother's for a playdate. I kiss each of them good-bye; three-year-old Julia on the forehead, two-year-old Lola on the lips.

I try to spend the last evening of my life at the movies, but I can't focus; the dialogue is lame and the actors too beautiful to be believable. Halfway through the film, I abandon my seat and escape to the lobby, where the scent of stale popcorn makes me both ravenous and nauseated.

I pick up my phone and tap out 411.

"Connect me to Doolittle's, please," I say with a surprisingly rational tone. I give the barman my order: A bison burger, waffle fries, and seasoned sour cream, to go. When I pull up to the sports bar, a teenager with a crooked fedora hat opens the door for me. Inside, the din of the nine-to-five crowd gathering over happy-hour drinks echoes throughout the restaurant, vying with ESPN for my attention. I give the hostess my name, and in exchange she hands me a deep plastic bag that crinkles with the weight of the food inside.

My last supper.

I drive down Diffley Road in the silent capsule of my car, the aroma of fresh fried potatoes invading my nostrils. I see the world through a new lens, as though I were floating with a bird's-eye view of the city below me. I watch the absurd rumbling of its inhabitants scurrying about, filling gas tanks, stuffing their faces with Krispy Kremes and designer mochas.

Will I miss any of this?

Nah.

When I pull into my garage, my bumper knocks a tower of Bounty rolls onto the floor. Another unfinished task on my to-do list: Replenish paper towel supply. Before I can guilt-trip myself, my gut growls, and I hurry inside to heat up the food. My foot taps in a nervous rhythm on the hardwood floor as my meal spins round and round in the microwave. The burger emerges overcooked and dry; the fries are soggy after soaking in their own grease for too long. I shove the half-pound patty of buffalo and the tic-tac-toe boards of potatoes two at a time into my mouth, barely tasting the flavors.

Food consumed, I turn on the television to distract myself with an episode of *Sex and the City*. I can't muster even one giggle; Miranda's pregnancy problems seem absurd given the impending events of the evening.

Back in the kitchen, I fling a cupboard door open to reveal the stash of medication I've stocked in preparation for the overdose. I grab the bottle of Percocet—postpartum leftovers—and roll it between my palms. Gazing like a lover at the death beads, the muffled clinking taunts me into a hypnotic trance. I pop the cap and inhale the powdery smell of the pretty blue pills.

What combination will do the trick? Will the painkiller alone be enough to knock me out? Do I take them all at once or little by little? I need advice on how to do this right—granted, anyone successful at suicide wouldn't be around to mentor me through to the other side.

I can't do it.

When I glance at a photograph of the girls and me from the previous Christmas, a strange survival instinct kicks in. I'm propelled, in some sort of primal state, to escape the pills before me.

I fling the garage door open in a fury and slam my ass down in the driver's seat. I jerk the car into reverse and speed down the road, barely obeying traffic laws. It is 6:18 P.M.; my mother must be bathing my daughters. Moments later, I stumble into her town house and burst into a blubbery blob of tears. My body dissolves into dry heaves as I gasp for air. Unable to speak through the strands of saliva and snot, I collapse into my mother's arms, safe from myself for the moment.

The rest of the evening passes in a blur. I sit on my mother's couch, alternately sobbing and dipping a crooked spoon over and over into a bucket of Coffee Lover's ice cream. Once the girls put on their pajamas, the four of us drive back to my house. My mother helps me get the girls in bed and offers to spend the night on my sofa. I'm not sure I want her there, but in my exhausted state, it's easier to agree than to argue.

Before I go to sleep, the guilt from the ice cream binge floods in, so I down five laxatives. All night, I run to and from the bathroom, making sure to turn the faucet and the ventilation fan on to disguise the sounds of my bowels erupting into the toilet bowl.

After my final trip to the bathroom, I notice my mother poking her head around the corner.

"Upset stomach," I whisper.

She nods and turns back toward the sofa.

"By the way," I say before I retreat to my bedroom. "I'll be up at four A.M. for my regular workout. Don't be startled by the noise."

chapter fifteen

Y Not?

My suicidal urges scare the shit out of me. To keep the depression at bay, I return to my trusty coping mechanism: Ana.

I still can't run and cycling is a snore, but Ana won't let me sit on my ass.

"Couldn't sleep either?" a fellow gym rat asks as he races me to the doors of the YMCA.

"Might as well stick to routine," I say.

"That's good," he says. "It shows you're dedicated."

"Or crazy," I mutter under my breath.

"Kind of early for a Saturday," the bearded Blondie says as he scans my ID card. He nods toward the clock: 5:05 A.M.

What do regular people do on the weekends? I can barely recall the lazy Saturdays of my past.

"Do you run like that every day?" a man in a yellow muscle T asks as I dismount the elliptical an hour later. I am about to point out that I wasn't running, I was elliptical-ing, but who am I to critique a compliment?

"Yeah," I say.

"Wow," he says, shaking his head with owl-wide eyes. "I mean: *wow*."

Ah, but even I am not the skinniest sprite at the Y.

There is a new girl on the fitness floor today. My Anorexic Idol is five feet, five inches tall and weighs about eighty pounds. She is so painfully frail that if she fell, she'd crack her skeleton clean in half. Her torso is beyond trim; her ribs jut out from beneath the skin, skin so thin it is almost translucent, like the wrapping of a spring roll. When she stands in profile, it appears as though her stomach had been hallowed out with an ice-cream scoop.

My Anorexic Idol exhibits the trademark contradiction of exercise addicts—so much oomph despite the emaciated state. Only women in pursuit of corporeal perfection possess this extreme energy level. She throws herself to the floor mat and thrashes her legs in frantic bicycle crunches, flattening a phantom tummy pooch.

My Anorexic Idol's pipe-cleaner body both disgusts and intrigues me. Watching her, I battle opposing urges: one, to shake her bony shoulders and shout, "Stop already! You're going to kill yourself!" and two, to high-five her with "You go, girl!" That degree of thinness requires a level of self-discipline that I aspire to.

Not that I don't get my freak-show share of attention.

"You've got that V muscle going on," a bicyclist in a hooded sweatshirt says as I complete a set of ab exercises. "I've never seen that on a female."

Of course you haven't, Ana smirks. *There's only one Super Woman.*

"I'm looking to lose ten pounds myself," he says, patting his belly. "Any tips?"

Just restriction, compulsive exercise, and sadistic torture. Laxatives work well, but barfing is better.

But anorexics never share their secrets, so I say, "Lots of produce."

In the weightlifting area, I lose myself in the one-to-ten rhythm of the bench press. Lift, lower. Lift, lower. One set turns into two, then three. I am about to embark on my fourth round when confusion floods my brain. I set the weights down, lean my elbows onto my knees, and suck down as much breath as I can. The Cybex machines look like space shuttle equipment. Have I landed on Mars? What I am doing? Where am I? *Who* am I?

Shh, Ana says. *It's too early to think. Keep lifting. One more rep. One more machine. Almost done.*

"Smokin' guns," a buff baldy says as he passes by me mid-biceps curl.

See? Ana says. *You're not sick. You're strong.*

I try not to shit where I eat; or, in this case, date where I work out. But when my running hiatus ends, and I return to the treadmill for daily ten-milers, the guy gym-goers flock.

"You should do Grandma's Marathon in Duluth!"

For weeks, Tri-Guy has sidled up to me at the Y with the same refrain. He's attractive enough—tall with a sturdy build and shy smile—though his brown hair is balding a bit. His eyes, while sparkling, are uneven; one seems stuck in a perpetual wink.

Today, we bump into one another in the weight room.

"If you ever want to have coffee sometime . . ." he says.

I look over my shoulder as I squeeze the life out of my inner thighs.

"Give me a call," Tri-Guy says and hands me his business card.

Coffee turns into lunch, then dinner. The only things Tri-Guy and I have in common are running and a mutual fascination with, well, me. Tri-Guy is gaga over the fantastical Erica Rivera. In his presence, I feel like a puppet performing the peppiest version of myself.

No more than five minutes after our good-bye handshake, my phone beeps with a message from Tri-Guy. "Not only are you beautiful, you're incredibly fun to be with," he gushes on my voicemail.

As I delete the message with one hand, I stuff an M&M's cookie in my mouth with the other. What did I do to impress Tri-Guy so?

I only shared the most mundane, minor details of my life; Tri-Guy isn't anywhere near knowing what makes me tick.

Tri-Guy is perfect on paper: a CTO of an up-and-coming technology company, a world traveler, and a triathloner (hence the nickname) with money to burn. There's only one problem: I don't want to jump his bones. For two dates, I employ my best conversational maneuvers to keep him talking. As long as his lips are busy recounting his latest business merger or African safari, I avoid making out with him.

On the infamous third date, Tri-Guy prepares an elaborate homemade spread, tailored to my Zone-style diet: shrimp cocktail, field greens, broiled salmon, and mango slices.

It's clear what's on the menu for dessert.

I am so tired—now that I'm running again, I don't stay up past 8:00 P.M.—that when Tri-Guy leans in for a kiss, it seems easier to submit to his advances than initiate the "I need to go slow" conversation.

After the regulatory tonsil hockey, I slink down into the marshmallow fluff comforter on Tri-Guy's bed. He undresses me and slides down my body. He kisses the inside of my thighs, working his way upward, buries his face between my legs, and I feel . . . nothing. If something is happening down there in the promised land, my body isn't picking it up on the radar. I can hear the sounds of oral sex and I see Tri-Guy's head bobbing up and down, tongue flicking in and out, but I can't break through the barrier to ecstasy.

I know when Tri-Guy penetrates me by the pressure in my pelvis, but there's no improvement in the pleasure department. The mechanics work, but the act is completely devoid of emotion. Tri-Guy is so quiet I worry that if I exhale too loudly he'll lose his erection.

I've never had bad sex before. Normally, I'm multiorgasmic.

But tonight, it feels as though Ana shot my genitals with a stun gun. The same ability that allows me to block out physical sensations—running on a stress fracture, leg-pressing weights heavier than my body, and ignoring gnawing hunger—comes back to bite me in the ass during my booty call.

My spirit slips out of corporeal boundaries, rises like steam, and hovers above me. I watch the learned lovers go through the motions below, but I am not present in any form.

After a few slow thrusts, Tri-Guy collapses on top of me.

He does not ask if I came.

I didn't.

"Stay over," Tri-Guy coos as we engage in the postcoital cuddle. "I'll make you eggs Benedict in the morning."

This—a man who wants me to stick around after sex *and* cook for me—is a rarity. This could be a bona fide relationship.

Tri-Guy stares at me with wide, eager eyes.

"We'll go running together," he says.

Game over.

Puh-lease, Ana moans. *Tri-Guy can't possibly run fast and far enough for a decent workout. Besides, eggs Benedict is known for its fattening Hollandaise sauce. Get the hell outta here before you blow up!*

I suddenly understand how commitment-phobic men feel. All I want is to dash out of the apartment, speed away in my SUV, and get home in time for *The Tonight Show.*

"I have a thing against overnights," I lie. In fact, it's been so long since I had a lover, I would give my left arm—not a leg; I need that for running—to wake up with a warm male body in the bed next to me. But Tri-Guy, as perfect as he appears to be, is not worth sacrificing sleep for.

"I understand," he says.

I scurry off into the night and shoot through my front door just as Jay Leno launches into his monologue.

The next morning, I run a kick-ass ten-miler.

Ahh, Ana sighs while I stretch. *A great run beats a great guy any day.*

"I'm going to break up with Tri-Guy," I tell my coworker Judy later that week.

"But Tri-Guy's *good* for you," she says.

"He's a person, not a prescription!"

"I think you're scared," Judy says. "Because a man is finally treating you right."

I *am* scared. Scared of how I'll maintain a romantic relationship without ruining my rigid eating plan and running routine. The imminent threats to Ana spin in my brain: There'll be late-night sex sessions, lazy Sunday mornings, catered office parties, family barbecues, rich desserts, and expensive wine. How will I have energy for running? How many pounds will a man cost me?

Ana has me firmly in her grasp. Like an abusive lover, she strips away my social support by convincing me I can trust no one.

They're out to get you, Ana warns, *or at the very least, they're going to destroy your diet.*

Because 99 percent of socializing revolves around food, I have to stay away from people to control my caloric intake.

Katrina, my sole remaining friend, is sitting across from me at Starbucks slurping a green tea frappuccino piled high with whipped cream and raspberry syrup. I don't drink blended coffee anymore—all that milk, so much sugar!—so I sip a lukewarm mug of house blend, coffee so bitter I can barely swallow it.

Katrina is a newlywed. When she's not bitching about her in-laws, she recounts quotidian minutiae of domestic life. Will she and her husband Matt use their tax return for a new deck or a new car? Which room of their custom-built home will they paint next?

Katrina talks. I try to listen. But Ana has control of my eyes. I trace the chubby outlines of Katrina's body, mentally shearing away the thick layers of flab, imagining a thinner, prettier, more appealing version of my only friend.

Katrina suddenly interrupts her own stream-of-consciousness rant. "Do you ever feel alone, Erica?"

Oh. It's my turn to talk.

"Uh . . . yeah, sometimes I do."

The more sincere response would be, "Do I ever not feel alone?"

Katrina sighs and something inside me settles; perhaps my friend will offer up some soothing words of wisdom.

"Yeah," she says. "Me, too. On the nights Matt works late, I feel really alone."

I nod. I offer up a whimper of sympathy. Inside, I seethe.

Our experiences of aloneness are not even in the same emotional stratosphere.

"Speaking of Matt, I've gotta stop at Bruegger's and pick up a bagel for him."

Game face time. I crack a smile and give her the obligatory hug. As Katrina's fat folds beneath my embrace, I comfort myself with this: I may not have a husband anymore, but I will never, ever, be obese.

"Where are you off to?" she asks.

"I've got a crazy busy afternoon," I say.

In truth, all I do is drive down the block to the bookstore.

Ana likes to pass the time reading recipes. There is a pistachio-hued armchair at Barnes & Noble that I claim as my anorexic hang-out. It isn't just the overstuffed upholstery that draws me to that particular spot; my favorite chair faces the Great Wall of Cookbooks. My shrine is made up of titles such as *The Seven Sins of Chocolate*, *Brownies to Die For*, *A Passion for Ice Cream*, and *Chocolate Obsession*.

Like a teenage boy who's stumbled across his father's *Playboy* collection, I flip through the brightly colored books with a squeamish, secretive enjoyment. Gazing at photographs of gooey cakes and cookies turns me on, makes my heart pump and the butterflies in my stomach go berserk.

Thinking about eating is almost as satisfying as physically doing it. I curl up in the chair like a snail, and loneliness washes over me like a warm bath; comforting and familiar, it lulls into sleep.

* * *

When I take off for my run at four o'clock in the morning, the sky is as black as a charcoal pit. Due to the recent heat wave, it's eighty degrees outside and the humidity is as thick as a fleece blanket.

I'm soaring down Wilderness Run Road and into the tucked-away oasis of a park when the bomb drops.

No, not from the sky. Not an A-bomb. Not Pearl Harbor, part two.

The blueberry bomb.

In my gut.

Last night, I stood before the fridge, searching for a substance to stuff down whatever yucky muck of emotions had bubbled up inside me. The sweetest substance in stock was blueberries. So I shoved handful after handful of the little blue orbs into my mouth. As the cold skin of the berries broke between my teeth, juice burst in sweet explosions on my tongue. In a matter of minutes, I had two pounds of blueberry bloat in my stomach, so I downed a few Correctol and went to bed.

Now the blueberries are fighting back.

The breath in my lungs plummets into my stomach and I double over. The blueberries have to come out, one end or the other. I duck behind a bush just before a river of liquefied feces shoots out of me in tandem with a stream of piss. The sludge slides across the grass beneath me, barely avoiding my sneakers.

When the dual streams stop, I stand, relieved and weightless. I barely give a passing glance to my surroundings—the only people up this early would be lunatics. Like me.

I pick up the pace where I left off, but my stomach sloshes inside my body like a cauldron of hot stew. I only make it one more mile before the bomb drops again. I scuttle into a pocket of evergreens on the edge of someone's backyard, squat, and let 'er rip. I feel a twinge of pride—though I've never had the runs *on* a run, I'm getting pretty efficient at this shitting by the side of the road routine.

By the time I arrive home, I'm completely drained.

Yet inside, Ana is cheering.

Jump on the scale! she screams. *Let's see how much weight you lost!*

I strip off my acrid shorts and sports bra, both soaked through with body fluids, and hop on the scale. The red needle hovers, then settles, on 104 pounds.

Holy shit.

It's never gone this low before.

In disbelief, I step on the digital scale as well: 111 pounds. Three beeps sound as my body fat is calculated: 5.5 percent.

That's, like, dead.

As I admire my divinely smooth, flat stomach in the mirror from every angle, a vibrant sensation radiates through my body. I feel as though I've been scraped from the inside out with a spatula, like a bowl licked clean of brownie batter.

Hollow. Empty. Pure.

"Thin enough now?" I ask aloud to an invisible Ana.

Not yet, she whispers. *Close, but not quite there.*

I recall a quote from *People* magazine: "The perfect anorectic is dead."

I wonder: How many more pounds until perfection?

chapter sixteen

The Mommy Meltdown

Beneath the summer sun, I turn into a lizard.

The signs that I've done irreparable damage to my body seep out. My skin sloughs off like scales; my spine erodes into a column of misshapen rocks. My hands turn red and ashy; the skin across my knuckles breaks open and bleeds. My teeth jut out from the jaw like a horse. My stomach develops a fine symphonic range; I can audibly trace the bubbles of digestion rolling through the intestines. My bowels belch and hiss and gurgle at random. My period is still MIA, twelve months and counting.

A gap breaks between my buttocks, a canyon so wide I can see straight through to the other side of my body. I can't keep my fingers from fondling the crack, from estimating in inches how much space I have between the cheeks. A dark bruise covers my tailbone, making it look as though I had forgotten to wipe after my last trip to the toilet.

When I stand, energy leaks from my limbs. I feel like I am losing blood through some unidentifiable hole in my body, though I can't find where to put my finger to plug up the flow. If I could, I'd live my life lying down, though I no longer need to be prostrate to catch up on my shut-eye. I can fall asleep anytime, anywhere: at the movies, at the bookstore, even during an eyebrow wax.

People stare at me as though I were a mangy animal on display at the public zoo. I resemble the bodybuilders of *Oxygen* magazine whose veins erupt from overtoned arms, faces fixed expressionless and hard, like baked Barbie dolls. I barely recognize my own reflection; my features—the sunken eyes, the asymmetrical lines etched in my forehead, lazy lips in a perpetual frown—frighten me.

I spend a lot of time in front of the mirror. Every curve and bone is subject to checks. Every morning I grasp my thighs from behind, grip the two handfuls of squishy cellulite, and pull them apart. Like a chaperone to two horny teenagers, I must keep my thighs as far apart as possible or something disastrous will happen. If all systems are go after a thorough self-examination, the day proceeds peacefully. Any shift or expansion, however, and optimism implodes in my face.

I am the mother of three children; two real, one invisible. It's clear who the prodigal daughter is. The scoreboard in my Game of Life reads: Ana: all, Julia and Lola: nothing.

Ana makes me a miserable parent. I can't care for my eating-disordered ego and raise kids at the same time. When I restrict, I'm a beast; the slightest sassiness, a single spilled Sippy cup, or a broken whatchamacallit sets me off.

The girls are testy, too. One morning, I unplug the TV before Blue finds her last clue.

Julia wails on a decibel level between a foghorn and fire engine siren. Mean Mommy explodes inches from the three-year-old's chubby face.

"WHAT. ARE. YOU. CRYING. ABOUT?"

Julia lifts her big green eyes, the irises drowning in tears, and says, "I want a new Mommy."

Your wish is my command. Mommy is replaced by a mummy.

The flat affect that overtakes my face spreads and infects my entire body. Even caffeine in copious amounts fails to rouse me, sending a chain reaction of twitches and tingles through my veins, as though my nervous system were trying to electrocute itself back into action. A dull buzz hums in my brain; my soul is comatose.

The girls and I are registered for Preschool Fun for Us at the Eagan Community Center. When the first day of class arrives, however, the girls sit transfixed by Nick Jr. cartoons on the couch. Once Dora the Explorer embarks on her trek to the gooey geyser, it seems cruel to turn the TV off.

I know I won't fit in with the other mothers, those women with marble-size diamonds on their fingers, inch-long lacquered nails, delicately highlighted locks, and waists even tinier than mine. Mothers who remember to pack organic juice boxes and hormone-free milk; mothers that potty-train their children before the second birthday.

I am not that kind of mother anymore. I sit in a catatonic state every afternoon on the living room floor as my daughters tumble around and empty out baskets of toys. I rarely interact with them. I observe. I make sure no one dies on my watch. I do not nurture. I do not cuddle. I do not participate in their play.

I'm satisfied if my daughters' shirts match their pants and their crooked bobs are brushed. The girls might lounge all afternoon in dirty diapers; even the rotting shit stench won't rouse me.

We rarely venture out anymore; when we do, it's for food. This self-imposed hibernation is enough to drive any mother crazy—that is, if I weren't nuts already.

"More please, Mommy," Julia requests in seamless Spanish. She pushes an empty yogurt container across the toddler table.

"Wow. You must be hungry," I say as I uncover another Trix yogurt.

Julia lifts the container to her lips and slams the neon goo down her throat.

"More please, Mommy."

"No, Julia. Two is enough."

"Mom-*eee*."

"Are you really hungry?"

"Yes."

"Okay."

Yogurt number three down the hatch.

"Grahams, please."

I drop the cinnamon graham cracker sticks onto her place mat. Julia places each one delicately on her tongue. She chews, then spits, a brown sludge onto her napkin. I watch from the counter as my daughter repeats the action with every last graham cracker.

Baby binges. Child-size chew and spit.

I bet they don't teach *that* at Preschool Fun for Us.

As though fitted with special ED glasses, my daughters can see Ana and BB lurking beneath my Mommy façade. The moments of clarity, when I realize that the girls are actually paying attention to the world around them, are increasing.

"*Palom . . . mitis! Palo . . . mentas! Palo . . . mitas!*"

Julia is pretending to have forgotten the Spanish word for "popcorn." It is Friday—aka Mommy-and-Me day—and we are at the Minnesota Zoo. The bad news: Ana plans our weekly excursions, which vary according to her appetite. The good news: At least we're out of the house and in the real world.

We used to go to the Children's Museum, where I sat on the parents' bench and stared at the Magic School Bus display blinking away. The flashing lights, the canned echo of an artificial thunderstorm, the giggles and shrieks of other people's toddlers put me in a hypnotic state.

Now the zoo is Ana's favorite place because it requires so much walking. The girls love the zoo, too, especially since the remodeled snack bar opened at the entrance. On a typical outing, I spend as much time watching the girls swallow giant bags of popcorn as I do admiring animals. My daughters' diets have devolved to gas station cookies, McDonald's ice cream, and an assortment of vending machine treats.

Julia shoves another handful of cheese popcorn into her mouth; half of the fluorescent cheddar kernels tumble to the floor. Every few minutes, she folds the top of the red-and-white striped bag down and passes it to me as though she were finished. Only seconds later, she pokes me in the ribs and begs the bag back.

Across the atrium, a mother whips her kids around and around in circles. They squeal in delight from their seats in the double stroller.

"That looks like fun," Julia sighs. She stuffs a bundle of popcorn into her mouth. "Mommy?"

"Huh?" I grunt in response.

"I wish you could be happy with us."

I love my daughters; I just don't know why they love me.

In my mind, Zombie Mommy is worse than no mommy at all, so I keep suicide simmering on the back burner; it's a wild card I hide in my pocket just in case life gets too hard. Because I can't guarantee I'll be around much longer, I keep my daughters at a distance. I don't want the girls to trust me too much; as long as Ana is my copilot, I'm unreliable. If time is the currency of love, I'm bound to go bankrupt.

If (or is it a question of when?) I die, the loss will be easier on my girls if their memories of me are bad ones. No one mourns a substandard parent, do they? Cesar will find another wife soon enough. The girls will grow up in their new family, so well mothered by another woman they'll forget I ever existed.

It feels like my daughters are holding me hostage.

My mother is doing her best to assist me with regular babysitting dates. One afternoon, on the five-minute drive from my house to hers, Julia and Lola fall asleep in the backseat. Neither my mother nor I want to wake them, so we let them stay asleep in the car while we sit on the couch and wait out the nap.

"You look nice," my mother says.

"Yeah, right," I say. My greasy hair is pulled back in a ponytail and tucked beneath a baseball cap, my shirt has a polka-dot design of coffee stains on the front, and I can't remember when I last washed my jeans.

"It would help if I knew what was wrong," my mother says.

"Isn't it obvious? My life is shit."

"You're overwhelmed."

"I'm beyond overwhelmed."

"Medication might be a good thing to ask your doctor about."

"How is that going to help, Mom?"

"I don't know . . . level out the mood swings?"

But my mood has been consistent—consistently depressed.

I stare straight ahead; in a recent feng shui attack, my mother painted the walls in optimistic lemon and tangerine hues. My presence here must be polluting her chi.

"You need to change your attitude," my mother says. "You have two daughters who love you."

"They love me because they have no other option."

"You are so ungrateful!" my mother sneers. "Do you know how many women want to have babies and can't?"

"Then they can have mine; I can hardly take care of them anymore."

The pull of the depression is so strong now, I feel like a sinking ship; throwing my daughters over the edge and into the lifeboats below seems like the only way to keep them from drowning along with me.

"Maybe the girls should be in daycare," my mother suggests.

"And how am I going to pay for that?"

"You can get another job."

"Doing what?"

"You can make good money waitressing."

"Yeah, working a crappy job for minimum wage would really help my depression!" I say sarcastically.

All the logic-boxing makes me dizzy. There are no clear-cut answers about where to go with my life—that is, if I want to go forward at all. Every option I follow in my mind leads to failure. Death seems like the only surefire solution.

I storm down the stairs.

"Where are you going?" my mother calls to me from the landing.

"I just want to get away!"

I sprint to the car, ready to fling the door open and wrench the girls from their car seats. Then I see their drowsy faces and their ruffled hair. They're so . . . adorable. Endearing. A momentary warm fuzzy melts something inside me.

My mother catches up to me. "Take a week off if you need to. I'll give you money. Where do you want to go?"

I don't even know. I'm too tired to do the tourist thing. Even packing a suitcase seems impossible right now.

Then I realize: I don't want to get away from Minnesota, or my daughters, or even my mother. I want to get away from *Ana*. No matter how far away I travel, she'll still be with me.

The girls shuffle in their car seats and open their eyes.

"I just want to go home," I say.

My mother returns the girls to me a couple of hours later, and we all act as if everything is back to normal.

Which, in a sick and twisted way, it is.

An average evening in the Rivera household looks like this: I am on the spinner in the basement, crying and sweating, trying to exorcise whatever dietary demon I devoured that day. Heaving, primitive cries rise from my throat, punctuated by multiple *fuck you*s to whatever deity might be listening.

The girls are upstairs in the darkened family room, watching their fourth video in a row. When their movie ends, the girls will whip off their clothes and chase each other around the house. They will fill their matching potties and splatter the piss across the bathroom walls like urinary graffiti artists.

I might bathe them. I might not. I'll dress them in one-day-dirty pajamas. If I have a modicum of energy left, I will recite—not read; my brain can't handle that anymore—*Goodnight Moon*.

Once they're asleep, I'll immerse myself in a scathing shower, sitting in the tub, knees to chest, crying and peeing until the water turns icy.

Sound dysfunctional?

Here's the trick: by the end of the night, I'm too exhausted from all the exercise to entertain suicide.

JOURNAL ENTRY

I let Ana drive the Mommy bus today. That way, I can stay numb while I wait for the heart attack that never comes. Maybe a hunger strike is the way to go, but it would take forever to die.

chapter seventeen

Eating My Words

As my body disintegrates, the writer in me emerges. While I was a casual poet in high school, my writing, along with the rest of my hobbies, was jettisoned when I married Cesar.

Now I'm the slave of a midnight muse and nocturnal inspiration. Many nights, I awake with a start, as though I've been bitten by an invisible insect. My hand shoots toward the bedside table and grabs a stack of Post-its and a pen. Even half-asleep, I compose full-page poems. The next morning, I rarely recognize my manic scribblings.

Words spawn more words. I write like I do everything else—in excess. I write standing at the kitchen counter while my daughters devour breakfast. I write in the car as I swerve like a drunk driver across the Mendota Bridge. I write at work when I should be redirecting adolescents' inappropriate boundaries. I write while I grocery shop, while I shower, while I shit. I write in my head all day long.

Soon I tire of my self-indulgent journaling habit and dive deeper into my poems. The poems expand and grow into essays. I wonder: Is there a memoir here?

To find out, I attend a writing workshop at the Split Rock Arts Program.

I'm in the spotlight; well, okay, there isn't a spotlight, they're fluorescent lights, and I'm not on a stage, I'm seated at a conference table. My classmates, the usual suspects for this kind of workshop, surround me. There's the cancer survivor with spiky hair and excessive enthusiasm for life; the middle-aged mother mourning the untimely death of her teenage daughter; the recovered heroin addict who almost jumped off the Golden Gate Bridge; the silver-haired shrink-turned-mystic. I am the youngest student here; I am also the thinnest. Both these facts buoy me from the fact that I am also the most inexperienced writer of the bunch.

As part of the class, each student is required to distribute a sample of his or her writing for commentary.

Today is my day.

My project, all ten polished pages of it, is a love story. The sample I've submitted describes a weekend I spent with a former lover, including a scene in which I prepare dinner for my sweetheart.

I look eagerly around the table with held breath as I await my classmates' responses.

"Who brought the cupcake?" Shrink-turned-Mystic asks.

In a flush of creative inspiration, I inserted a cupcake into one scene and described eating it in detail. While the dinner is true to life, the dessert is pure invention. I don't feel guilty about the little white lie, because the cupcake serves as an edible metaphor.

I blush as a ripple of wrinkled faces turn toward me.

"Actually," I say. "There was no cupcake."

A choir of gasps fills the room.

"You mean . . . you made it up?" Mourning Mother whimpers.

"I thought writers could embellish in memoir," I say. "As long as the scene is emotionally true."

Jaws drop and heads shake. From their devastation, you'd think I just fabricated the death of my dog.

"I can't believe you didn't eat the cupcake," Mourning Mother says with a wobbly chin.

A cacophony of whispered insults rises from the table like flour from a bakery vent. Accusations of dishonesty echo through the room. I feel like I've been dropped in an estrogen-infused version of the film *Twelve Angry Men*.

"It's just a cupcake," I say.

"But it was such a focal point of the chapter," Recovered Addict says.

"You've completely lost your credibility with me as a reader," Cancer Survivor says as she readjusts her pink-ribbon visor.

"Sorry everybody. Jeez," I say, raising my hands like a convict.

"No, this is good," author-instructor Paulette Bates Alden says. "It brings up the issue of honesty in writing."

Deliberation ensues about the disclaimer necessary to excuse the cupcake's inclusion. The suggestions range from a footnote to a prologue to scrapping the memoir label altogether and rewriting the story as a novel.

"I'll cut that part out," I say. "I can eat the cupcake in another book!"

Cancer Survivor slaps the manuscript down on the table and sighs.

"Anorexia is written all over this," she says.

"Excuse me?" I say as I pull out the Coleman cooler that travels with me everywhere. I don't usually eat in front of my peers, but the stress is making my stomach grumble. I need to crunch on something.

"Your best writing is about the food. You describe the pastry you ate with more detail than you do your lover."

"I was probably craving something sweet, and writing about the cupcake was the next best thing to eating one."

"I have to ask," Cancer Survivor says. "Have you had personal experience with eating disorders?"

"When I was younger, sure," I say as I snap a bare celery stick between my teeth. A cacophony of *ah-ha*s echoed around the room. "But that's under control now."

"Uh-huh," someone mumbles.

Cancer Survivor looks at me as though she could shoot arrows with her eyes. Her voice thunders above the din as she says, "Write *that* story. See where it takes you."

On my way home from the Split Rock Arts Program that day, I cross the Ford Bridge. The Mississippi River rushes beneath me, the sun shines blindingly white-hot above. Inside my head, angry voices swirl and conjure up comebacks I could have spat at the writers' roundtable. The cupcake debate doesn't bother me; the focus on the food does. I'm writing a love story, damn it! Why isn't that coming through?

Something explodes inside me and I release a scream so loud and fierce it feels like I'm giving birth. I hit the steering wheel, curse, and swerve.

Then I realize why I'm so pissed off: I've been caught. Whether my subject is a cupcake or an eating disorder, it's impossible to lie in writing. The truth seeps out between the lines and readers will recognize it even if the author doesn't.

JOURNAL ENTRY

It is becoming harder and harder to separate the writer in me from Ana. Is she keeping me from developing my talents?

I take Cancer Survivor's advice. It's time to expose Ana on the page. On the last day of the Split Rock Arts Program, my class convenes for a formal reading in the basement of the Coffman Union. The theater is called The Whole, though with its army green walls and artistically placed graffiti, "The Hole" would be more fitting.

When my turn at the podium arrives, I prop up my laptop and tightly clench my fists so my classmates won't see how hard I'm shaking.

Like the bad sex experience a few months before, I'm out of my body, hovering somewhere between the ceiling and the stage.

I read:

> *I am composing a pact. Yesterday, as I bounced on the elliptical machine in my musty basement, depression, my constant companion, crawled up my weary legs and perched on my shoulder as it has done every day since my divorce.*

The words tumble out of my mouth despite my quivering tongue. The voice that erupts from deep within me is at first unfamiliar; it is angry, yet strong.

I take a shallow breath and continue:

> *I imagine my depression—and it is, truly, uniquely mine—in the form of the Grim Reaper; drowning in a black velvet cape with a face too blurry to make out. The depression reminded me, in its monotone mumble, that my life is miserable, that there are no more pleasures in store for me. I told the depression that I understood its despair, its unrelenting urge to throw in the towel and dissolve into obliviousness, to disappear, even if only to see who the hell would notice that I'd gone.*
>
> *I've taunted death in the past with depression's best friend, anorexia. I've starved myself to skin and bones, scraped out my insides with laxatives, and dared my heart to break down with daily 10-mile runs. I'm not dead yet; but I'm not alive, either.*
>
> *So I made a pact with my depression and anorexia. This is the pact: write it all down. Get my pitiful existence on paper. If, upon completion of my documentation, my life is no better than it is at this moment, I will let them win. I will let them take me. I don't know who will come out victorious in this battle; perhaps none of us will. The hopeful voice*

*inside says this is a safe wager; that chances are, by the time I finish
writing this memoir, I will have met a new Prince Charming, gradu-
ated with my Master's, found a fulfilling job, and have some new athletic achievements under my belt.*

*The depression smirked at the hopeful voice, knowing that it would
not be destroyed so easily. I've had many, many bursts of hope in the past
and none has been explosive enough to free me from the bonds of my bosom
buddies. For now, they are both still here, peering over my shoulder at
these pages, and no amount of running or eating or hoping has lessened
their grip on me.*

And so it begins, my story.

When I finish reading, I'm sweating and my cheeks are scalding.
When I look up at my classmates, a dozen shocked faces stare back
at me. The room is dead silent.

"Thank you," Paulette says.

My eyes connect with Cancer Survivor; she smiles knowingly
and nods. When I return to my seat, Shrink-turned-Mystic taps my
knee and whispers, "You have a gift."

That afternoon when I drive home over the Ford Bridge, something explodes inside me again—not anger, but energy. My whole
body hums with self-assuredness. I'm finally speaking my truth.

JOURNAL ENTRY

In *The Writer's Life*, author Julia Cameron says going sane looks
a lot like going insane. I struggle to differentiate between the
two states, but I'm certain I don't want to waste any more of my
life on Ana.

After the workshop, Paulette schedules conferences with each attendee.

"I don't know you well, Erica," she says in her sweet Southern accent, "but I can tell you're smart. You have everything you need to be a writer."

She encourages me to apply to the University of Minnesota as a non-degree-seeking student in the Creative Writing Program. I start filling out the paperwork that same day, but I won't be notified for weeks regarding the university's decision.

Half a summer of uncertainty remains; sufficient time, I assume, to exorcise Ana from my life.

chapter eighteen

The Downfall(s)

The physical downfall comes first.

I'm charging along Penn Avenue, only a block into my running route, at 4:45 A.M. The path is dark, save for a flashing construction sign near a pothole. I leap off the sidewalk, into the street, and over a curb.

Then I go down.

This isn't the kind of fall where I watch myself flying through the air in slow motion, completely helpless as I await the inevitable splat on the sidewalk, and later wonder how one second seemed to last so long.

This is the kind of fall where I don't even realize I tripped until I'm facedown, spread-eagle, on the concrete. My Discman is several feet in front of me, the Alanis Morissette CD spit far beyond it, and the batteries are scattered across the street. When I stand to retrieve my music, I see my palms are streaked with scarlet scratches. There is also an inch-deep, quarter-size wound on my knee. Blood oozes down my leg, and I think I can see the ivory tip of a bone.

Ana and I don't debate about whether or not to log my mandatory ten miles today.

Injury is no excuse for skimping on calorie burn, she tells me.

The run must go on.

By the end of the route, the sun is rising and I begin to pass other early-bird exercisers. I imagine the sight from their eyes: a broomstick-thin woman bleeding from the hands and knees, running like a hunted animal. No one stops, or even slows, to ask if I'm all right.

Not that I want help. Ana is still invincible, after all; it's this damn body that's so unreliable.

The financial downfall follows.

The bills have been piling up for months. I'm beyond living paycheck to paycheck; most of my divorce settlement is gone, and I'm subsisting off loans I won't be able to pay back for years, perhaps decades.

I've taken retail therapy to the next level. My closet is filled with clothes that still have the tags on, shoes I've purchased solely to match certain purses, and more belts than I have pairs of pants. After exhausting the space in my closet, I hit up arts and crafts stores for trinkets and doodads to decorate my house.

My friends at Wells Fargo don't consider my spending problematic, so why should I? Every time I overspend, they charge me a nominal fee followed by a letter congratulating me on my newly increased credit limit. As long as the cards keep swiping, I won't stop shopping.

I haven't hit rock bottom yet, but I'm catapulting toward it without a parachute to slow my descent.

Credit Consolidation Services is *so* not my scene, but I'm too broke to pay for a financial adviser. Instead, I sign up for a free appointment with a credit counselor. I await my appointment among welfare mothers and homeless men in a lobby that reeks of cheap hair products and body odor.

A chubby man in a wrinkled dress shirt calls my name and leads me into a basement office.

"Let's see what you've got," Patrick says as his computer hums to life. I spread my credit cards across his desk like a poker dealer.

"Starbucks Visa!" he exclaims. "I didn't even know they made these."

"Every store has a charge card now," I say.

"What is the interest rate on this?" he asks.

"Twenty-nine point nine percent."

"For *coffee?*"

"Is that unreasonable?" I ask.

Patrick shakes his head and flashes me a condescending smile.

"The first thing I tell my clients about coffee is that it's the equivalent of a pack-a-day cigarette habit."

"Exactly," I say. Finally, someone who understands how addictive java can be!

"What I mean is: Brand-name coffee does major damage to your budget. As such, it's the first thing you need to cut."

I grimace at the thought of a day sans caffeine fixes. Maybe I'm not ready for a financial reality check yet.

Patrick punches each credit card balance into his computer and calculates how much it would cost to pay off my debt over a five-year period.

"Before I can consolidate these cards," he says, "you have to prove you'll be able to pay the monthly fee. Let's make a list of your expenses."

His fat fingers hover over the keyboard, awaiting my monetary confessions. Shame wells up inside me. "I haven't always been this irresponsible!" I want to say. "I'm not a diva; I'm depressed. I'm trying to spend my way to a better mood."

I stay silent. Patrick doesn't care how I got into this hole; he just wants to get me out.

"Medication costs?" he asks.

My voice trips over my tongue; I spout off a few unintelligible sounds and finally mutter, "Nuh-uh."

"Is there anything else you'd like to say about that?"

I'd like to say that frappuccinos *are* my medication—they're that essential. My daily Starbucks pit stop is my motivation to get out of the house in the morning, to run an extra mile when I'm exhausted, to shuttle my kids from one family-friendly outing to another.

"No," I say with a sigh. "There's nothing more to say about that."

When we finish the budget, Patrick tells me I'm spending $2,000 more a month than I earn.

"Time to trim the fat," he says. He looks over my spreadsheet. "Can we cut the health club membership?"

I shake my head. "No can do. I'm a runner."

"Can't you run outside?"

I shoot him an indignant glare.

"Not when it's twenty degrees below zero," I say. "The YMCA is nonnegotiable."

Patrick's eyes return to the spreadsheet.

"You'll have to eat out less."

"I don't eat out."

"Then spend less on groceries; use coupons, buy what's on sale."

"I don't skimp on nutrition."

"No more seventy-five-dollar facials. Get haircuts at the beauty school. Trade massages with a friend. Carpool to school. Sell your house. Work more. Spend less."

"Hallelujah!" I want to scream. "Why didn't *I* think of that?"

The conversation has catapulted into the realm of absurdity. It's like me telling Pudgy Patrick to run ten miles a day and subsist on salads.

"Nice suggestions," I say. "But they're unrealistic."

Patrick slides the spreadsheet into a file folder and slaps it shut.

"I can't help you until your spending is under control," he says. "Either you make some changes or our next appointment will be to discuss bankruptcy."

I'm too tired to work more. I'd die without the Y. Since I stopped dating, my weekly visits to the spa are the only times I'm touched.

The sole suggestion of Patrick's I can put into practice is selling my house. After my divorce, my mother gave me an open offer to cohabitate, so I make arrangements to move in with her as soon as the house sells.

Then I call my Realtor, Kathy.

"You've lost more weight!" she exclaims when she shimmies her way through my front door.

And you haven't lost a pound! Ana replies in my head.

"Have I?" I say.

I don't think I look thinner, though I certainly look worn out. The last time Kathy saw me, she was handing me the keys to my dream house. Today my hair is held back by a headband and I'm dressed in the same baggy sweats from my morning workout.

"Stress," Kathy says with a diagnostic nod and a frown.

As Kathy leads me through the presale paperwork, she switches back and forth between reading and prescription glasses; when she gets fed up with the fine print, she puts on both pairs at once. If this were a sitcom, canned laughter would be echoing through the room.

But this is my life and it's far from funny.

Kathy hands me a stack of papers in triplicate. I sign them all without reading a line.

"Okay!" she says in her foghorn voice. She flips through her calendar. "How's Sunday for an open house?"

"That's so soon," I say. I'd been hoping for at least another month to stew in my denial.

"The market is miserable, Erica. We have to act fast."

Kathy cradles her black leather folder in one hand, a poised pen in the other.

I sigh. "Yeah, Sunday's fine."

"Don't worry," Kathy says with a pat on the arm. "You'll get your degree, find a steady job, and soon you'll be buying a bigger, better place than this."

"Promise?" I want to ask. I force a smile that must look as fake as it feels.

"See you Sunday!" Kathy says as she trots down the walkway. "Make sure the lawn's ready!"

In the weeks to come, my cell phone rings incessantly with requests for showings—yet there are no offers. Not one. Though my house is immaculately clean and charming, it is in need of repairs—namely, new windows.

Every evening when I slog through the foyer, I notice signs that strangers have been in my home. The entryway lights are ablaze and the thermostat reset. A dining room chair is pushed back, a kitchen towel askew, a closet door ajar, the porch screen unhinged.

In the master bathroom, the toilet lid is upright and a pungent stench hangs in the air. It is this detail that irks me the most. If you are bold enough to shit in my house while I'm out, couldn't you at least take the pains to conceal it?

I picture the temporary ghosts who have wandered through the halls, reclined on my bed, rearranged my furniture, browsed my bookshelf. I picture them redecorating the bedrooms in their imaginations and whispering theories on why I'd want to sell such a cozy house.

After a month of daily showings, Kathy calls with news.

"We have an offer!" she says.

"Great," I say without an ounce of enthusiasm.

Kathy describes the contract: ten grand less than my asking price with a closing date one month away.

"Who's the buyer?" I ask.

"A single mom, like you! Small world, huh?"

"Yeah."

"Her father's the one paying for the house. He lives upstate, but he'll drive down to sign the papers and write the check. So . . . what do you think?"

Who cares what I think? I'm out of options.

"I'll take it," I say.

I flip my cell phone shut and burst into tears.

chapter nineteen

What's Up, Doc?

Do you feel that your life is manageable?

My pen hovers like a helicopter over the intake form at the Riverside Wellness Office. This should be a simple yes-no response, but I'm stuck. How honest do I want to be? Should I own up to my incapacitated state now and skip a looming interrogation from the MD?

My pen nosedives toward the blank boxes. I check yes.

Dr. Anderson is an anorexia expert and preferred medical provider for the Center for Eating Disorders. Aside from a physical, what I really want from this appointment is permission to pig out. Ana, however, insists on maintaining the starvation status quo. The tug-of-war is under way.

A nurse calls my name and leads me through a door, down a hall, and onto a scale. As I slip off my flip-flops, she peruses my chart.

"Oh," she says, lowering her voice with embarrassment. "I won't weigh you now."

She ushers me into a treatment room and wraps a blue cuff around my arm. Blood pumps through my limbs and my heart gallops in my chest. I shouldn't have had that second cup of coffee.

"Eighty-four over sixty," the nurse says. "Very good!"

The numbers sound low to me, but if she says they're good, they must be.

Another nurse knocks and enters with a tray of hypodermics. She gingerly slides the tray across the counter as though it were a plate of roasted quail.

"Nice veins!" she says when she eyes the brilliant blue piping down my arms. "That's what I like to see!"

The parade of providers continues. The next knock announces Dr. Anderson's arrival. He floats in like a monk, his white robe undulating like a ribbon. He is tall and gangly, aged like a sickly tree. His horse face displays the flattest affect I have ever seen.

"Weight," he says, motioning toward a scale in the corner of the room.

I place one big toe on the black base.

"No. Backward."

I clench my fists and step onto the scale. It is one thing to skip the weighing altogether so as not to upset me; it is quite another to refuse Ana the measure of her success. Granted, I already weighed myself at home today—twice—but it never hurts to compare my scale's accuracy to the high-tech readouts.

"I see Jane Hampstead is your emergency contact," he says as he jots down the digits. "She's a nurse, isn't she?"

"Yes," I say. "She's my mom."

Dr. Anderson's face brightens for an instant. "Yes! Now I see the resemblance."

Questions collide inside my head and prevent my lips from moving. How much does this man already know about me? What is his history with my mother? Is this a setup?

"How old is your brother now? Where is he going to school?"

Deadpan, I answer the questions, miffed that my health has taken a backseat to my family tree.

Dr. Anderson presses the cold O of the stethoscope to my chest, his forearm flattening whatever breasts I have left. The rush of blood floods my ears and drowns out my heartbeat. My shoulders tighten and fold inward, Ana's self-protection from this corporeal spy.

I want my heart to give Dr. Anderson a show. I want it to stop, to flutter, to somersault. I want to get caught and be sent away.

"Lie back, please," he says.

Dr. Anderson's hands move across my protruding stomach. He tap-taps each of the four quadrants as though he were playing a bongo drum. His fingers reach for my wrist and push down hard to find my pulse.

Auditory input expands in this frightening yet exciting silence. The second hand of the doc's watch ticks like a church bell at noon; the pager on his hip vibrates to life against my knee; a buzzer sounds just outside the door; feet shuffle in the hallway. A charged, ominous energy fills the room.

Dr. Anderson is going to call my mother. He's checking me in. The cavalry is coming!

"Forty-eight," he says when he drops my wrist.

Isn't that almost *dead*?

Dr. Anderson leans casually against the wall.

"How is treatment going?"

"One step forward and two steps back," I say.

Dr. Anderson's frown curls into a grin. "You mean: two steps forward and one step back."

"That's what I said."

"Mm-hmm." Dr. Anderson makes a note in my file. "Any questions for me?"

Only a thousand. Like: Am I thin enough yet? Can I stop restricting now? How do I escape Ana?

"How much weight do I need to gain?" I ask.

"That's personal," he says. "It's so hard to put a number on it."

But that's what weight is all about! Numbers, numbers, numbers!

"When people stop obsessing about food and eating, their weight will return to its natural state."

Ana makes me nod my head with a serious "I understand."

Inside, incarcerated Erica is shrieking. Can't he see? I'm crumbling. I'm a jigsaw puzzle in need of reassembly. I am imprisoned in my body; Ana is the unwavering warden. Haul me off, hospital gown and all, to a place where professionals in starched scrubs will care for me, where my sticky fingers won't find another box of Correctol, where there are no Sauconys in sight.

I want to incite just one fucking emotion in Dr. Anderson. I want the finger-shaking threats, the phone calls home to alert the mother ship: "Hampstead, we have a problem!" I want Dr. Anderson to take my chin in his leathery hand, squeeze my cheeks together, and bellow, "If you don't eat a hamburger tonight, you're going to have a heart attack!"

Why doesn't anyone want to help me?

Dr. Anderson and I stare at one another in silence.

"Keep doing the Center for Eating Disorders," he says, and *whooshes* out the door.

I follow Dr. Anderson's orders and return, tail between my bruised tailbone, to the Center for Eating Disorders. This time, I'm assigned a new therapist: Dr. Shania McDermott.

As soon as I crumple onto her salmon-colored couch, she says, "You look like shit."

You gotta love a shrink who doesn't beat around the bush.

To avoid Shania's concerned expression, I stare at her computer monitor, where animated tropical fish squiggle between green reeds. I have the same screen saver at home; Dave installed it shortly before we broke up. I wonder who installed hers.

"Erica?"

"Hmm?"

"Can you see the reality of the situation?"

"If I look so bad, why hasn't anyone commented on it?"

"Your family sees you every day; they might not notice. To me,

it's obvious. Your hair is thin. Your eyes are dark. You look exhausted. You look like you need to go back to Mendota Hospital."

"I don't want to do inpatient."

A half-lie. I'm starving, sunburned, and exhausted. I wouldn't
mind a weekend away on a hospital ward.

"You're not going to *want* to do it," Shania says. "But you should
go anyway. I'll help you make the call."

This is what I've been waiting for: someone to put her foot down
and say, in no uncertain terms, that I am a wreck. But Ana won't
admit that my shit-together façade is starting to stink.

"You have so many big transitions coming up," Shania says, referring to the upcoming move to my mother's house and my pend-
ing U of M application.

"*Exactly,*" I say. "I'm too busy to commit to a treatment plan."

"Think about what maintaining the eating disorder has cost
you."

I do: my education, my social circle, my romantic prospects, my
daughters' toddlerhoods. Hundreds of hours wasted sprinting and
spinning to nowhere.

Ana has eaten up my entire *life.*

And yet.

"That moment in the morning," I say. "When I look in the mirror and see the washboard abs . . ."

In my mind, I replay the daily split-second when I stand before
the mirror, sweaty and flushed after my workout, and my body tingles with satisfaction at the reflection.

"*Nothing* compares to that feeling. Nothing."

JOURNAL ENTRY

It's easy for Shania to want me to recover; she's on the "other
side," the side of health and happiness. I don't trust that my
circumstances will improve if I give Ana up. Ana is all I have at

the moment and she has been faithful to me as everyone else fades away. Ana is always fluttering just beneath the surface, ready to embrace me with open arms and cradle me with her sadistic comfort, the comfort of numbers that I can control— pounds, mileage, calories. My future is unknown, but if I can keep my weight stable, I'll feel safe.

To prove to Shania that my physical health isn't as bad as it seems, I schedule a follow-up exam at Mendota Hospital.

I like Dr. Walker right away; her cherry-colored lips and mother-hen physique remind me of my kindergarten teacher. Instead of disgusting, her stomach fat looks soothing; I want to snuggle up in the flabby folds and listen to her gut gurgles.

"Any unusual stress?" Dr. Walker asks as she brushes a lock of thick blond hair from her forehead.

"My life is all stress, all the time," I say.

I sit back against the hard plastic chair and clasp my hands across my lap.

"Any depression or anxiety?" Dr. Walker asks.

"Depression."

"Any thoughts of suicide or hurting yourself in any way?"

Yes. Every day. All day.

"No, nothing like that," I say.

"Just feeling down . . . ?" Dr. Walker says in her smooth soprano tone. Her voice trails off as though dangling a verbal hook.

Ana doesn't bite.

"Yeah," I say, twirling my earring around and around between my fingertips.

Dr. Walker quizzes me on a checklist of symptoms.

"Sleep?"

"Not enough."

"Feeling faint?"

"Occasionally."

"Headaches?"

"Once in a while."

Dr. Walker scribbles on my chart. I sneak a peek at the basic stats: heart rate, fifty-two; blood pressure: ninety-two over sixty-one. I can't make out my weight.

"So?" I ask. "How am I?"

Dr. Walker rocks back and forth in her chair.

"You're at the point, Erica, where you can choose: inpatient, day program, or outpatient."

"I qualify for inpatient?"

"Your BMI is almost as low as your original assessment," Dr. Walker says. "And as long as you're missing periods, you're too thin. You need to restore weight."

Dr. Walker keeps talking in her lullaby tone. I nod, I crinkle my forehead in mock concern, I smile politely. But I can barely hear her over Ana.

What a fucking failure. You've fattened up since December. You haven't maintained your discipline. You're not skinny—you're a slacker!

"Take a couple of days to think it over," Dr. Walker says, passing me a business card. "And give me a call."

I tuck the white-and-purple printed card in my wallet, knowing I'll chuck it at the first garbage can I pass. If all I need to do is eat, I can do so on my own, without experts breathing down my back.

"Don't put too much importance on what setting you'll be in," she says. "In the hospital or at home, you need structure to overcome this."

Dr. Walker stands and shakes my hand.

"Food for thought," she says and shuts the door behind her.

It's barely been twenty-four hours when Dr. Walker tracks me down.

"Erica," she says on my voicemail. "Your labs came back and I'm concerned." She sputters a blue streak of medical jargon I don't understand. "What that means is: your liver is leaking."

I hold out the phone in front of me, eyes wide with disbelief.

My liver is leaking? What the fuck? Doesn't that happen only to fall-down drunks or cancer-riddled geezers?

"This condition can be reversed," Dr. Walker continues. "But only if you improve your nutrition. If you have any questions, call me."

I *do* have a question, but it is one I'd never ask: Will it kill me?

After the liver-leaking announcement, my eating disorder morphs form. The Binge Bitch (BB) returns in an attempt to replace Ana and keep me alive. As though my body knew I wouldn't survive if I lost any more weight, the urge to stuff myself assaults me on a regular basis.

When BB takes over, I am at her mercy. When BB sends me on a mission, I drive any distance, drop any activity, and devote hours of time to appease her. She rips the steering wheel out of my hands, steers the SUV to the closest supermarket, fills another plastic basket with her favorite foods, signs the credit card slip, and unloads the groceries from the trunk. I am simply a bystander, an observer, completely out of control.

This isn't textbook emotional eating. I'm so numb that I transform every unidentifiable feeling into hunger. Hunger is a problem I have a surefire solution for, even if it is an unhealthy one.

Food is the ideal balm to self-soothe. When in the altered state of consumption, I detach from reality. My failed marriage, career confusion, superficial friendships, subpar parenting—all evaporate as my attention burrows itself in my taste buds. For those few moments, as the crispy coating of an M&M or a swirl of frosting dissolves on my tongue, the only world that matters is in my mouth.

Then the guilt kicks in and the chaos that BB creates shifts my distress from something ethereal (disappointment? loss? guilt?) to the concrete (shoving a birthday cake down my throat). My feelings of rage, disgust, and frustration finally make sense—who wouldn't hate themselves after eating so much crap?

chapter twenty

How to Binge: An Instruction Manual

Binges start in the brain.

Because you can't pick your thoughts and emotions like entrées at a Chinese buffet, something ugly is bound to bubble up inside you eventually. One effective way to cleanse yourself of these unpleasant experiences is to stuff the thoughts and emotions down, then shit them out.

Try it. You'll like it.

The true enjoyment of a binge begins in the meticulous planning that goes into it. Build up the anticipation over a period of time—though not too long or the urge will dissipate.

Fixate on a food. You must be specific. What brand? What flavor? What consistency? What temperature? Define the requirements with iron rigidity. Accept no substitutes. Pick your poison and hunt it down.

You can play games with the binges. A favorite way is to challenge fate. For example, as you walk to the mailbox, say, "If there's nothing life-altering in the mail, I'll binge." When you open the box and find a Victoria's Secret catalog, rest assured: this is absolutely enough justification to stuff yourself.

Bingeing is a specialized science, and the eater's recipe specifically tailored to the troubling emotion at hand. The Angry Binge is built on crunch: nuts, chips, dry cereal. The Lovesick Binge is pure sugary softness: ice cream, cake, caramel, marshmallows. The Self-Loathing Binge is the worst, a purely desperate act, when you eat whatever you can get your mouth around: stale cheese crackers, sugar-free Life Savers, fruit snacks stolen from your children's lunch boxes.

Start with a small portion of your forbidden food. If you are going off the dietary deep end, it better be for something you denied yourself during the many months of anorexia. Tell yourself that you will eat your treat like a normal person, guilt-free. Tell yourself you are in control. Initially, you will believe these lies. Don't despair; the inhibitions will evaporate exponentially with each bite.

After you polish off one portion, you have reached the crossroads. Do you stop and stay normal? Or do you indulge and go wild?

Life is short. Suffering is inevitable. Go with the latter.

Forget utensils; you have to use your hands. You must make this eating experience as primal as possible.

Get really gross with your binge food. Sniff it. Grope it. Lick it. Poke it.

Worried about your waistline? There are few loopholes big enough to slip your fat ass through.

Calories from binges do not count if you:

- Eat in the car

- Eat standing up

- Eat with your coat on

- Eat in the bathroom

- Eat off your child's plate

- Eat in secret

- Eat something healthy first

- Divvy up the food into piles before you eat it

- Do not know the nutritional content of the binge food

- Exercise after you eat

- Have a laxative chaser

- Are remarkably productive, creative, or otherwise brilliant afterward

Binges, like sex with a new lover, are always over too quickly. If you still have leftovers—and until you get good at this bingeing thing, you will—wet them, stuff them down the drain, hit the disposal, annihilate the evidence.

If guilt kicks in when all you have left are crumbs—and please, eat these too, if you are so inclined—head for the medicine cabinet, where you will surely have a month's supply of so-called gentle laxatives. *Warning:* They are not gentle if you down half a box. In only twelve hours, your digestive system will be completely clear of all the crap you compacted into your gut. Expect to lose one to five pounds in water weight and fecal matter.

Breathe a sigh of relief.

Rinse and repeat.

In the monthlong interim between selling my house and moving in with my mother, I unsuccessfully try to hide BB's dysfunctional behaviors from my daughters.

BB demands medication, in the form of sugar, all day long. To keep my food addiction alive and kicking, I convince myself that there is an invisible barrier between the front and back seats of my car. Today, my girls watch on as I chew and spit an entire box of Cinnamon Toast Crunch in the library parking lot.

"Don't eat it all," Julia says from her car seat. "You'll have a tummy ache."

"Who wants a twist cone?" I ask as I scrub the crumbs off my cheeks.

"I don't want ice cream, Mommy," Julia whines.

"We're going to get a twist cone and that's that," I say, as though she'd just refused a balanced meal.

The lazy-eyed McDonald's cashier remembers us; we're frequent ice cream eaters. He hands both girls a twist cone according to body type: short and wide for Julia, tall and skinny for Lola. I thank the cashier with the smile of a perfect mommy surprising her children with an impromptu ice cream cone.

"Help, Mommy!" Lola shrieks as we take our seats outside on the patio.

My daughters are my accomplices. This is our MO: I give them the ice cream and they, believing the cones to be too big, beg me to shave a layer off the two-toned treat. I never order a cone for myself—Ana doesn't eat ice cream, after all—but BB reassures me this isn't ice cream eating, it's helpful parenting.

My tongue swirls around the soft serve until it has shrunk to half its size. Back in Lola's hands, she lifts it high above her mouth and nibbles on the cake cone—the only part she likes.

"Look!" she says as melting chocolate and vanilla dribble down her arm. "My ice cream is crying."

"Why is your ice cream crying?" Julia asks, her chin now stained with an ice cream beard.

"Because she misses her mommy."

My heart clenches like a fist inside my chest. I hate that unfettered honesty in children, especially when I'm trying to self-destruct.

"Don't be silly," I say. "Ice cream cones don't cry."

Julia reluctantly slurps the chocolate top off her cone. My legs bounce in a nervous jig as I await her declaration of satiation; then, behind her chubby cheeks, I see sadness so profound I want to cry myself. Julia is not happily throwing back the treat like her sister, who has a sugar-rush sparkle in her gap-toothed smile. Julia is eating as though coerced to do so.

This is a form of abuse, Ana says. *You're setting your daughters up for obesity.*

Ice cream abuse? BB scoffs. *No such thing.*

Julia hands me her saliva-slicked cone with a disgusted scowl on her face.

"My stomach hurts," she says. "I want to go home."

BB continues to use my daughters as decoys.

"Let's get a doughnut for tomorrow morning," I suggest one evening after pumping gas. Julia and Lola hop out of their car seats and race into the Holiday gas station ahead of me. They point at the Krispy Kremes decorated with red, white, and blue patriotic sprinkles. I drop two squishy rings into plastic bags and fill up the biggest cup I can find with decaf coffee.

This is the last moment I remember inhabiting my body.

BB's in control now; she steers me toward the freezer section, slides open the frosted door, and grabs a pint of Ben & Jerry's fudge brownie ice cream.

How hard would it be to scoop out just the brownie bits? she wonders as I spin the pint around and around in my hands. Then another container catches BB's eyes: Dove brownie affair, featuring chocolate chunks and a hard circle of chocolate ganache at the top of the container.

Yum.

BB must be famished; neither the 1,200-calorie count nor the seven-dollar price tag deters her from the purchase.

In truth, the flavor of ice cream is irrelevant; BB craves the excitement, the naughtiness, the delicious frenzied feeling of rushing home to do something bizarre with dessert.

Who am I to stand in her way?

Back home, I make a beeline for the kitchen sink and dump the pint of Dove upside down. The hockey puck of chocolate ganache slides out with ease; I eat it standing over the sink as the rest of the ice cream slinks into a strainer to melt.

The sooner you get the girls to bed, BB reminds me, *the sooner we get back to our ice cream project.*

I'm drying the girls off after their bath when a voice bellows behind me.

"Heeelllooo. . . ."

I spin around to find my brother hanging on the frame of the bathroom door. BB's voice was so loud in my brain, I hadn't even heard him come in.

"What are *you* doing here?" I ask.

"Mom said you needed a babysitter."

"Mom's wrong," I say. "I don't work tonight."

Shane shrugs. "Okay. I'll just take off then."

As I dress the girls in their pajamas, I hear the fridge door slam.

"I'm taking a diet Mountain Dew!" Shane yells up the stairs. "See ya!"

It's not until he leaves that I remember the strainer in the kitchen sink.

Oh, shit.

Did my brother discover BB's ice cream project?

I can only imagine how the melting mess in the sink must have looked through his eyes.

Oh God, I really *am* a freak.

Stop thinking, BB interjects. *And start eating. You'll forget about this in no time.*

She's right, though it takes the pint of ice cream, six caramels, and three chocolate bars.

The girls are in bed and BB's done swallowing, but the binge doesn't have to stop. I can still spit.

I remember a few hidden treats in the glove compartment of my car. I scamper barefoot through the garage, lean over the passenger seat, and stuff a chocolate chip granola bar, a molasses cookie, and a package of Skittles into my mouth. I mush it all together with my teeth and spit it into the black abyss of the garbage can. By the time I hock my last loogie, my stomach gurgles acid, my head aches, and my throat is raw. I feel like the lowest, most pathetic form of life on earth.

But that's just me.

If we hadn't exhausted our sugar stash, BB would happily chew and spit till the sun comes up.

Friday evenings are the worst. While my peers are primping to go out and get drunk in smoky bars or wiggle their overinked bodies at downtown clubs, I am watching *Blue's Clues* DVDs and folding midget laundry. As I haul another basket of pinks and purples to the girls' closet, an ambiguous ache hits me with sledgehammer force.

Must. Medicate. Now! BB demands.

I consider sneaking off for a treat later, when the girls are in bed, but the BB waits for no one. If I put off eating, I might actually experience an emotion, and those are too dangerous to handle alone.

"Let's go to McDonald's!" I trill to the girls, hoping my excitement proves infectious.

"Grandma already gave us ice cream," Lola says.

I clench my fists and grit my teeth. Of course she did! The ice cream obsession must be genetic!

"We'll go really fast and come right back," I say.

Before they have time to tantrum, the girls are in their car seats, barefoot and naked, save for their diapers. Thank God for drivethrough.

The key turns in the ignition.

Click. Click. Click.

No. No. No.

I remove the key and shove it back in.

Click. Click. Click.

The car sounds like it's clearing its throat but never reaches the cough that would send the engine humming.

"The car's broken!" Julia says.

I am getting my ice cream, car or no car, BB says.

"We'll walk," I say.

"Ok," the girls reply in unison. Four little feet slip into sandals and the garage door opens with a moan. A gust of hot air and the brutally bright sunset blast across our faces. The humidity is thicker than Silly Putty.

"Give me your hand!" Julia says, rubbing up against my leg. "Let's go!"

I imagine the half-mile trek with two tired toddlers. Even I am not that crazy.

"No," I sigh. "It's too hot and too far away."

The girls' innocent eyes stare back at me, silently questioning whether I am really aborting Operation Ice Cream.

"Oh well," I say. "No ice cream today. But we can still watch videos!"

Television—the remote-controlled kiddie tranquilizer.

Back inside, I cue up a new Angelina Ballerina flick that transfixes the girls immediately.

Angelina will be pirouetting for thirty-two minutes, more than enough time to bike to the store for something sweet.

The girls haven't moved an inch since I plopped them down on the couch. They don't even notice that I've left the room. I may as well be invisible.

Thirty minutes of rodent ballet recital remain.

Back in the garage, I wiggle my helmet on, fling my leg over the side of my bike, and roll off into the street. The tightening of my glutes as the wheels spin beneath me feels so good, it's almost redemptive.

Three minutes later, I speed through the aisles of Walgreens like an Energizer Biker Bunny. BB is over the ice cream craving now; she needs something more substantial—s'mores.

Fate is smiling on me; graham crackers are BOGO, a bag of marshmallows costs only a dollar, and king-size Hershey bars are on sale.

The plastic bag of goodies dangles from the handle of my bike as I glide toward home. Saliva slips from the corners of my mouth in anticipation of my binge. Inside, I gloat.

So there, God! You thought you were going to stop BB by side-lining my car? Who has the last laugh now?

In the middle of my spiritual brag-fest, the bag bursts. A cloud of graham cracker dust erupts, the marshmallows scatter, and the chocolate bar shatters on the street beneath me. I hit the brakes and whip my face from side to side, seeking witnesses for this God-produced booby trap. The steamy suburban streets are empty.

The bag didn't get tangled in the tire spokes or slip off the handle. The bag didn't tear; it *exploded*. Shrink Shania's once-spoken words echo in my head: "Sometimes everything seems like a sign." This incident couldn't possibly have any deeper meaning than the simple laws of physics . . . could it?

I salvage half of my s'mores stash from the ground and, with some creative knot-tying, I close up the hole in the bottom of the bag and continue on my way.

A few wheel revolutions later, my excitement turns to terror. Will I arrive home to find my girls' heads split open after a fall from the couch? Will they be screaming in traumatized horror at my absence? Will they be flattened in the street after trying to follow me on foot?

When I wheel up to my house and shed my riding gloves and helmet, all is silent. "Julia? Lola?"

I stumble inside, heart thumping, and take the stairs two at a time.

"Girls?"

There they are, sleepy and sunburned, sprawled across the sofa, their eyes still glued to the TV screen as the Angelina Ballerina credits roll.

They're unaware I even left.

"Come have some s'mores!"

Faster than a short order cook, I top cracker after cracker with chocolate and mounds of Jet Puffs, microwaving the sandwiches until the marshmallows expand to ten times their original size. The girls plod down from the den and take their seats reluctantly, as though I were serving cold pea soup. They pick and poke at the s'mores, venturing only a bite. Lola hardly swallows before she's on her feet, heading toward the wastebasket.

"I'll take that!" I gasp, intercepting her faster than a world-cup soccer player.

I reheat the two plates, convincing myself that I will sit down at the table like a sane person and enjoy two s'mores. Then I will stop.

I'm swallowing my second s'more when Ana gets scared.

Wet it! she says. *Wet it all before you eat . . . s'more!*

This doesn't have to be a binge, I respond calmly. No harm done.

No harm done—yet! BB growls back.

It's a race against time; Ana versus BB.

I turn on the tap and dump the marshmallows down the disposal. The hot water dissolves them into slimy pellets. The graham crackers go next.

But the chocolate . . .

I shift into damage control mode: one hand crams the mouth with Hershey's, the other stuffs the sink.

During my s'mores demolition mission, the girls chase each other around and around the dining room table, erupting in peals of laughter. Julia suddenly careens into me and wraps her entire body around my thigh.

"What are you doing, Mommy?"

I am up to my elbows in soaking wet s'mores at the sink. Melted chocolate is smeared like shit across my cheeks.

"Just cleaning," I say. "Almost done."

After the girls go to bed, I remember I have to call my stepfather, Jay, about my defunct car. But first, I have to test a hunch: now that the binge is over, my car will start.

I put the key in the ignition and the engine roars to life.

Hooray! BB rejoices. *We can go get that soft serve cone now!*

But even I don't have the energy to continue the caloric tirade.

JOURNAL ENTRY

I've learned my lesson: Don't chide the Big Guy. He is, perhaps, the one being more bullheaded than me.

chapter twenty-one

What Flavor Is Your Parachute?

I don't want to be a counselor, but I wouldn't mind the structure that graduate school would provide. While I await the decision from the U of M's writing program, I take one final stab at my master's in marriage and family therapy at a prestigious downtown university.

Thirty wannabe therapists, all fresh faced and overly enthusiastic about how they're going to save crumbling marriages from divorce, surround me. My classmates are dressed in crisp, pleated suits. They eagerly raise their hands to answer questions, their wrists dripping with expensive jewelry. Their robotic heads nod in unison and their expensive pens scribble in the margins of their programs as the dean drones on.

I'm supposed to be paying attention. This—a student orientation mapped out in fifteen-minute increments from which presenters do not waver—is the kind of environment I once thrived in.

Not anymore.

The room is gray, the Power Point presentation is gray, the professors are gray—or they could be, mumbling in monotone about the university's high academic standards, the grueling program requirements, and how fortunate we are to be here.

"Of over two hundred applicants," the dean says. "You were the chosen ones."

I'm not listening.

As Mr. Peanut smiles back at me from a ripped package of salted nuts, I calculate the calories in the twelve cashews I just ate—and try my damnedest not to think about the leftover sheet cake outside the door. I nibble my cashews, drink a few cups of decaf coffee, and make it through the three-hour orientation sugar free.

When the students and staff all go home for the evening, I stay behind in the atrium.

Whew, Ana says when I spot the janitor wheeling his giant garbage can down the hall. *He must have chucked the cake. Temptation eliminated.*

Curiosity may have killed the cat, but it beckons to BB. She wants to see if any cake remains on the refreshment table. I tiptoe down the hall, peek around the corner, and there, alongside the stacks of paper plates, plastic silverware, and navy blue napkins, is the cake.

I approach the pastry as though it were a sleeping dragon.

And I stare.

My eyes trace the rise and fall of the frosting borders and ponder the chocolate layer of pudding on top. I've never tasted a cake like this; it might be a once-in-a-lifetime opportunity.

I serve myself a sliver of cake. The tines of my fork disappear into the fluffy layers of the dessert and ease a piece past my lips.

You don't really like the cake, Ana hisses.

She's right; the cake is too crumbly for my taste. But the sensation of frothy mocha frosting dissolving on my tongue, light as cotton candy, is orgasmic.

The whirr of a vacuum cleaner echoes down the hall; if I'm going to do this, I better be fast. The fork, as though possessed, runs around the edge of the cake, scraping up every last lick of frosting. With a flick of my wrist, I drop the brown glob onto my plate.

The plan is to overdose on the icing in the car, so I modestly cover the plate with a napkin and carry it downstairs. As soon as I hit the dark streets of Minneapolis, wind shoots down the avenue and whips the napkin off the cake. I am a frosting thief, exposed.

A homeless man with a nappy afro and crooked expression approaches, mumbling to himself, his vacant gaze shifting from the ground, to the sky, to me. It's hard to say which one of us looks scarier; my own eyes are as wild as a werewolf's. I grip my plastic plate as though it were a lifesaver. If the bum mugs me, I will happily surrender my keys, my wallet, my clothes; but never, ever, my sugary treasure.

"Holy shit!" he exclaims as he passes me. He stops and spins around on his heel. "You gonna eat all that?"

As soon as I turn the corner, I grip the frosting in my fist and stuff it in my mouth. The icing dissolves instantaneously on my tongue. I eat. Repeat. Eat. Repeat. My ecstasy brings on momentary blindness; after a few swallows, I look down and see I have scraped the plate clean.

The guilt kicks in by the time I hit the freeway. Ana is an excellent accountant and knows the nutritional content of food to the milli-calorie. A slice of this kind of cake—or a few handfuls of frosting—clocks in at 1,000 calories.

Time to even the score between the overeater and the exerciser in me. I audition options to burn off the binge. Run again? Too late. The elliptical? Too much exertion. The spinner? Bingo. Spinning, after all, is almost like sitting.

When I stomp into my house, Shane, startled awake, jumps up from the couch.

"I need to work out," I say.

My brother-turned-babysitter looks at the clock; it's 10:30 P.M.

"Go to bed," he says with a shake of his head.

"But I just ate a ton of cake. I feel all mushy."

"Go to bed!" he barks and slogs off down the driveway.

*   *   *

A few nights later, the cake craving calls to me again. Not just any cake will do. It's time for the big guns now: Turtle Bread Company. Never mind that the legendary bakery is in south Minneapolis, a thirty-minute trip from home. With a few shortcuts and my lead foot, I'll pick up a slice and be back to the burbs in no time.

Before I go, I poke my head into my daughters' bedroom. Their snores puncture the sticky summer air.

"I'll be right back," I want to whisper. "Mommy just needs a little dessert."

As I back out of the darkened driveway, I think of my cherubs deep in dreamland. What surprises me as I steer toward the sunset is not that I have left the toddlers alone, but that it is so *easy* to do so.

The sky is fading to a bluish black when I pull up to the bakery on Chicago Avenue. My steps turn into skips as I approach the door.

I pull the gold handle; the door doesn't budge.

I pull again. No go.

Then I see the sign: *Closed*.

It's 9:03 P.M. One less stoplight and I would be sliding a forkful of chocolate-frosted ecstasy into my mouth right now.

BB is too stubborn to be dissuaded. Forget a single *slice* of cake; she's going whole hog now. I fantasize about a posh concoction with frosting draped around the edges like Christmas garlands and topped with brightly colored balloons. I imagine taking the bulbs of buttercream into my mouth and sucking them down, in all their food coloring acidity, one by one.

As I drive back down the parkway, I scan the Yellow Pages in my brain for a bakery that will be open this late on a Sunday. Ten minutes later, I'm hustling up to the pastry case at Babb's, one of the few twenty-four-hour grocery stores that remain in the Twin Cities.

My hands tremble, my shoulders shake, my heart thumps. I squint and scowl, examining the desserts longer than decency allows, stroking the glass like a convict trying to caress a lover through bulletproof glass.

I take my place in line, anxiously avoiding eye contact as though I were about to hold up the joint. The same baker as always, a hunchbacked woman with German accent and silver hair, is assisting a Ken and Barbie couple in their selections. Their arms—his beefy, hers twiggy—are flung casually over one another's shoulder. Ken has a bag of Chinese take-out in his hands; Barbie has a bouquet of hot-pink tulips in hers.

I haven't even ordered yet and already I feel weighted down. I stare more hungrily at the sweethearts than I do the sweets. My heart can't take Ken and Barbie's PDA any longer. It's been so long since I shared greasy Chinese with someone, so long since someone bought me flowers, so long since anyone *touched* me.

I'd give up sugar in a second to spoon with a man.

BB forces my attention back to the bakery case, my safe place, where I cannot be denied nor rejected.

Gimme a dessert already, and I'll numb that pain up for you, she coos.

But the fruit tarts that shimmered only moments ago beneath the yellow light, the fluffy apple fritters that resembled goose-down pillows, the thin white wedges of cheesecake that called to me with their crisscrossed caramel drizzle—all have lost their allure.

I recall a magazine article that said the pleasure centers in women's brains react *more* intensely to the taste of chocolate than they do to sexual stimulation. But not only is there no chocolate on display; there's no cake. Not even one.

"Can I help you?" the German Grandma asks.

I open my mouth but flail for breath as though having an asthma attack.

"Don't . . . you . . . have . . . any . . . chocolate . . . birthday . . . cake?"

"No," she says with a sympathetic head shake. "But we have these."

She pulls out a tray of simply frosted, unexciting cupcakes.

I want to smash the glass. I want to grip her stumpy neck and snap it in half. I want to roar, "A cupcake?! A *cupcake?* You think *that* dinky pastry is going to satisfy the Binge Bitch? Are you insane?"

"No, thanks," I say curtly, already turning and pushing my way past the other customers.

I'm desperate for a carbohydrate hit now. I pace the aisles convinced I can find the perfect substance to quell whatever ambiguous discomfort rumbles in my belly. I prowl through the frozen food section with a predator's eye.

BB considers, then rejects, the following items for her inevitable binge:

- Ben & Jerry's Chunky Monkey ice cream (too cliché)

- Pillsbury chocolate chip cookie dough ice cream cake (too fattening for such a late-night binge)

- Häagen-Dazs dark chocolate almond bars (too elegant for the swine-like process of a binge)

- Pepperidge Farm chocolate layer cake (too much patience required for thawing)

By my third round past the freezer cases, I realize I am not alone; a Jackie Chan look-alike is also perusing the ice cream novelties.

Now, I don't possess a plethora of knowledge about the male psyche, but I know that guys rarely buy ice cream unless they have a girlfriend suffering from PMS at home. This man is not on an urgent errand; he lingers, like me.

Then I see his headset—I am being followed by an undercover store employee! My fellow foodie is ensuring I don't slip a pint of Cherry Garcia down my sweatpants.

Offended more than frightened, I pick up a box of Klondike 100-calorie ice cream sandwiches and head toward the registers. *That* should keep the Babb's cop off my back.

"I don't know about these one-hundred-calorie packs," the cashier says as he slides the box across the scanner. "How can you be satisfied with one wimpy sandwich?"

"The way I figure," I say in a sultry tone, as though sharing some erotic secret, "is that even if you eat the whole box, you haven't ruined your diet."

He bursts into dorky guffaws but stops when he sees I'm serious.

"I never thought of it that way before," he says.

Of course he hasn't. Only BB's devotees calculate how regretful you'll be if one serving turns into six.

I pay for my decoy dessert and drive across the street, to Festive Foods. I hate shopping at this trailer trash grocery store, but it's 10:00 P.M. already and the bakery is self-serve.

I'm perusing the selection when a voice bubbles up behind me.

"I know a woman who used to date a cake."

A frazzled blond woman with big black gaps between her teeth stands behind me.

"Every Saturday night," she continues, "she'd shut herself up in her apartment and eat a whole cake."

"Whatever gets you through the day," I say and drop the first plastic dome I see into my green basket.

No sooner do I heave the grocery bag onto the passenger seat of my SUV, than my nervous system hurtles into overdrive. My mouth fills with saliva, my fingers quiver, my pulse quickens. My plan is to eat the cake at home, at my dinner table, in peace, but I only make it three blocks before I swerve onto the side of the road. Cars whiz past with a flurry of honks, drivers throw obscene gestures my way, but as soon as I pop the top off the cake, the rest of the world disappears.

With ferocious fingers, I separate the cake layer by layer, packing the pastry by the fistful into my mouth. Each layer is a distinct experience: bitter chocolate frosting, whipped mocha mousse, crisp

Oreo crust. The consistencies clash; the flavors cancel each other out. The cake looked better than it tastes. When I return to reality and see the crumbs scattered across the car seat, a bomb of regret explodes inside me. I long to cry but can't.

The streets are vacant now as I flick on my turn signal and merge onto the freeway with a carb-induced calm. At least my medicinal binge is effective; by the time I reach home, I am inoculated against the pain of another weekend as a single woman.

I return to a peaceful house. The clock's pendulum swings, soft and steady, on the wall; the blades of the ceiling fan spin hypnotically; the Winnie-the-Pooh night light in the hallway casts muted shadows across the carpet. I crack open the girls' door; they are as identically serene and asleep as when I left them.

It isn't until the BB's tirade is over, after I've cleaned the car and am about to drop the frosting-smeared dome into the Dumpster, that I notice the pastry's official name: Confusion Cake.

When I receive an acceptance letter from the University of Minnesota's Creative Writing department, I have to decide: Do I stick with shrink school or do I forge a new path as a writer?

"Am I wrong to give up the counseling degree?" I ask my father.

"It sounds like you wouldn't make much of a living as a therapist," he says. "If you're going to get in debt for a master's degree, it better be in a career with financial security."

"Like creative writing?" I say with a half-smile.

"That's the idea?" he asks. "To be a writer?"

I nod. "I've been told I have talent."

"Hmm," my father says with his trademark unemotional expression. "What about a job in human resources? Something with good insurance and a retirement plan."

I imagine myself holed up in a dark cubicle for the next forty years.

"I'd kill myself," I say.

My father raises his eyebrows as if to say, "Yeah, right, my little drama queen."

JOURNAL ENTRY

Feel like biting my head off today. Could I be the first person in the world to decapitate herself?

"Your dad told us you wanted to kill yourself," my mother says at our next child exchange.

"Yup," I say. Why beat around the bush? Why bother with denial?

"What would make you want to do that?" Jay asks as he places a heavy hand on my shoulder.

"I'm depressed."

"That doesn't mean you can't have fun!" Jay says.

My mother shoots her husband a sideways glance and grimaces. "It would help if you had a plan for the future," she says.

Fuck plans. The *plan* had been for me to be married, to be a mother of three, to be a licensed marriage and family therapist, to be putting the finishing touches on my dream home.

"So what's the plan?" my mother asks.

"To run away," I say.

"With the circus?" Jay chuckles.

"The circus has no use for me."

Ana may be fast, but she's as flexible as a lead pipe.

"Why not take a full-time position at Teen Transformation?" my mother asks.

I've considered this option only because TT is BB's dream job. As key keeper, I have access to foods I would never buy for myself. Not only am I allowed to eat, I earn $11.75 an hour stuffing my face. But Ana refuses to go full-time; forty hours a week at TT is guaranteed to make me fat.

* * *

"What *stanks*?" Andy, the newest addition to the TT roster, asks over dinner.

"Sorry," I say, motioning to my salad. "It's tuna fish."

Andy crinkles his nose in disgust. "Do you eat healthy all the time?"

"Pretty much."

"I bet you go home and eat a bunch of junk food every night!"

"I try not to," I say.

In public, I'm in-control Counselor Erica; in private, BB has possessed my body.

After dinner, the staff chauffeur clients to the community center for swimming. I am assigned to stay back alone to answer the phones.

TT is blissfully quiet tonight, save for the hum of the stainless-steel refrigerator, the *swish* of air-conditioning through the floor vents, and a mild grumble in my stomach.

I'm bored, BB whines.

I don't want to self-destruct, so I try distraction instead. I pick up a magazine, but the sentences on the page are mere symbols, incongruent figures, illegible words. Nothing makes sense; I am instantly illiterate.

Let's do a food project! BB says.

Now that the seed is planted, the binge is bound to sprout. I swing the food cupboard door open and ponder four shelves of potential gut-stuffing substances. I begin with the least offensive offering: peanut butter sandwich cookies. I eat two, seated at the table, my attention focused on the experience. The cookies are nothing special; the best part is the imitation peanut butter center. Then it occurs to me: Why waste calories on the cookies if I can just eat the peanut butter?

Here we go again.

In an instant, I'm munching my way down each side of the plastic tray, splitting each cookie in half, sliding the shortbread beneath my front teeth, sensually slipping the peanut butter across my tongue. I repeat the process over and over, stacking the naked cookies like poker chips on the counter.

There is something Zen-like about bingeing. The repetitive motion, along with the fat and sugar filling my tummy, lull me into a sweet state of relaxation. Mouth meditation.

When I've licked one tray of cookies clean of their peanut butter centers, I return to the cupboard for another. When the cookie tower threatens to tumble over, anxiety scorches my throat like acid reflux. How many cookies have I licked clean? How many cookies are in a package anyway? Sixty? That's a *lot* of peanut butter filling.

As long as you don't swallow, BB reminds me, *you're not cheating on your diet.*

Time to switch over to the chew-and-spit routine. I crunch the cookies into a mushy pulp in my mouth and spit into the sink. Salivating like a rabid dog, I polish off package number two in record time, leaving lumps of masticated cookies in the sink. The bliss is so fleeting; I want to rewind and relive the cookie consumption over and over, want to feel my tongue eternally coated in peanut butter.

Footsteps clomp on the concrete steps outside as the TT residents approach.

Shit.

The shortbread tower is slated for immediate demolition. I must obliterate any evidence of my cookie tirade. With one sweep of my arm across the kitchen counter, I knock the empty trays and plastic wrappers into the garbage can and toss a bundle of paper towels on top to camouflage the refuse.

The cookie skyscraper collapses into the sink, but I don't have time to start the disposal.

With a *click-click-click-click*, a coworker enters her code into the security system outside—my last warning of the incoming rush of adolescents.

The door opens and a cacophony of pubescent voices erupts.

I pretend to unload the dishwasher.

The clients burst through the entryway with snarled swimming hair, damp towels tossed across their shoulders—and post-exercise appetites.

"Can you open this, Erica?" Victor, TT's dweeb-of-the-week, asks as he jiggles the knob of the food cupboard.

I open the cupboard, leaning against the frame casually as though I were immune to the temptation of the brightly packed products inside. Victor slips his whole body behind the door and rummages. There is urgency in his search; he shuffles and shakes every package on the shelf with determination.

"What happened to all the peanut butter cookies?" he whines, his gaunt torso folding in on itself.

How is it that these kids can't remember chore assignments, medication dosages, bedtimes, or basic hygiene, but they memorize the contents of the snack cupboard?

"Huh," I say with a half-assed scan of the cupboard. "They must be gone."

Victor pulls his head out of the cupboard and pushes his duct-taped glasses back onto the bridge of his nose.

"But I'm the only one who likes them!" He scratches his scalp, huffs, and crosses and uncrosses his arms. "They *have* to be here!"

As Victor gives the cupboard one more look-see, I reach into the sink behind me and push the cookies down the drain. Before I can start the disposal, Victor emerges, shaking his head and sighing. Then his gaze falls onto the garbage can and his eyes widen, as though he just acquired X-ray vision.

The frantic gallop of my heart seizes. I prepare to execute a line-backer block to keep him from Dumpster diving and discovering the empty cookie trays.

Victor snaps his head back to me. "Oh well," he says. "I must have imagined them."

Great, I think. *Instead of healing my clients, I'm fueling their hallucinations.*

The next day, I awake with a carbohydrate hangover. My body is a bloated flotation device. My eyes are puffy, bright red pimples burst in an arc across my forehead, and my shoulders slump with the weight of regret.

When I arrive at work, TT is awash in a foul odor. Did someone puke on the carpet? Did a boy pee on the bathroom walls? Did a girl get her period and forget to use a pad?

"What's that smell?" I ask no one in particular.

"The disposal is backed up," Marjory, one of my superiors, says as she slides out from beneath the sink. "Someone jammed a bunch of leftovers down there."

"Damn kids," I say and slink away.

chapter twenty-two

Back to School

When fall semester at the U of M starts, I realize how self-absorbed I've been all summer.

After so much time alone, to be around other people—especially fellow writers—is like a rebirth into society; the Creative Writing Program is my midwife. As soon as I introduce myself to the class, my spitfire personality returns and I slip back into the student role as though I never left the classroom.

My classmates are *real* writers with publication credits, literary contacts, and aspirations of bestselling books. In comparison to them, I'm so far behind. Because of Ana's antics, all I have are pages of pity-party and very little publishable material.

I've been writing under the assumption that true artists keep one foot on the dark side of life to be interesting. The writers who surround me are men and women of all ages with normal lives and day jobs and kids; none of them appears to rely on addictive substances for inspiration. They aren't mired in depressing projects about childhood trauma; one guy writes pop songs and another girl writes funny bits about her family's Christmas tree farm.

The revelation that good writing is based on skills, not psycho-pathology, means that I don't need to rely on an eating disorder for material anymore.

After receiving all the syllabi, I walk to the bookstore to stock up on my assigned reading. Energy hums across the field between the English Department building and the student center. People are sprawled on the still-green grass, book spines broken open before them, backpacks abandoned against tree trunks. Buses rumble by, voices chatter on cell phones, teammates high-five. Swarms of students push past me with wobbly towers of books in their arms.

I stand still. I am in my element. I am in heaven.

I must look absurd, frozen in the middle of the educational chaos, my jaw dropped in awe. I admire the highlighters in every hue, sniff the fresh notebook paper, and try out a mini stapler with a satisfying *tap-tap*. This is so much better than hanging out with Ana and BB! Instead of scouring grocery store shelves for a pleasure-inducing taste, I wander the aisles of the bookstore in search of memoirs, short story collections, and poetry anthologies. Stacks and stacks of books—so much to learn, so little time! I want to hunker down between the cash registers and read myself to death.

I pass the backpack display and peruse the high-tech laptop bags. Then I see it: the backpack equivalent of my soul mate. It is a sassy black and hot pink combo with multiple zippers, pull-out handle, and wheels. I roll the bag around the sales floor, amazed at how smoothly it moves. Then I check the price tag: $79.95. Too pricey.

As I turn to leave, I trip over another backpack on the floor—an ugly brown-and-orange-striped bag. This one is half the price, though it doesn't have wheels. Then I see the make-or-break feature: a detachable cooler compartment. I rip open the Velcro seal of the cooler and stuff my hand inside to estimate how much food would fit in there.

A turkey wrap, an apple, a bottle of water, Ana estimates.

I stand between the two bags, a simple decision suddenly bearing the weight of the world. Where do my loyalties lie? With the bag that allows me to cart around school supplies without hurting my back or with the bag that will sustain Ana's strict diet?

It's time to put my money where my mouth is.

I snap up the handle on the hot pink bag and wheel it to the cash register. Price be damned, this is a present to the writer in me, a thank-you to myself for getting serious about something other than eating and exercise.

"What a cute little stapler," the elderly cashier says as she rings up my school supplies and textbooks. I slip my credit card across the counter before she can tell me the total. It isn't until I'm walking toward the exit that I glance at the receipt.

Granny Cashier didn't charge me for the bag.

I look down at my backpack buddy on the floor. Should I say something? Is it stealing if I don't?

I hug my textbooks to my chest with one hand and steer the handle of the bag with the other. The blood pounds behind my eardrums. Will an alarm sound when I pass through the glass doors? Will the security staff stop me?

The bag rolls behind me as I pass between the sensors.

Nothing happens.

I wheel into the nearest bathroom and snap off the tags.

"Thank you, thank you, thank you," I say to the Backpack God.

When I reach my car, I load my new bag into Lola's car seat; it fits perfectly.

"You and me, baby," I say to the bag in the rearview mirror. "You and me."

JOURNAL ENTRY

For the first time in a long time, I'm not thinking about eating or exercise. I just want to wander and watch the movement on campus, to absorb the intellectual eagerness of the students by osmosis. I can feel my brain expanding already.

Learning is as close to God as I can get.

School is going to be my salvation.

The move to my mother's is looming.

Whereas previous moves lit a fire inside me, inspiring all-nighters packing boxes, this move is different. I'm not moving somewhere bigger or better. I'm regressing to dependent daughter status.

I don't know how my mother feels about *me* moving in, but she's ecstatic about spending more time with her granddaughters. I try to focus on the upside of our multigenerational arrangement—perks like having a babysitter 24/7, Jay's home-cooked meals, and animal companionship in the form of their golden lab, Max. Maybe my mother will teach me a thing or two about parenting. Maybe evening out the adult–child ratio will relieve some of my stress. Maybe having housemates will make me feel less lonely.

Yeah, right.

Ana's slightly less enthusiastic about the uprooting.

The scariest part of living with my mother is I won't have Ana and BB to lean on. An eating disorder won't survive in the basement of my mother's town house; no more twilight runs, no more late-night binges over the garbage disposal, no more tubs of waterlogged peanut butter down the drain.

I've put off packing for as long as possible. Whenever I look around my overdecorated house, I can't imagine boxing up my pretty possessions and sending them off to a frigid storage locker. It's easier to deny the move altogether. As long as I don't pack, I won't have to move.

But I'm down to the wire now and unless I want to wander around my mom's place naked, I have to pack some clothes. There isn't room at my mother's for my whole wardrobe; there isn't even a closet in my basement abode yet. In his spare time, Jay is crafting a makeshift clothes rod from four poles and planks of leftover wood.

I stand paralyzed in my all-white, walk-in, California Closet. My eyes roam over the array of tops, bottoms, boots, and bags stocked from floor to ceiling. As I deliberate about what I want to go with me, I am inundated with unknowns: How long will I live at my mother's? Which seasons of clothing will I need? Then there's the question of sizes: Do I box up the 2's and the 4's in the hopes that I maintain my size 1 figure? Or do I bring a variety of sizes along in case I gain weight?

I don't want to give my body too much breathing room to get bigger. If only one thing remains constant among the flux in my life, it should be my weight. So I compromise, leaving the 2's on hangers and dropping the 4's on the floor, my system to indicate what goes to my mother's and what goes to storage.

Half my clothes—the ones I bought on impulse when I was at my skinniest—still have the tags on them. I unhook item after item from the hangers until I reach the sexy section of my wardrobe: a long line of stringy tops with lace borders and little bows; a stack of low-rider jeans; a collection of flirty skirts.

And the red pants. The pants I bought last year. The pants I never had occasion to wear. I haven't had a first date in three months; I haven't had sex in six; I haven't had *good* sex in almost a year. And now, even if a man were to appear, the infamous red pants are too small to squeeze into.

If I send the revealing clothes to storage, am I transmitting the wrong message to the universe? Or I am romantically jinxed already?

I barely make it through one side of the closet before a tidal wave of sadness smacks into me. The pain—a hot, clenching sensation in my gut—knocks me to my knees. I grasp at the silky fabrics, bawling, imagining the kind of woman that would wear such flirty camisoles and sharp blazers: A woman with a bursting social calendar and impressive résumé. A woman with well-behaved children and a savings account. A woman who Has Her Shit Together.

The kind of woman I'm supposed to be by now.

* * *

When I fail to finish packing the closet, I call in the reserves.

My mother comes over to discuss the logistics of moving over dinner, though I'm the only one who's eating.

"Maybe Shane would pack up my stuff if I paid him," I say.

"Your brother is busy," my mother says as she takes a seat across from me at my dining room table. My *brother* is busy? *My brother?*

I stab at an asparagus spear tumbling from atop my veggie burger.

"He has school and football, you know," my mother says.

And I have work, kids, depression, and an eating disorder. If anyone is too busy, it's me.

I hate admitting to my mistakes. I hate needing help, period. But I can't hold back any longer. A couple tears stream down my cheeks.

I hate crying in front of my mother. I also hate eating in front of my mother; this is the only discomfort I can do something about. I push my half-full plate away and look up at my mother. Her figure is blurred by my watery eyes.

"If I have to pack even one more box, I am going to have a nervous breakdown," I say.

Ten minutes later, she has my brother, stepbrothers, their friends and girlfriends, scheduled to pack up my house on Saturday. Because there's only room for the essentials—winter clothes, a volume of Anne Sexton poetry, my laptop, and my treadmill—at my mother's house, the rest of my belongings are boxed up and sent to storage.

On the morning of the closing, I win the lottery.

When the mechanical voice on the phone informs me I have tagged two numbers and the Powerball, I *whoop!* aloud. I rush to the nearest gas station with the preposterous hope that I've won enough money to save my house. The cashier, a sweaty man rattling

Spanish into a cordless phone, smiles when he sees me with my ticket. He covers the receiver and asks, "Got a winner?"

"I think so."

"Let's run it and see."

He shoves the ticket into a machine.

"Five dollars," he says. He pops open the register with a *ching* and counts out the bills.

"Don't bother," I say, grabbing two packages of Chex Mix and a big bag of peanut butter M&M's. "I've already spent it."

Kathy careens into the Coldwell Banker Burnet boardroom in her usual frantic manner. She reaches for the candy bowl in the center of the table and scoops up a handful of Halloween-themed chocolates.

"Are you nervous?" she asks as she unwraps the chocolates one by one. "I'm nervous."

Kathy nudges the candy bowl toward me.

"Help yourself," she says through a mouthful of brown goo.

"No, thanks," I say. I'm still full from my M&M's and Chex Mix feast, eaten en route to Kathy's office.

"Incredible," she says with a shake of her head. "I wish I had your willpower."

She chomps audibly on her chocolate.

"I don't know about you," she says. "But this deal has been making me crazy."

"You have no idea," I say as my finger does figure-eights on the polished tabletop.

"I really hope the buyer doesn't back out."

Forty minutes later, a weathered man in a plaid shirt and suspenders sits down across from me.

"You sure are lucky," he says after he shakes my hand. "I wrote the offer without ever having seen the place. When my daughter told me how nice the house was, I trusted her."

"It *is* a nice house," Kathy says with an insincere smile.

The buyer glares at Kathy.

"It needs major repairs. I never would have bought it if I'd seen it with my own eyes ahead of time."

I keep quiet, my fists clenched beneath the table. *Just sign the papers*, I silently will him. *Let's get this over with.*

"But what can I do now?" he sighs. "My girl's in love with that house, rotted windows and all."

The buyer readjusts his John Deere cap and scribbles his name on the triplicate forms in front of him. He pushes the papers toward me.

"You sure are lucky."

"Now that you're here," my mother says, "We can take better care of you."

She's trying to cheer me up about moving into her house, where I am allowed to stay for one rent-free year. The girls happily settle into the spare bedroom upstairs, which my mother has painted pink and decorated with Barbie decals. Their setup is plush; the girls even have a view of the pond out their window.

In my bedroom—aka the basement—there are no windows. The basement is finished by construction standards only, meaning that it is insulated, heated, and has functional lighting. Two walls are an ugly concrete gray by nature or filth, I'm not sure. The other two are covered in opaque plastic, yellow insulation bursting from the seams. The view from my bed is a mess of old mattresses, abandoned baby toys, and leaky paint cans. A labyrinth of pipes and slats of wood lines the ceiling. I feel like I'm sleeping inside the skeleton of a starving beast.

My bed is beneath the living room; more precisely, my head rests just below the familial sofa. This is Jay's favorite hangout, where he beaches his barely-bathrobed body on the beige leather. There's no sound buffer between the upstairs and the downstairs, and I can hear every shift of body weight, every root beer can click, every scratch of newspaper pages turning. The chains on the Tiffany lamps jangle when tugged, and the sofa-recliner's footrest snaps when kicked back into place. Jay is obsessed with surround sound. Night after night, I fall asleep to the growls of football announcers, to bombs dropping on televised wars, to the echo of unidentified farts above my head.

chapter twenty-three

A Family Affair

At first, it's a relief.

Back in my mother's house, I feel like I'm sixteen again. My only responsibility is to load and unload the dishwasher; on my worst days, even that task is overwhelming. Parenting is my part-time job, and I treat it like most teenagers do their employment: indifferently. Looking busy doing nothing is hard work; it is a role I play Mondays, Wednesdays, Fridays, and every other weekend. On the remaining days, the girls are with Cesar.

My mother does more than help out; when I'm under Ana's spell, my mother mothers my girls. There are times I wonder if my daughters would be better off relying solely on her for survival, as of the two of us, she's the financially secure, emotionally stable one.

My mother, the martyr, immerses herself in parenting, take two. Maybe she is trying to make up for her absence in my childhood. She is bathtub lifeguard, hall monitor, potty trainer, kiddie chef, and breadwinner all rolled into one. She scours the racks at Unique thrift store for clothing; she buys slightly used games and books from Once Upon a Child. At night, she does the pj power struggles and scratchy backrubs. I read the girls three stories in a voice reminiscent of automated telephone recordings.

Thank God for joint custody; I can hardly handle my kids every other day, much less 24/7. My free time, however, is not spent recharging my batteries but building the empire of my eating disorder.

If I'm going to be miserable, I might as well look fabulous doing it. If I'm going to be depressed, I might as well appear productive. Anorexia eliminates the anxiety-inducing lack of structure in my life; on my kid-free days, I spend up to four hours exercising. Run at 4:00 A.M., yoga at 10:00 A.M., swimming at 2:00 P.M., weightlifting at 4:00 P.M. Stick a movie, hot-tub, or massage in the middle of my day and I successfully avoid living my life.

"Aren't you going back to work?" my mother asks a few weeks after I've settled into my basement abode.

Why bother? There's no mortgage to my name and my mother doesn't demand any money from me. She foots the daycare bill, she buys the groceries, she pays for utilities. My only expense is fuel, as in food for me and gas for my car.

"I'm taking some time off," I say. "I'm exhausted."

"You're running at 4:00 A.M.; of course you're exhausted."

I'm thankful for my mother's doormat nature now. She doesn't demand I stop exercising; instead, she watches the girls in the mornings so I can sleep in and run later.

I've completely let my perfectionist standards slide; my only goal during the residence with my mother is to generate twenty-five pages of solid writing for graduate school applications.

Someday I'll get my shit together again. For now, I'm in survival mode.

I try to steer clear of my mother's kitchen. It both intrigues and disgusts me; like a culinary car accident, I can't turn away. Some mysterious magnetic field pulls me in and welds my feet to the cheap tile floor.

Food is strewn about on countertops, abandoned where last consumed. The cupboards are a jumbled, colorful chaos that boasts nutritional indifference. And yet, there is an uncanny sense of control here, as evidenced by jars of Skippy super chunk with only a spoonful carved out, a block of Muenster cheese with only a sliver missing, a half-full carton of Whoppers.

Alone in my mother's kitchen, a fever crests inside me. Like a frantic squirrel on a scavenger hunt, I open and shut doors, shuffle packages, eager to store edible treasures in my stomach for a hibernation period that never comes.

Jay has his own issues with food—namely, he eats too much of the wrong kinds of it.

"What are you getting into in there?" my mother asks from her seat on the living room couch.

"Nothing," Jay calls back from the kitchen. Though he's hidden from view, the crinkling of a plastic bag gives him away.

"You're not dipping into the Honey Grahams are you?" she asks.

Jay sighs in the gruff way that warns of an impending outburst.

"I'm trying to," Jay says. "But I can't get the damn bag open!"

Occasionally, my mother and Jay swap the watchdog role.

"Don't touch that cereal!" Jay warns my mother one evening when he sees her pouring a bowl of Honey Nut Cheerios.

"Why not?" she asks.

"I want to try that new Italian place tonight," Jay says.

My mother, already in her pajamas, looks down longingly at her cereal.

"Fine," Jay says. "If we're not eating out, I'm making tacos."

"I just want Cheerios," my mother says, hugging the bowl close to her and settling back into the couch. I'm at the computer with my back turned on both of them; I may as well be invisible.

The kitchen erupts in culinary cacophony: pans sizzle, cupboards slam, plastic packages rip, chunks of cheese hit the chopping block. As Jay bangs away on dinner, Mom turns up the volume on the TV; she channel hops between Comedy Central and CNN. Back and forth. Louder and louder.

"Dinner is ready!" Jay screams.

My mother is deep into *The Daily Show* and does not respond.

"Aren't you going to have some tacos?" Jay asks; his tone of voice implies it's not a question.

The silence is loaded; I know my mother is thinking up ways to avoid eating her husband's greasy feast without upsetting him.

"Maybe I'll have a little," she says.

"Is that a yes or a no?"

"Yes . . . I guess."

"I've got dessert, too!"

"Uh-oh," Mom says when she sees the carton of Breyer's double-churned ice cream. "You shouldn't be eating that."

He shouldn't be eating artery-clogging ground beef or half a pound of shredded cheese, or twelve-inch flour tortilla chips slathered with salty salsa either, but Mom has to pick her battles.

"I buy one container of ice cream a year and I get the fat ass comments?!" Jay exclaims.

My mother whimpers an apology. Jay plops down on the sofa beside her and imitates an estrogen-infused voice: "Thanks for buying groceries and making supper, honey."

Jay eats his tacos and my mother eats her Cheerios as Iraqi combat wages on the TV screen.

"Did you buy this stuff?" Jay asks me as he peeks into a take-out container on the kitchen counter the next day.

"Nope," I say.

I don't know what's inside, but the smell of it tells me it's fried. Jay pulls out a handful of chicken strips and French fries.

"Huh," he grunts. He leans up against the counter—his favorite way to dine—and pops each breaded twig of chicken into his mouth. He licks his fingers audibly between bites. "This is good stuff."

My mother's way of making up with her hubby is to fatten him up. Along with the Finger Lickin' Good chicken strips, there's a fresh tub of turtle ice cream in the freezer, a super-size jar of Skippy on the countertop, and—Jay's favorite—a large loaf of cheap white bread by the toaster.

I'm convinced eating disorders are contagious. Like the strep throat we swapped incessantly as children, the exercise addiction and binge eating Ping Pong between my brother and me. When I was anorexic, he was obese. Now, as I gain weight, he's whittling down.

It's hard to say when the transformation started. There wasn't a formal announcement of a health kick, but as soon as he discovered football in high school, he slimmed down and bulked up.

At twenty-one years old, he is so fit that I'd date him if we weren't related.

When I see my brother, Ana and BB call to me straightaway. Shane's conversation topics turn exclusively to exercise, to what he's eaten on a particular day, or to the vitamins and supplements he hocks to athletes. He doesn't just go to the gym—he walks the two miles there.

Shane pulls up to my mother's house one evening unexpectedly. There's a new bumper sticker on his crappy car: "Be kind to animals. Kiss a rugby player."

"How's Shane-ski?" my mother asks when we gather in the kitchen.

"Pumped," he says. "I sprinted five miles, uphill!"

My admiration of my new-and-improved buff Bro borders on envy. Fitness has always been *my* domain; now he's gaining not only muscle mass, but my mother's hard-earned approval as well. Shane is pissing all over my pride territory.

"I brought you that list," he says to my mother.

Shane's Webster-size textbook on sports nutrition falls with a thud on the table. What happened to my brother, the one who couldn't be bothered to read—not even comic books—for the first eighteen years of his life because of dyslexia?

"Approved foods," my mother reads. "Cottage cheese."

"You have that one covered," I mutter.

"Eggs, hummus, and turkey breast," my mother continues. "Sounds doable."

She shuffles off down the hall to show Jay the new diet rules.

"How's your training going?" he asks me, referring to the up-coming Twin Cities Marathon.

"My sports medicine doc says I need more protein."

"I've got a recipe for you," he says.

I raise my eyebrows. My brother may kick ass in the gym, but not in the kitchen.

"If it's a smoothie, I'm not interested," I say. Smoothies are his specialty.

"This isn't just any smoothie," he says. "It's a chicken smoothie."

I barely contain my gag reflex. "You're kidding."

He shakes his head. "It's really good."

"Tastes like chicken?"

"Ha ha. Don't knock it till you've tried it."

Shane sets a big box of plastic bottles onto the counter.

"If you won't try the smoothie, do one of these," he says, motioning to his stock of nutritional products. "I've got it all: weight loss supplements, colon cleanses, protein shakes, energy enhancers."

"I'll stick with my own form of carbo-loading, thanks," I say, returning to my chips and salsa at the table. I wave the Tostitos bag in front of his face. "Want some?"

"Err . . . uh . . . okay," he says.

Instead of reaching in and grabbing a handful of chips, he snatches the bag and plops it in his lap. Hand to mouth. Crunch and stuff. He eats hurriedly, as though a linebacker were about to tackle him. Minutes later, all that remains is a spattering of broken triangles in the bottom of the bag and a red smear around the salsa bowl.

"I don't know why this crap sounds so good to me right now," he says, shoving one last chip into his now-frowning mouth.

"Blame it on Mom," I say.

"Blame it on Jay; he's the one who buys all the junk food."

Shane rolls down the top of the chip bag and heads for the kitchen. He sticks his whole head into the fridge like a body-builder ostrich. He rips two mozzarella string cheeses between his teeth as though they were as tough as beef jerky. Then the microwave whirrs to life as he heats up a Tupperware of leftover sausage alfredo. He twirls and twists the dried-out pasta, gloppy beige sauce, and oily pork around his fork, then slurps it down in seconds. For dessert he attacks a loaf of cinnamon raisin bread over the sink, folding slice after slice into his mouth. Crumbs accumulate amongst his golden stubble.

"I thought you didn't eat bread," I say.

"I don't. Bread is evil," he says, twirling the bag closed. "But I'm going to lift weights; I have to fuel up."

Shane swings the freezer door open and digs around until he unearths a bag of frozen berries. The berries *plunk* like rocks into a glass, which he tips back like a tequila shot, swallowing the fruit in a second. No chewing required.

Just when I think my brother is done bingeing, he goes haywire. He flips open every cupboard, searching for . . . something. I want to tell Shane to stop. I want to remind him that whatever he craves—emotionally or otherwise—is nowhere near my mother's cupboards.

I know. I've checked.

Watching my brother binge sparks BB's feelings in me: the rabbit-speed heartbeat, the blossoming of sweat beads around the hairline, the tingling between the thighs. I want to binge, too. I want to immerse myself in those moments when BB tells me any calories consumed will magically dissolve later.

"Don't you have anything good?" he whines when my mother wanders back into the kitchen.

I could tell my brother about the tray of cherry cordials that Jay bought on a camping trip, the ones that melted on the car ride home, the ones that Jay refused to throw out and froze instead. When I found them, the chocolates were squished and mashed together, hardened in crooked rows, leaking with gooey cherry syrup.

I could tell my brother how I've been peeling the cherries from the paper wrappers one by one late at night. I could tell him how delicious the cherries taste after I defrost them in the microwave. I could show Shane their disfigured chocolate casings, but there is only half a tray left. I want to save the naughty treat for myself.

Shane hangs one arm over the freezer door, the icy air wafting over his sweaty face.

"There's a Frosty in there," my mother says.

Shane pulls out a yellow paper cup with the Wendy's emblem on the front.

"How old is this?" he asks.

My mother cringes. "At least a week?" she says.

"Gross!" I say, though BB's been eyeing the ice cream since it made its appearance. The only reason I haven't eaten it already is that its absence would be too obvious.

"The grosser, the better," Shane says.

Oh. My. God.

My brother has just spoken BB's favorite mantra.

Shane chips away at the Frosty, his spoon like a jackhammer, until the cup is empty.

"I'm going to take a hot-tub," he says, opening the fridge one more time. "I just need a snack to take with me." He pulls out a yogurt and snaps a banana off the bunch on the counter.

As he saunters, bare-chested, down the stairs, I shake my head. I don't know how he does it, but he is in great shape.

"How does Buca sound?" my mother asks when we discuss plans for an adult-only restaurant dinner.

As an Italian restaurant that specializes in family-style (read: excessive) dining, Buca is a dangerous place for BB. The restaurant serves entrées on platters, not plates. It's the kind of venue people use for wedding celebrations or graduation parties—not a casual dinner for three.

My mother must read my perplexed expression because she says, "I have a coupon."

Of course. God forbid my mother pay full price for a meal.

"Fine," I say.

If Ana gets her way, I won't eat at all.

"I'm dying for a salad," my mother says as we peruse Buca's menu later. "But order whatever you want."

"We have to try the bruschetta," Jay says.

There is already a basket of bread on the table and I know from previous visits that the bruschetta comes in a pizza-size pan with a thick layer of parmesan cheese sprinkled on top.

"That's a lot of carbs," I say.

My mother and Jay look at me as though I just cursed.

"Have we decided?" the waiter asks when he appears with my mother's gin and tonic.

I haven't; the debate is still raging in my head. I'm sick of salad; I already eat it twice a day, every day. But almost every other entrée is noodle-based and dripping in melted mozzarella. I rock back and forth in the booth, my hands beneath my thighs. My palms start to sweat as I estimate how many inches one meal will add to my waistline.

Jay orders the bruschetta and an Italian salad—all big enough to share.

The waiter nods and turns to my mother.

"The spinach salad," my mother says.

"Jay just ordered salad, Mom," I say.

"I'm in a salad mood."

"I think we have enough salad," Jay says.

"Spaghetti, then," my mother says.

I raise a pointer finger in objection. "I don't eat pasta."

With one sentence, Ana eliminates 99 percent of the menu.

The waiter stuffs his notepad and pen back in his apron pocket. "I'll come back in a few minutes," he says.

"I want roasted chicken," I say. It's a dish that potentially pleases both Ana and BB; though the generous portion of poultry is prepared with oil, it is served with grilled vegetables. As far as I can tell, it is the lowest-carb, lowest-calorie item on the menu. It will also leave room in my stomach for dessert. Everyone should be happy.

"Let's get the special," Jay says. "Chicken breasts stuffed with sausage."

"I'm not so sure about the stuffed part," my mother says. "Lemon chicken sounds better."

"Two chicken dishes sound redundant," I say.

"How about pizza?" Jay asks.

"Spinach pizza!" my mother says enthusiastically.

Somebody shoot me, please.

We order the roasted chicken and the spinach pizza. No pasta in sight.

"The chicken is so cute!" my mother says when the waiter brings out the food. I've never heard poultry described as cute before. "This is such a yummy place!"

How would she know? My mother nudges lettuce leaves around her plate. She barely nibbles half a slice of pizza, a bite of a chicken wing, and one tomato off the top of her bruschetta.

Jay, on the other hand, uses his bread crust like a sponge to lap up every last drop of oil and sauce on his plate. I've barely begun to chew my chicken when my mother cranes her neck for the waiter.

"We'll need some boxes," my mother says as she pushes her mostly full plate away.

While we wait for the check, Jay pulls out a flossing instrument from the front pocket of his flannel shirt. As his eyes wander over the black-and-white photographs on the wall, he works the pick between each tooth, then wipes the removed chunks of food onto his napkin.

"Are you flossing at the table?" my mother asks.

"Is that wrong?" Jay asks.

"It's disgusting," I say.

"It's like a toothpick," he says. "People still use toothpicks."

"They shouldn't," I say. "It's bad manners."

The waiter returns before Jay and I begin bickering in earnest.

"Dessert?" the waiter asks.

I regret having ticked Jay off; he's my ally in overindulgence. If anyone was going to lobby for and share a dessert with me, it'd be him.

Can't you feel how tight your pants are? Ana asks.

A few bites of apple crostada won't hurt, BB says. *It's fruit, after all.*

Yeah, just like French fries are vegetables, Ana says.

"We've had enough," my mother says before I can opine.

Speak for yourself, BB says.

As soon as we get home, Mom plops down on the sofa with a bowl of Cheerios.

Though I can't stand being around my mother and Jay so much, I depend on their presence to keep BB in check. BB thrives on my isolation. Like a vampire that comes out exclusively at night, BB is active only when I'm alone.

"Coming to the game?" Jay asks as he backs the Jeep out of the driveway. My brother is in the state football playoffs tonight and everyone in my family will be in the stands to cheer him on.

Everyone, that is, but me.

"Nah," I say. "I'm gonna take it easy."

"Are you running tomorrow?" my mother asks from the passenger window.

The gunshot start of the Twin Cities Marathon is only twelve hours away and I haven't decided if I'll run the 26.2 miles from downtown Minneapolis to the Capitol in St. Paul.

"I don't know," I sigh. "I'll see how I feel in the morning."

My mother and Jay wave good-bye and the Jeep disappears down the street.

Fuck taking it easy. BB has a full night ahead of her.

As soon as the 'rents are out of sight, I take the stairs two at a time to the kitchen and snack surf. As methodically as a serial killer scoping out a victim, I examine the buffalo wings in the fridge, the ice cream selection in the freezer, the cereal offerings in the cupboard. I settle on a party-size bag of Tostitos and a fresh tub of guacamole. It's a semi-healthy combo and as close to carbo-loading as I'll come before the race.

I lounge on the couch, losing myself in the crunching rhythm as chip after chip slips between my lips. The contrast of cool guacamole and the sandpaper surface of the Tostitos scratching the roof of my mouth is delicious. After a dozen dips or so, I consider stopping.

But I can't; I'm eating on autopilot. My entire arm disappears into the bag over and over again until I come up with a handful of air. In only ten minutes, I've devoured every last chip and half a pound of guacamole.

Nice work, Ana growls. *Now you've really fucked up. How are you going to run a marathon tomorrow with all this rumbling around in your gut?*

The next morning I awake from my guacoma with the psychological dead weight of the previous night's binge. Whether I feel like running or not is irrelevant; I am calorically in debt. I need to run at *least* 26.2 miles to undo the damage.

Taking off at the starting line, my stomach feels like a five-pound fanny pack of flab. My thighs are massive blocks of ice and my calves ache with each thunderous step.

At mile three I stumble into a Porta Potti and drop my pants to pee, but my body shakes so hard I can barely force the stream into the toilet. I want to quit already.

That's it, lazy ass, Ana hisses as the plastic door slams shut behind me. *No more potty breaks. You run until you cross the finish line. Now get going!*

This race is known as the Most Beautiful Urban Marathon in the country, and the Twin Cities lives up to its namesake this October day. The scenery consumes me: the leaves glitter gold and crimson in the midmorning sun, the odor of roasting woodchips wafts down the parkway, and the ripples of the Mississippi shimmer beneath the Franklin Bridge. I lose myself in the hip-hop sounds on my Walkman, vowing to finish the race before America's Top 40 ends.

BB is happy to run for the free food. A bearded man doles out bananas from a wicker basket, roadside adolescents toss Cliff Shots my way, and fellow runners share orange wedges midstride without breaking pace. There are more treats offered on the sidelines—Life Savers, gummi bears, gumdrops, even hamburgers—but Ana won't let me stop for a taste test.

So focused on burning off last night's binge, I don't realize how fast I'm running. When I cross the finish line, I feel . . . nothing. No joy, no pride, no relief. If anything, I am disappointed. Part of me didn't want to finish at all. Part of me was hoping that this would be the day when my body would finally wave the white flag and force me to collapse.

Once again, my body proves indestructible.

I follow the other finishers like a sheep as organizers herd us through various checkpoints. Volunteers slip a medal around my neck, remove the timing chip from my shoe, and direct me toward the bag pickup. When I collect my belongings, the bright-eyed woman behind the table exclaims, "Did you race? You look great!"

I am flat-faced, unexcited; hell, I've barely broken a sweat. My singlet and compression pants are dry.

"Go get some food!" the woman says, waving toward the lush green lawn in front of the Capitol.

A massive buffet featuring fruit, bagels, muffins, and yogurt is spread out beneath a party tent. My body aches to replenish the 2,600 calories I just torched, but I walk down the line with my jaw wired shut. When I reach the last table, I stop dead in my tracks— there is a full sheet of thickly frosted marble cake. If there were ever a time to indulge in sugar, it would be now, when my body is in a carb-deficient state. There's no one around; I could cut a humungous slice and find a secluded spot on the grass to stuff my face.

You don't deserve to eat, Ana says. *Not after all the junk food last night.*

I turn away from the cake and pick up a banana instead.

"How'd you do?" another runner asks as I board the bus home.

"Three fourteen ten," I say.

"Wow," he replies, shaking a spiky-haired head. "That's, like, an eight-minute mile!"

Actually, it's seven twenty-four, Ana says, *but who's counting?*

I can't take credit for my kick-ass performance. I didn't run the marathon—my eating disorder did.

My mother calls me after she sees my results online.

"You qualified for Boston," she says in a voice appropriate for delivering positive HIV results. "But you don't really want to do that, do you?"

Boston? I wasn't trying to qualify for the most prestigious marathon in the world. I just wanted to burn off a binge.

* * *

"What's that?" a chubby woman with curly hair asks as she peers over my shoulder.

"The Twin Cities Marathon emblem," I say. I hold up the design of my soon-to-be tattoo: a runner wedged between two leaves and 3:14:10 printed beneath.

"What a great idea to put your bib number on there!" she says.

I force a smile. I'm too shy to tell her what the numbers really mean.

"I ran the marathon, too," she says. "I'm doing New York next. How about you?"

"Maybe Boston," I say.

"What's the qualifying time?"

"Three forty."

Her eyes widen. "Oh, God," she says with a laugh. "I'll never make it. My time was four forty-five!"

Probably because you're so fat, Ana sneers.

My tattoo artist leads me back to his lair. Tyler is a pasty-skinned blond with a string-bean body. As he prepares the needle, I admire the boxing paraphernalia and skeleton sketches on the walls.

I recline on a leather chair and Tyler brings the tip of the needle to my skin. "Blue on top, orange on bottom, right?" he asks, indicating the leaves.

"Err . . . yeah," I say. I forgot to bring the official TCM brochure, so I'm relying on a black-and-white photocopy and my memory for the color scheme.

"You're sure?"

"Absolutely." Absolutely *not*, but I don't want to wait any longer to get inked. Who cares about the colors anyway? They're only going to be etched on my ankle for all eternity.

"Here goes," Tyler says. "Let me know if you need me to stop."

"I've had two kids," I say. "I can handle it."

As soon as I get home, my new tattoo still hidden beneath a

bandage, I rifle through my file folder until I find the TCM brochure. The emblem is on the cover, in color: orange leaf on top, blue
leaf on bottom.

I smile at my mistake. It seems fitting somehow that the tattoo
is upside down.

chapter twenty-four

The Learning Curve

The U of M writing program is not for lightweights. I'm working with acclaimed authors like Madelon Sprengnether and Deborah Keenan. My courses, in poetry, creative nonfiction, and memoir, respectively, are workshop-based, meaning I will submit samples of my writing to my peers to be critiqued in a weekly roundtable. This isn't the Minnesota Nice kind of feedback. This is hardcore.

Meanwhile, the wolves inside me are at war again. Ana and BB team up to sabotage my writing. As soon as I flip open my laptop, Ana attacks with a tingly sensation that starts at the back of my neck and spreads down my limbs; she makes my heart race and armpits sweat. The only way to relieve the anxiety is exercise. Most days, I spend more time working out than I do working on my writing.

When I finally manage to get something down on paper, Ana infiltrates my poetry between the lines.

NOT ANOTHER DIET

Bread is the staff of life
But carbs are the cane

Atkins beats me with
Until my body
Breaks free
From its fatty coating

I suspect my writing isn't as brilliant as it seems, so I ask for feedback from Professor Keenan before my turn at the round-table.

"It's a funny thing, this writing," I say when I sit down across from her one afternoon. "Last night when I printed these poems out, I thought they were pure genius, but now that I reread them, I realize they're crap."

My self-effacement falls flat; Professor Keenan doesn't laugh.

"How many do you have?" she asks.

"I brought five poems today, but I have four hundred more at home."

"You wrote four hundred poems so far this semester?"

"Some I wrote over the summer."

"Bring them in," Professor Keenan says.

"What?"

"Bring them in next week."

"Are you sure?" I ask. Even *I* don't want to reread four hundred of my own poems.

"You want to apply to the MFA program, don't you?"

"Yeah."

"It's competitive. You're going to need really strong work to win a place here."

"I'm just in shock that you're willing to read them all."

"That's what I'm here for."

I know Professor Keenan will give me her honest opinion—and if it's negative, I know she'll let me down gently.

A week after I hand in a phone-book-size stack of poems, she returns them to me with a typed cover letter. Among her comments, she writes,

You are in what my friend...calls "the trauma loop"—your poems feel ferocious, sad, repetitive, struggling, honorable, and almost all deeply self-referential . . . you are writing the same poem, over and over again.

Professor Keenan recommends I focus on nonfiction essays instead, but Ana's nonexistent attention span makes sticking with one stanza—much less an entire paragraph—excruciatingly difficult.

A day in my life as a wannabe writer looks like this:

4:00 A.M.: Wakeup call to Joni Mitchell's song *Blue*; not exactly the optimist's anthem.

4:45 A.M.: Set out on ten-mile run like a match has been lit beneath me. Every moment of my muscles' throbbing is delicious. I'm high on endorphins and writing inspiration floods my brain.

6:10 A.M.: I'm done with the run and resolve to sit outside and pound out at least a page of literary masterpiece.

6:15 A.M.: Too chilly to write outside. I'll just change out of my sweaty clothes first, then write down ideas for the Great American Memoir.

6:30 A.M.: The girls are still asleep, and it's too quiet, so I turn on the news for background noise.

6:40 A.M.: Whoops. Inspired by a health segment on the news, I take a break from writing and knock off a few ab exercises.

6:45 A.M.: My stomach is rumbling now. I was supposed to eat within a thirty-minute post-run recovery window. I'll eat quickly, then write down that brilliant idea . . . if I can remember what it was.

7:00 A.M.: The girls are awake and screaming monkey sounds. I better get them ready and settled in front of the tube, then I'll write.

8:00 A.M.: The girls are ready but I haven't decided what to wear today. The weather is unseasonably warm and I don't have preapproved clothing combinations on hand. This could take a while . . .

9:00 A.M.: Nine already? The girls want a snack now and, come to think of it, so do I. While I'm in the kitchen, I'll pack a lunch for myself so I can have an uninterrupted eight-hour writing day at Starbucks.

9:40 A.M.: Cesar is running late to pick up the girls, so while we're waiting, I'll just respond to a few e-mails.

10:00 A.M.: The girls are gone now, but my so-called quick e-mailing has turned into a major information expedition on Google re: Joni Mitchell's creative process.

10:30 A.M.: I'll begin award-winning writing spree shortly. I'm feeling chilly again, so I'll just heat up a cup of coffee before I go.

11:00 A.M.: Major construction requires detour through Minneapolis to get to St. Paul.

11:20 A.M.: I'm finally sitting down at my favorite Starbucks with a frappuccino.

11:30 A.M.: It must be man-in-midlife-crisis day. I've been approached by three of them who ask about my computer (what the hell do I know about screen resolution?), what I'm writing, and how they can publish their memoirs, too.

12:00 P.M.: Ugh. Total writer's block. Nothing of substance coming out. Out of eight waking hours, I've written for only thirty minutes. I'm extremely good at avoiding writing, and when I do write, very good at avoiding the project I'm supposed to be working on. Maybe I haven't lived enough yet to write the Great American Memoir. I'm going to turn off the laptop, go have some book-worthy experiences, then write.

12:10 P.M.: Scratch that; I'm too hungry. Going over to campus for lunch instead. Class isn't until 4:45 P.M. I can write later.

As soon as I set foot on campus, my focus drifts from academics and I fixate on food. The walk from the parking ramp to the English Department is a rigorous exercise—in self-restraint. In only ten minutes I pass Chipotle, Bruegger's Bagels, Dairy Queen, Subway, Sally's Sports Bar, Ben & Jerry's, Chinese Buffet, and Big 10 Pizza. The succulent aromas of formerly forbidden—and now binge-friendly—foods commingle in my nostrils, inflaming my appetite.

I feel like a bottomless pit; the hunger just won't go away no matter how much I eat. Even after today's lunch of chicken salad tossed with walnuts, feta cheese, and apple crisps, I'm still starving. Considering the other options at Panera—honey buns and bagels—I decide a second salad will do the least damage.

"The first one was just an appetizer, huh?" a wiry old man asks when I sit down with my encore entrée.

I force a smile and a dry "Ha-ha." He straightens his apron, slings a damp towel over his shoulder, and clears the table next to mine.

The second plate of romaine can't fill my cavernous stomach, so I approach the register for the third time and ask for a baguette.

"You mean an extra piece of bread?" the cashier asks with a scratch of his head.

"No," I say. "I want a whole baguette. To go."

To go to a corner booth and binge, **BB** clarifies.

"Oh!" he says. "Of course."

He hands me a wheat baguette—as tall as two-and-a-half-year-old Lola—sheathed in a paper bag. I settle into a booth butted up against the wall. From my belly-button up, I look like I'm studying. Beneath the table, my hand is peeling off the crust of the baguette like a scab, then slipping it in my mouth as nonchalantly as a piece of gum. When I'm done, all that's left in the bag is the squishy innards—the high-carb part, or so says BB—of the baguette.

This is how BB distracts me from writing. It's as though her job were to keep my self-esteem as low as possible. If I'm shit-faced ashamed of myself, I won't take risks in my writing. The urge to stuff myself increases with the intensity of my work; on the days I'm slated to present a new piece to my peers, I refuse to show my face in class until I'm high on carbohydrates. I binge my way down the street: chips and guac, chicken tacos, a twist cone, a chocolate waffle bowl, an M&M cookie. My binges, and the resulting weight gain, form a buffer, a flabby armor, to protect me from literary criticsm.

Today is no different, but Ana's worried I'm getting a paunch, so I pop a few laxatives to move all that fibrous wheat through my system as quickly as possible. Moments after the sweet pink pills drop down my throat, my stomach churns.

I close my eyes as the chemical cyclone gains strength in my gut.

"Are you meditating?" a man in a pin-striped suit asks as he passes my table.

My mouth is as dry as, well, bread crust.

"No," I wheeze.

"Dreaming up the next Google?"

"More like taking a nap with my eyes open."

He laughs and keeps walking.

When the seasick feeling subsides momentarily, I pack up my stuff, toss the bread in the garbage, and make my way toward the restroom.

"Wow!" the towel-toting geezer says as I pass by. "You eat fast! Must be in a hurry."

"I have class," I say. In an hour and a half, that is.

Head bowed, I hide my face behind a curtain of hair, bracing myself against the wall as nausea sweeps over me. I wouldn't mind losing my lunch, but I want to get to the bathroom first.

I pass a booth where a tall, thin blond reads with her chubby brunette daughter. There is a decadent, half-eaten brownie between them. The pair looks like me and Julia, ten years from now.

"Mom?" the girl asks as she folds a corner of her paperback down. "What does *cope* mean?"

"Read me the sentence."

"She knew she could cope until morning."

"It means she could hang on. She could deal with her pain until the next day."

I wish I could deal. I feel like I'm hanging on by my fingernails.

I thought moving in with my mother would make *me* a better mother; instead, it strengthens my alliance to Ana. In my all-or-nothing mind-set, I am the shittiest parent on the planet. Rather than do a mediocre job at raising my children, I jettison the responsibility all together.

One morning, my mother interrupts my treadmill run at 5:45. Lola, limp and lethargic, is in her arms.

"Just so you know," she says, "they're awake."

"Uh-huh," I say, not bothering to remove my headphones. She should know Mommy doesn't clock in until 7:00 A.M.

"Lola's temperature is a hundred and three," she says, tentatively stepping closer to me. "I don't know if you want to do something about that."

"Like what?"

"Someone should see her."

"Why?" I ask. "All they'll do is charge twenty bucks to say, 'It's a cold; it'll go away in a week.'"

"She was up all night coughing; didn't you give her any medicine?"

"She wasn't coughing when I put her to bed," I said. "So I didn't give her any."

"*She wasn't coughing* when you put her to bed?!"

"No."

My mother shoots daggers at me with her eyes. "Then you weren't watching."

I'm watching now. I'm watching as Julia begins the day with grapes. Just grapes. No syrup-soaked pancakes, no peanut butter and jelly waffle, no pleas for Lucky Charms. Her face falls and her eyes redden.

"My mouth hurts," she whines. "My stomach hurts. My knees hurt." The pain slithers down her body as her fever peaks.

Lola's complexion, already the lightest shade of pale, fades to an almost-translucent tone. Her voice sounds husky and rattles with phlegm. Two green boogers crawl like caterpillars down her nose.

"I'm cold, I'm cold," she says, shivering, all the while sweating through the Teletubbies costume she refuses to take off.

I put the girls in wrestling holds to get the decongestant down their throats. They scream and kick as I tuck their heads beneath my chin and force their mouths open with my fingers. I squirt the medication along the edge of their gums, plugging their noses so they swallow. Lola spits it out at me; Julia vomits it back up.

While I wash off at the kitchen sink, my mother hunches over a page-long note she's writing for Cesar. It is a detailed account of how to care for the girls over the weekend.

"Mom, you are not giving that to him."

"He needs to know what to do," she says.

"He's an adult," I say. Unlike me, Cesar has common sense when it comes to parenting. "He can figure it out."

I can't wait for Cesar to take over; I stand by the front door and watch for his car out the window.

My mother comes down the stairs, cradling Lola.

"Don't treat her like a baby," I say.

"Stop being so hard on me," my mother says.

Now my eyes shoot daggers.

"You are being so rude and disrespectful," she says.

"I haven't even said anything!"

"It's all in the silence, Erica."

The silence between my mother and me is now the loudest sound in the house.

Though we live only a staircase apart, we haven't spoken in forty-eight hours.

Tonight, my mother and I cross paths at the kitchen. There are no mandatory pleasantries, no dull synopsis of the weekend's events, no jokes, no nagging, not even a "You've ruined my life!"

This is not the silence of family members so comfortable with one another that they feel no need to chat; this is a charged silence, the kind that, if broken, would explode in a shock-and-awe campaign of emotion. Every old hurt would be unearthed and anger would spurt, unstoppable, like lava.

"What's going on, Erica?" my mother finally asks as she leans a hip up against the stove.

I rinse the remnants of my lunch from a Tupperware at the sink, the water whisking Romaine and radicchio leaves down the drain.

I think: A shitload.

I say: "Nothing."

"Anything I can do to help?" she asks.

I think: "Yes. Turn off the goddamn TV."

I say: "No."

When I had my own house, there was no blaring television.

There was easy-listening music in the mornings, sunset vistas in the evenings, fresh food all day, a routine that my daughters knew and followed. There were open windows and peace after 7 P.M. Here, the chaos ramps up a level when the sun goes down.

Jay interrupts our passive-aggressive chat to prepare dinner. He glides between the stove and the countertop, alternately dicing then dropping vegetables and hunks of mystery meat into a pan. The stench of the stir-fry coats the walls as it half-sizzles, half-burns on the stove. The scent of sweet-and-sour sauce will be imbedded in my hair, my clothes, stuck to the inside of my nostrils all night.

My mother's mind has already jumped from Jay's food preparation to leftover storage. Jay is oblivious to my mother's apathetic appetite; he cooks every night for the two of them, though he is the only one who eats. I know my mother will barely pick at his Asian creation; rather, she will move the goop around her plate for a few minutes, claim satiety, and pack up whatever Jay doesn't gobble down. No one will reheat the food all week; mold may blossom before they throw it out.

"It's so hot in here," my mother says as Jay gives the stir-fry a final shimmy in the pan.

He slides the slimy vegetables onto clean plates and chuckles. "Welcome to hell."

Later that night, a pile of file folders appears on my desk. I move them aside and scoff loudly enough so my mother will hear me across the room. I can't stand when she tries to pawn her clutter off on me.

When she fails to turn her attention from the TV, I clear my throat and say, "Um, Mom? What are these folders doing here?"

"It's just some old stuff I found," she says, flipping off the TV and hoisting herself off the couch. She turns away from me and walks slowly across the room.

"And I would want this because . . . ?"

"For inspiration. For writing," she says over her shoulder.

"I have more than enough to write about," I say, keeping my gaze fixed on my desk.

I can't see my mother's face, but her voice wavers when she says, "It just doesn't seem fair. We're letting you live here rent-free and you're writing mean things about us behind our backs."

While it's true that a lot of what I write about my mother and Jay is negative, it's just journaling, not meant for public consumption. Besides, how would my mother know what I'm writing about unless she's snooping through my stuff?

"It's pretty presumptuous to think that all I'm writing about is you and Jay."

My mother is standing at the edge of the room now, half-turned toward me, half-turned toward her bedroom.

"You know, I used to blame Grandpa Stuart for everything," she sighs.

"And he probably deserved it," I say.

I can't tell from my mother's nonresponse if she's ignoring my comment or didn't hear it in the first place.

"Then I learned to take responsibility for my future," she continues.

"That's nice," I say.

"It just doesn't seem fair . . ." My mother's voice trails behind her as she walks down the hall.

I don't hate my mother; but the fact is, she's hurt me more than once. The additional strain of raising two girls under her roof hasn't strengthened our fragile relationship. And while I understand her fear of being virtually dragged through the mud, what she doesn't comprehend is that by writing, I'm exorcising the anger that has been simmering inside me all these years. By writing, I'm emptying myself of all the mother-daughter emotional muck so we can start fresh someday.

But she doesn't get it. As I watch her float, so thin and phantom-like down the hall, I wonder if she ever will.

*　*　*

"Where are the girls when you have class?" Professor Keenan asks me one evening after class.

"With my mom," I say.

"Does she help you out a lot?"

"She's practically my co-parent."

"Does she live close to you?" Professor Keenan asks.

No one at the U of M knows I live in my mother's basement; thus far, I've avoided any discussion of my living situation with my peers.

"Oh, yes," I say. "She's *very* close."

"How nice."

It *was* nice, especially when I could barely care for myself, much less two preschoolers in the throes of asserting their independence. But what once felt like help now feels like a hindrance. Instead of relieving my depression, my mother's over-involvement makes me feel useless.

I'm invisible. I'm dispensable. I'm Stand-in Mommy.

I'm also jealous.

I see how happiness explodes on my daughters' faces when they're with "Gramma-bamma." My mother teaches them silly songs, tickles them until they can't breathe, and assembles princess puzzles for hours on end.

There are days when I feel up to the Mommy Challenge, days when *I* want to heat up the mini hot dogs Julia and Lola love, days when *I* want to help them get dressed, days when *I* want to sign them up for swimming lessons. My efforts feel like too little, too late; my mother has already taken care of everything.

"Help, please!" Lola calls one afternoon from the bathroom; this is the cue that she just pooped in the potty.

"I'll help you," I say, poking my head in the door and reaching for the Baby Wipes.

"No! I. Want. Grandma."

I'm not even worthy of wiping my daughter's ass now?

* * *

As the semester goes on, all of my relationships are sent through
the writing wringer. My primary poetry topic is my own shitty
mothering.

CRY BABY

Eight a.m. and I'm back in bed
"Blue" coos in stereo
Preschooler feet come pounding
Are you crying Mommy?
No, my darling

Rubber Ducky glares back at me
Fetal form on bathtub floor
Shower steams too long
Chickpea face
Pokes through the curtain
Are you crying Mommy?
No, my darling

One day she'll come waddling
And worried
Flip back flannel
Kiss cold cheek
Are you dying Mommy?
No longer lying
Yes, my darling.

After I finish reading this piece in the workshop, I can't bear to look
at my fellow poets' faces. The silence in the room could burst my
eardrums.

Professor Keenan takes a deep breath and shudders. "That poem is whacked," she says.

A few students chuckle uncomfortably.

"In the best of ways," Professor Keenan clarifies. "Other comments?"

Todd, the most intimidating writer in the class, adjusts the pencil behind his ear and says, "Completely frightening."

The poet with multiple publication credits strokes his gingerbread-colored beard and says, "Creepy."

"It's almost Plath-like," a plain but pretty brunette says in her Southern accent. "And publishable."

I should be proud of the reactions to my poetry, but BB refuses to accept praise. Even if my peers give me props for my writing, she wants to stuff. As soon as class is over, she steers me to the corner market for carbo-loaded snacks. Then, in an isolated corner of the Engineering Atrium, I devour a loaf of pumpkin chocolate chip bread, fistful after fistful of caramel popcorn, and a sleeve of ginger snaps. Five laxatives later, I go home, my ego—and all evidence of my binge—down the crapper.

JOURNAL ENTRY

I think I'm trying to stuff down the writer inside. When I make myself sick, my work stagnates. In *The Writer's Life,* author Julia Cameron said she used to rely on booze and cocaine to fuel her writing. Eventually, she realized the chemicals were impeding, not enhancing, the creative process. I might be at that point; but how do I give up food?

I'm convinced some substance in my diet lowers my inhibitions and sets BB free. Is it artificial sweeteners? Hydrogenated fats? Sodium? If only I could pinpoint the culprit and eliminate it from my meals, my frantic overeating would be cured. I try a half dozen dietary cuts: no carbs, no coffee, no carbonated beverages, no chocolate, no candy, no ice cream. Nothing works.

I think my problem is food.

Silly girl.

The problem isn't food. It's me.

chapter twenty-five

Prozac Popper

JOURNAL ENTRY

Why is society surprised when artists go off the deep end? You can only dip into the dark side of human nature so many times before you get wet yourself.

Depression returns in big, black waves, reducing me to an immobile blob. All day long, I count down the hours until I can pop a sleeping pill and hit the sheets. My twice-a-month head-shrinking sessions with Shania aren't enough. When I spend more time horizontal than vertical, I submit to psychopharmacology.

Dr. Swan is the psychiatrist at the Center for Eating Disorders, and she's as dainty as her name implies. She reminds me of Snow White: petite, with mousy brown curls delicately tucked in a clip at the crown of her head. She doesn't walk me back to her office; she sashays with subtle elegance, like Jackie Kennedy.

"Take a seat," she says in a voice as soft as cotton.

Dr. Swan's office is the epitome of order. Everything is in its proper place; even the few papers she has left on her desk are perfectly stacked atop one another. There are photographs of her two children on a corkboard: one is a preschool-aged girl—a spitting image of the MD—with a wide, precocious smile. The other is a bald, blue-eyed baby, though I can't tell from the gender-neutral onesie if it's a boy or a girl.

"When did the depression come back?" she asks.

"It's never gone away," I say. "Since my second daughter was born, it's been there."

I silently complete the calculations: two and a half years. I've been under this damn melancholic rain cloud for as long as Lola's been alive. Postpartum depression—the psychological equivalent of stretch marks.

"Can you describe what the depression feels like?"

I shake my head. There are no words. Winston Churchill once likened depression to a black dog, but dogs are endearing. This is a menacing presence, some sort of demon.

Even if I could describe it, Dr. Swan wouldn't understand.

"Let's give Prozac a try," she says.

"Can't I have Wellbutrin instead?" I ask.

When I ran out of the drug a few months back, I didn't refill the prescription. I wanted to believe my depression was situational, not chemical. I wasn't defective; my lifestyle was. But I'm still depressed, and if I have to be medicated, I might as well get a manic boost out of it.

"If the eating disorder is active, Wellbutrin could cause a seizure."

At this point, I wouldn't mind if it did.

"Any questions about side effects?" Dr. Swan asks.

Forget life-threatening side effects like seizures; all Ana wants to know is, "Will I gain weight?"

Dr. Swan sighs. "Prozac is weight neutral. In fact, it's the only antidepressant approved for binge eating disorder."

Sold! If I can eliminate those daily 1,000-calorie carb-fests, I could lose at least a couple pounds a week.

"So how long till this kicks in?"

"Four to six weeks."

A month is an eternity to wait to feel better, but compared to two years of gloom, it's only a wrinkle in time.

"Are you okay with this?" Dr. Swan asks, waving her prescription pad in the air. The colossal rock on her third finger sparkles in the sunlight.

"At this point, I'll try anything."

"No," Dr. Swan says. "What I'm asking is: You're not going to overdose, are you?"

Not right away, Ana says. *We have to lose some weight first.*

I make a sound somewhere between a gasp and a giggle.

Dr. Swan blushes. "Sorry," she says. "I have to ask if someone's suicidal."

Dr. Swan doesn't know me well enough. I always laugh when I lie.

Within a day of popping the first green-and-white capsule, I feel better. Is this a placebo effect? All in my head? Who cares! The signs that something has shifted are minute, but I notice.

The artificially induced energy helps me troll through the dull tasks of daily life. I get out of bed with only one alarm. I respect the speed limit. I arrive on time to my appointments. I do all the mundane tasks I've been neglecting: the bank deposits, the library book pickups, the toenail cutting, the car vacuuming.

The renewed productivity feels good—for about a week.

Then worry overwhelms me. Is this my future? This monotonous ticking off of to-do lists?

Prozac forms a thick, invisible barrier between my brain, my body, and the rest of the world. My senses cocoon themselves in a fuzzy old bathrobe. At least with the mood swings, I felt *something*. The pain reassured me I was alive. Now, oblivion is my default response.

JOURNAL ENTRY

I continue on the robot track. I don't know who gets me where I need to go, but somehow I just show up. I am like everyone else now. It is unbelievably blah. Nothing bothers me and that's exactly what bothers me.

Ana has been bubble-wrapped; the body battle is over. The numbness seeps from my brain, down through my heart, and lodges firmly in my stomach. If I had trouble identifying satiation signals before, it is impossible now. My tongue can't detect taste, only temperature and texture.

Yogurt: cold and smooth

Peanut butter: lukewarm and chunky

Grapes: chilled and firm

Coffee: hot and thick

To Shrink Shania's delight, I do what I am told. I indulge in unlimited restaurant meals: sizzling shrimp fajitas, log-size omelets, gyro feasts. I do not deny myself dessert. There are so few pleasures in life—especially since Prozac has extinguished all my passions—that food becomes my only comfort.

Peanut butter is my new best friend.

My penchant for Parker's Farm honey roasted crunchy is a full-fledged addiction now. The pretty pink label screams to me: *Eat, eat, eat!*

My ritual is well established: First, I allow the peanut butter to soften to a malleable consistency. Then I peel back the plastic barrier from the container, like a teenage boy breaking through his first virginal hymen. The peanut butter is supple and slippery, ready to be penetrated. The sweet, nutty concoction coats my tongue and slides down my throat like spackle, smoothing over the rough spots of my soul.

Like a crackhead or alcoholic, I have to up my intake regularly to achieve a palpable high. What was once one tablespoon of peanut butter turns into a quarter cup, then half a tub. Thank God they don't sell my substance of choice in industrial-size containers or I'd eat myself to a peanut buttery death.

Shania does not believe me when I tell her I eat a half a pound of peanut butter a day.

"That's the eating disorder talking," she reassures me. "It only *seems* like that much. I'm sure it's the equivalent of a peanut butter sandwich. Or two."

Or six.

Like chain smokers or alcoholics, I wear my obsessive-compulsive peanut butter habit on my body. My stomach softens, my thighs jiggle, my face is a hydrogenated oil spill. But even weight gain and a pimply complexion do not deter me from indulging every day.

"I can't believe the Skippy is gone already!" Jay moans to no one in particular one evening.

It's my fault; Babb's ran out of my Parker's Farm drug of choice and in a moment of desperation, I settled for Jay's Skippy instead. I pretend to be immersed in the task of putting the girls in their pajamas down the hall, hoping that my nonresponse will render me innocent of the peanut butter crime.

A few moments later, my mother leans up against the doorway. "Did you finish off the peanut butter?" she asks.

I nod silently, too ashamed to make eye contact.

"I thought so," she mutters to herself and pads back down the hall.

On the next grocery list, Jay's handwriting reads: *Peanut butter.* SMALL!

* * *

"What's wrong?" my mother asks one night when she finds me crouched over the computer so tensely my shoulders touch my earlobes.

"I ate half the apple pie," I say. I'd come home that evening to find a fresh dimpled pastry tucked away, untouched, in the corner of the kitchen. One sliver turned to two, and though I tried to rein in BB with rules (eat only the filling or just the crust), I made it halfway around the pie before the bellyache began. Had I not needed to explain the missing dessert to my mother, I would have devoured every last bite.

"Don't worry," my mother says. "It's my fault. See what happens when I go grocery shopping hungry? I'll get rid of it."

My mother enlists Jay to do the grocery shopping; considering his penchant for junk food, it's hardly a deterrent for BB.

When I pull the Fritos corn chips down from the top cupboard, I only want to *look* at the back of the bag. I like to read snack packages. Blame it on creative curiosity—perhaps I could make a career writing blurbs for Frito-Lay?

"Sometimes a lightweight snack just isn't going to cut it. Fritos Scoops Corn Chips are strong enough to stand up to the challenge . . . Whether digging into a thick cheese dip . . ."

Hmm, good idea.

". . . or eating them all alone . . ."

Are the Fritos or the eater alone? It's open to interpretation.

". . . nothing satisfies like Fritos."

BB has to see if the product's claims are true. At the table, I munch and crunch and lick my salty fingers until there is barely a handful or two left at the bottom of the bag. The debate begins: Do I discreetly dispose of the corn chips in the basement garbage bin? Or leave the measly leftovers in the cupboard and risk confrontation later?

I leave the bag, unashamed of my identity as snack snatcher.

The next day, I notice an addition to the grocery list in Jay's handwriting: *Chips. Buy 2, hide 1.*

Pre-Prozac, I could binge to my gut's delight without gaining weight. Now, medicated, my waist expands along with my dietary repertoire. No matter how much exercise I do, I can't keep the scale steady. Before long, I have abundant breasts, a puffy tummy, and junk in the trunk.

I do not enjoy my voluptuous body; I ignore it. After a cease-and-desist on the tummy checks, I leave the scales to collect dust in the bathroom corner. Fresh from the shower, I no longer wipe steam from the mirror. I dress in my makeshift closet, far from my reflection.

I cannot escape my clothes, however, and consistently exhaust the sizes: the 1's won't rise past my knees, the 2's refuse to button at the waist. I'm reduced to the infamous jeans wiggle, flinging myself on the bed, kicking and cursing until the button slips past its hole, like the woman in the Special K cereal commercials of the 1990s.

The dryer is shrinking my clothes behind my back. At least, that's what I tell myself. My mother's antiquated appliance creates crop tops from my sweaters, capris from my pants. It has to be the dryer.

I am not fat. I am not fat. I am not fat.

"Mommy," Julia says. She pokes at the flab seeping out above the waist of my pants. "You're getting too big."

Earth to Erica! Ana says. *You're fat!*

JOURNAL ENTRY

There are moments when my body looks all right: curvy, lus-cious, like a woman should. Then there are other moments when my stomach feels so huge that I despise myself and can't wait to return to the safety and satisfaction of anorexia.

"Mom's cooking must be good!" my mother's neighbor says when we cross paths at the mailbox. She grabs her cheeks with both hands and squeezes hard, demonstrating how chubby my face looks now. "You're getting fat!"

I decide to knead my wobbly bits away.

"Calves and shoulders as usual?" my masseuse, Heidi, asks at my next appointment.

"And quads," I say.

Heidi smiles, her eyes tracing my body up and down.

"Anything else I need to know about?" she asks.

I cock my head in confusion. I've been seeing Heidi for six months. What more could she need to know?

"No."

It isn't until I glance at my naked reflection that I understand: Heidi suspects I am pregnant.

JOURNAL ENTRY

I feel as though I'm carrying a 30-pound sheath of peanut butter blubber over my real body. I wish I were pregnant, if only to justify how fat I am.

"I like women with curves," my brother says when I ask for his honest opinion on my weight. I'm debuting size 4 pants at our cousin's wedding. "You look better this way."

My smile can't disguise my disbelief.

Jay comes up behind me and surprises me with a grizzly bear hug. "I'll rub your back later," he says.

"No, thanks," I say.

"Doesn't it hurt?"

"No. Why would you think that?"

My stepfather traces a finger down my spine. "Because you have a back brace on."

I barely hold back a drama-queen outburst.

"It's not a brace," I say. "It's a *girdle*."

I rely on the metal-boned contraption—which was once reserved for only the clingiest of special-occasion dresses—on a daily basis now.

That night, Julia catches me releasing my rolls of blubber from the girdle.

"What's that?" she asks.

"It's to control my stomach," I say.

Julia puts a finger to her mouth like a doctor diagnosing a rare disease.

"You need to eat one time a day," she says.

If only I could.

The depression is so overwhelming, I'm desperate for distraction—even if it is self-destructive. If I quit numbing out with binges, if I stop obsessing about food, I'll have to acknowledge what a disaster my life is and feel the melancholy all day, every day.

Rather than resist BB, I offer myself up to her. I'm even grateful for her arrival. If I don't get a shot of serotonin in the form of simple sugars, I'll reach not for carbs but for the pills in my medicine cabinet. The choice comes down to chocolate or death. I choose the lesser of the two evils. My binges keep me alive.

Eating is my armor; food is my pain reliever, antidepressant, and sedative all rolled into one. It lifts my spirits, keeps me company, and puts the love-hungry monster inside me to sleep. If the post-binge serenity I feel doesn't quell the suicidal urges, I silence the depression with, "I *can't* kill myself tonight; I have to burn this fat off first!"

JOURNAL ENTRY

I bury my feelings in my body until I can find a safe place to release them. That place never materializes, so I stuff the grief down as much as I can. One day this dam is going to burst and I will drown.

Eating and exercise are the primary sources of pleasure in my life; but now, due to Prozac, I'm gaining weight, and it's affecting my running. My calves feel like two slabs of metal; I'm sure the stress fracture is not only back, it's spread to both shins.

"Legs acting up again?" Dr. Ken asks as he rolls his chair toward me.

"I did the hop test," I say, extending my gams. "And I barely passed."

"You did the hop test?" he gawks. "If you learn all my tricks, you won't need me anymore!"

Ahh, but you're such sweet eye candy, I think as Dr. Ken's fingers work their way up my freshly shorn skin.

"How many miles are you doing these days?" he asks.

"Ten miles, every other day, on the treadmill."

"Ten miles? I did six on Sunday in front of a dozen TV screens and I *still* thought I'd die of boredom!"

Dr. Ken palpates each shin, then turns his back to me to make notes in my chart.

"So what are you doing with your . . . health?" he asks.

When I don't answer right away, he spins around in his chair.

"Weight-wise, I mean."

"I've gained at least twenty pounds since I last saw you."

"Yeah . . . how did that happen?" he asks.

"A lot of peanut butter."

Dr. Ken smirks.

"I'm not kidding," I say.

"How much did you weigh before the eating disorder?"

"One hundred forty, one hundred forty-five."

"And were you happy?"

I bite my lip and slouch down. "Who knows."

Dr. Ken scoots his chair back and folds his hands behind his head.

"How do you feel about your weight now?"

"I hate it."

"I was afraid you'd say that." Dr. Ken takes a deep breath as though preparing for The Big Talk. "You look healthy now. You look strong. And by the way, when it comes to racing times, thinner does not mean faster."

I nod.

"Listen," he says, pointing to my legs. "These aren't stress fractures. But to prevent injury, you should add a Boost shake daily and take one day off from exercise per week. Sound manageable?"

"Sure," I mumble.

"Really?"

"No."

"Why not?"

"I eat too much."

"Erica." He sighs. "Weight gain won't cause more injuries."

"*I* know that, but the anorexic part of my brain doesn't believe you."

"Can you access another brain in there?" he asks, tapping his pen against his head.

"I'm trying."

"I challenge you to stay at this weight," he said. "You don't have to gain, just maintain. If you can do that, I wager you'll run faster and longer."

I raise both eyebrows up to my hairline.

"Can you tell I don't believe you?" I say.

Dr. Ken notices my TCM tattoo and lifts my ankle up for closer examination.

"Proud enough to make it permanent, huh?" he asks.

"I may never run that fast again!"

"TCM was not your best marathon."

"It was my only marathon."

"You have many more to come. There's some untapped potential there," he says, waving his pen at my legs. "If you stay healthy."

JOURNAL ENTRY

My prediction that my running would suffer with weight gain has come true. Am I a better mother when I'm well-fed? Yes. Am I a better writer with a full belly? Yes. But am I happier? No. I'm still miserable, just about different things.

"What keeps you going, besides running?" Shania asks at our next session.

"Binges," I say.

"And your daughters."

I know I'm supposed to agree with her; after all, motherhood is meant to be every woman's ultimate reason for living. But Shania and I are beyond the polite bullshit stage, so I say, "Yes and no."

"What do you mean by that?"

"Everything I love—running, writing, the girls, men—also makes me miserable. It's like I have this hole inside of me and nothing fills it up."

"Your problem is that you don't know when enough is enough," Shania says. "You don't need to be full to be satisfied."

This is the crux of it: I'm always reaching for something bigger, better, sweeter, sexier, but ultimately out of reach.

"If you put yourself in this all-or-nothing mind-set, you're going to be disappointed," Shania says. "You need to shift your expectations—not lower, just shift."

Can I fall in love with a man who doesn't make my heart flutter? Can I relish shorter runs? Can I feel accomplished regardless of how many pages I write? Can I eat moderately and still enjoy every bite?

Do I want to live like this forever? Or should I end it all now?

There are no clear answers.

"If I can't have everything I want, what's the point of living?" I ask.

"Nothing outside of yourself will make you happy, Erica. Only you can do that."

"Isn't it obvious I'm incapable of filling my own hole?"

"That's why you're here," Shania says. "I have no doubt you can survive this."

"I know I can," I say. "The question is whether or not I want to."

"Suicidal?" Dr. Swan asks when I reappear in her office for a Prozac follow-up.

"No," I say.

"Anxiety?"

"No."

"Exhaustion?"

"No."

"That's improvement, isn't it?" she asks.

I don't even have the chutzpah to raise my eyebrows.

"The medication may not have taken full effect yet. Can you stick with the Prozac for another three weeks?"

It's as if I have to choose between being sad and being skinny. How many pounds is happiness worth?

"Sure," I say. She hands me a refill order. I'm not planning to continue with my multicolored capsules; I'm going to wean myself off soon. But I will fill one last prescription, if only to save the pills for a future overdose.

"Hi there!" the chipper pharmacist at CVS says when I stop in at 9:00 P.M. that night. I slide the prescription slip toward her.

"Let me get you some—" She stops mid-sentence and looks up at my tear-stained cheeks. "Let me get you some of *that*."

As she putters behind the counter, I roam the incontinence aisles for the other half of my nightcap. My bedtime cocktail is a Prozac and Correctol.

"All set," the pharmacist calls. She hands me a paper bag. "I hope it works out for you."

"Me, too."

While Prozac quells the manic urges to be active, it also silences my muse.

I sit. And stare. And bitch. And curse the heavens.

This writing thing is harder than it looks.

Without Ana's starvation high, I have to *work* at being cleverly creative.

But still I write, building an essay word by word with the exhausting effort of a bricklayer, until I finish. In my next nonfiction class led by Madelon Sprengnether, I read my first antidepressant-enhanced essay.

"After the first two lines, I was willing to listen to whatever you had to say," Professor Sprengnether says.

My peers shower my writing with compliments in workshop.

"This is so raw," someone else says. "But relatable."

"I admire how you can weave humor into these serious topics."

"A little polish and this is complete!"

Though the writing doesn't *feel* better, the feedback is improving by leaps and bounds. At the end of the semester, I receive my final grades: A's in every single class. A perfect 4.0.

I collect a series of recommendation letters from my professors, edit my twenty-page piece on depression, and order transcripts from my former academic days. I seal it all in a bright white envelope and address it to the University of Minnesota's English Department. I watch the envelope drop with a thud into the post office slot. All those papers are as precious to me as my daughters' letters to Santa are to them.

chapter twenty-six

Ho-Hum Holidays

A few days before Christmas, I wind my SUV through the ritzy neighborhoods of Eagan in search of some display of holiday spirit. Julia and Lola are in the backseat, singing along to Jason Mraz on the stereo.

When the "love, love, love" lyrics fade, Julia says, "That song is about love. And I love you, Mommy."

"I love you, too," I say.

"I love you more," Lola says.

An argument ensues about who loves whom more.

"We all love each other," I say, struggling to keep my temper in check. "Stop fighting."

The girls gawk at the elaborate light displays on the neighborhood lawns. As we pass mansion after mansion, I glare with envious eyes at husbands perched on ladders, stringing icicle lights across gutters. Inside the foyers, wives drape garlands across banisters, their big diamond rings catching the glow of chandeliers. With a sting of nostalgia, I think of how only two years ago, I was decorating the Dream House with Cesar, how every room exploded red and gold, how I felt enclosed in a womblike coziness.

"When are we going home?" Julia asks when we pull up to my mother's house.

"We are home," I say. "We're living with Grandma for a while."

"I want to go to the new house."

"Someone else lives in the new house now."

"We have to find that house again and tell those people to leave."

Not even four years old, Julia has lived in eight different homes. As a child, I moved twice—within city limits and as part of a four-person family—and even those moves left an everlasting impression on me. I can't imagine what all this uprooting is doing to my daughters.

"I remember the last day at the new house," Julia continues with a sigh. "I was on the swings and Grandpa did an underdog."

An "underdog" is my father's trademark move on the swing set. He comes up behind Julia, pushes her swing as high as he can, and runs beneath her just before she comes swinging back down, her feet barely clearing his head.

I cringe and silently wish my children had amnesia. I don't want them to remember any of this.

"We're going to look for a new house soon," Julia continues. "Because Grandma's house . . ."

Her voice trails off, but my imagination ends the sentence for her: " . . . isn't home."

I'm glad I'm not the only one who's tired of the mother-daughter-grandma love triangle.

"I called Cesar," my mother says one afternoon, "to tell him that I'm going to the daycare Christmas party."

"Great," I say.

"Cesar said he didn't have any gifts planned," my mother says. "He said you were going to take care of it."

"I did take care of it," I say, reminding her of the Dora the Explorer and the Go, Diego, Go! action figures I bought on sale for $3 each. I already wrapped and labeled them so the rented party Santa could surprise the girls.

"Just those?!" my mother gasps.

"That's what the invitation said—one small present for each child."

"Well, I was worried that the other parents are bringing bigger presents," my mother says. "So I bought a mermaid doll for Julia and an elephant for Lola."

Because we're talking on the phone, my mother can't see the monstrous expression of anger on my face. She's not only one-upping me in the caretaking department—now she's winning the gift-giving contest, too.

"You don't have to do that, Mom."

"Better safe than sorry," she says. "By the way, don't feel like you have to go to the party or anything. I'll just bring the girls home when it's over."

Could I be any more unnecessary?

Christmas can't end fast enough: I am fed up with the holiday spirit and forced cheerfulness. At 9 A.M. on Christmas morning, I pull into Cesar's driveway, expecting the girls to burst from the door, eager to inform me of Santa's visit.

Julia and Lola toddle down the steps as though it were any other day.

"Aren't they excited?" I ask Cesar. He shrugs.

My daughters aren't old enough to be jaded!

As soon as we buckle in, the girls begin to argue.

"Today is baby Jesus' birthday!" Lola shrieks.

"Julia's birthday!" Julia says.

They go back and forth and back and forth until I intervene.

"Today is Jesus' birthday, and Julia's birthday is on Friday," I say. "There will be presents either way."

My mother snaps photos as the girls unenthusiastically unwrap their gifts. Each toy is *ooh*ed and *aah*ed at for a moment, then discarded. After a half-assed holiday meal of ham and au gratin potatoes, the girls settle into a mind-numbing Teletubbies video. I see sleep weighing down their eyelids.

"Nap time!" I say.

"Nooo . . ." they whine.

I need to sleep. Correction: I need to escape. But with nowhere else to go and a house full of witnesses, I can't rely on BB to put me in an altered state.

"Let's all sleep together in Mommy's bed," I say.

Smiles burst onto my daughters' faces and they scamper to their room to collect their belongings.

We crawl between the buttercup sheets and cover up. Julia clings to a Dora the Explorer comforter, Lola drowns beneath a Precious Moments quilt, and I cocoon myself in a fleece blanket the color of Pepto-Bismol. Lola refuses to use a pillow, Julia rolls hers up, and I drool onto mine as we await exhaustion to overtake us.

Julia's ragged fingernails drag across my forearm and Lola alternately clasps, then swats, my hand. Julia grinds her jaw back and forth, the teeth crunching and wincing. We blink silently at one another, at the wall, at the ceiling, and without knowing quite when, we sleep.

When we awake hours later, we all have a shiny scrim of sweat along our hairlines from the body heat. Julia wraps her drumstick arms, so thick and delicious I am tempted to bite them, around my neck. Her face hovers close to mine and her long lashes brush up and down against my cheek.

For a moment, my cave feels like a cozy wolf den.

"Don't speak," I want to say as I reach for my notepad and pen. "Wait for Mommy to write this all down."

chapter twenty-seven

New Year's Resolutions

"Are you hungry, Mommy?" Julia asks one night as I serve up her bedtime snack of Cocoa Krispies.

Mommy is always hungry.

"I already had a snack," I say, mentally cataloging my just-finished binge of three servings of strawberry shortcake, two graham crackers slathered with peanut butter, and a banana.

"But are you *still* hungry, Mommy?"

When it comes to eating, Julia has ESP. As her cereal clinks into the bowl and snap-crackle-and-pops when the milk hits it, I think about how long it's been since I've eaten a bowl of cereal. But no. This is the girls' snack time, not mine.

I sigh and smile as chocolate-soaked milk dribbles down Lola's chin. It would feel so good to sit down and have a bedtime snack with my daughters like a normal mother.

Don't you dare, Ana says. *Cereal is off-limits*.

Fuck you! I reply in my head. *I'm having Cocoa Krispies with my kids*.

"I would like some cereal," I say.

"Okay! Come sit next to me!" Julia says.

Warning! BB says. *One bite and you'll release the beast!*

I turn my back on the girls to serve myself a bowl of cereal. Somewhere between the cupboard and the counter, I slice up another serving of strawberry shortcake, grab a handful of dried cranberries, down two more graham crackers, a container of yogurt, and add a few spoonfuls of peanut butter to the tally.

In a sick guess-the-binge-food game, Julia shouts out each item, though she can't see what I'm eating.

"I smell yogurt!" Julia says.

How does she *do* that? The yogurt is plain, nonfat, and as far as I can tell, scentless.

"I smell grahams! I smell peanut butter!"

I can't smell most of my food even when it's right in front of my face!

At some point during the binge, my daughters disappear. I'm so busy stuffing, I never sit down with them.

Julia's voice echoes down the hall and shocks me back to consciousness.

"Mommy!" she says. "It's reading time!"

"I'll be right there!" I say.

The guilt hits like a tidal wave, and I have to purge. But how? The night before, in a vow to rid myself of BB, I threw my laxatives in the garbage.

"Mommy!"

"I'm coming!"

Back to Dumpster diving, back to ripping open stinky garbage bags and blindly searching for the snap-crackle-pop—of Correctol.

Thank you, Mommy, BB says. *Thanks for saving these for me.*

"What do you want to do differently next year?" Shania asks at our last session of 2006.

"I want to stop the laxatives," I say. "They make me feel like shit. No pun intended."

"Are you prepared to not poop for a few days?"

I giggle; sometimes Shania is too blunt even for me.

"That's the tough part—I get so bloated if I don't use them."

"You will poop again," she says.

"I can't believe we're having this conversation; it's absurd."

"You have no idea how many times I've had to say this, but: I promise you, you will poop again."

"I know."

"Do you have some laxatives you need to wet?"

Will shrink wonders never cease?

"You know about *wetting*?" I say.

I thought that food soaking—a binge prevention strategy—was Ana's invention.

"I know eating disorders inside and out," Shania says. "Don't take this the wrong way, but your eating disorder is not that unique. Have you ever looked around the waiting room? Women like you go through here all day long."

Well, then.

"Any plans for New Year's Eve?" she asks.

"New Year's hasn't been a holiday in my life for a long time."

"So nothing out of the ordinary?"

"Me, eating Julia's leftover birthday cake in the bathroom, alone, then asleep by eight."

Shania tightens her lips as though I'd told an inappropriate joke.

"I wish I were kidding," I say. "But I'm not."

I'd planned to giggle my way out of eye contact, but I can't. As soon as I look into Shania's speckled eyes, I start to cry.

"How does it feel to say that?" she asks.

"Pathetic."

The tears gain strength and snot runs down my face.

"It's not pathetic," Shania says. "It's lonely and sad, but not pathetic."

As predicted, on the last night of the year, I secretly hack off a quarter of a Barbie fairy sheet cake and escape to my bathroom. I turn the exhaust fan on so the clink of silverware against the plate won't alert my mother and Jay to my binge. Seated on the toilet, I shovel spoonful after spoonful of frosting into my mouth.

The only ball dropping on my New Year's Eve is a hunk of pink buttercream into my gut.

"Grandpa, I have a question for you," Julia says as she leans over the violet centerpiece of the banquet table. My father's retirement party at the Legion Hall is winding down; waiters clear dinner from beneath the heat lamps at the buffet.

I have eaten a bit of everything: an oily breast of rotisserie chicken, a spoonful of vegetable medley soaked in butter, salad with full-fat ranch dressing, half a white roll, and a lump of mashed potatoes. Julia has eaten a pat of butter and a few bread crumbs.

"Yes, Julia?" my father asks from the other side of the table.

"Where is the cake?"

My father laughs in the hearty Scandinavian way that makes his belly bounce.

"There isn't any," he says. "We ate cake at work."

Wrong answer.

A mix of anguish, pain, and misunderstanding coats Julia's face; she looks as though she's been spanked.

This is a really bad time for a tantrum. My father's coworkers are about to begin their speeches. A man who looks like he belongs on a Harley is adjusting the microphone in front of us, tapping and test, test, testing.

Mommy Me to the rescue. "I have trail mix in my car!"

Not only will trail mix satisfy Julia's sweet tooth, it will keep her busy during the coworkers' farewells to my father. Julia and I snatch up a few plastic cups from the bar and zip out to the parking lot, where I dole out the edible activity. Back inside, Julia presents a cup proudly to Lola, who bounces up and down on her knees like a toddler Tigger.

My mother sits down across from us and watches as both girls meticulously pick out the M&M's, the milk chocolate chips, and the white chocolate chips.

"I don't even know why I buy it," I say. "All they really want is the chocolate."

"I do the same thing," my mother says. "But all I eat are the nuts."

"No," I say, gearing up as though this were a political debate. "The nuts are last. Even the raisins come before the nuts."

"No," she insists. "The raisins are the worst part. I hate the raisins."

A silent epiphany overtakes me. For the last month, I've been picking out and eating the raisins from my mother's box of Grape Nuts trail mix cereal in secret. No wonder she hasn't mentioned the missing raisins! She is probably grateful that someone is schlepping them behind her back.

"That's so messed up," I say. "Does everyone eat it that way?"

"That's the fun of it," my mother says. "The picking out the good parts."

Fun indeed. What is this—a fucked-up family pastime?

Later that night, I am splayed on my stomach in bed, the bag of Happy Trails mix spread across the comforter. I smooth my hand over the rubble, searching for M&M's and chocolate chips. I must eat the chocolate first. It is the rule of the universe.

And so it begins. Pick, pick, pick. When the milk chocolate is gone, I move on to the next challenge: white chocolate. I don't even like white chocolate, but it's silly to discriminate. Besides, the point isn't pleasure; it is to consume, to kill time, to drug myself into a sugar stupor so I can fall asleep. The point is to escape the reality that I am twenty-five and living with my mother.

I devour the raisins.

Then the slivered almonds.

Last, and certainly least, the sunflowers seeds.

When all is said and done and chewed and swallowed, I berate myself for my swinelike nature. A sense of dread fills whatever space is left in my stomach and guilt sets in. I cry. I write up resolutions to take effect tomorrow. I head to the toilet and give hurling the Girl Scout try. Giving yourself the finger is supposed to be the most effective purging method, but in my experience, it doesn't get the job done.

Purge plan B: toothbrush-down-the-throat technique.

Nothing. Not even a dry heave.

This calls for desperate measures—sucking on zinc tablets until I gag—though all I manage to upchuck is a glob of barely digested brown goo. As I watch the slimy lump drop like a bobber into the toilet bowl, I ponder its calorie content. Five calories—max.

Laxatives are the last resort; shitting my guts out proves the only route to redemption.

JOURNAL ENTRY

I hate that my body and I are waging war, but I hate even more that it is winning.

Bingeing has become as automatic as breathing. My days are driven by getting high, coming down, and planning for the next fix. I anticipate the binges like normal women do dates. I ruminate about the what, the when, and the where of my next culinary encounter. Will I go all the way? Just fondle the food or allow it access to my mouth? Spit or swallow? Will this one-time tasting turn into a long-term relationship? Will I abandon my favorite food down the line for something more scrumptious?

But the binges have passed the point of enjoyment; even the

cortisol-charged excitement has waned. Food has lost its magical powers to make everything all right, and I am hit with a harsh reality check: No amount of sugar or starch will make the pain subside. It is both a freeing and a frightening realization. I don't want to eat; I just want to be hungry again. I have no choice but to change.

chapter twenty-eight

Taos Transformation

It's a new year and I'm ready for a fresh start. The perfect opportunity presents itself when I apply for and receive a scholarship to attend a memoir-writing workshop with my authorial idol, Natalie Goldberg. The workshop is in New Mexico—a state I've never visited—and I haven't had a solo vacation since I went to Spain as a teenager. I should be excited; instead, I'm scared. It's not my writing ability that makes me feel wary; it's the challenge of maintaining my weight in an unfamiliar environment. Meals are included in the workshop and I'm terrified. How will I rein in BB at a thrice-daily buffet? My clothes barely fit now; what will happen after a week of overeating?

Ana gets her own suitcase. Of all my baggage, hers is the heaviest and bulkiest, stuffed with tools to fight my body expansion. For one-week away, Ana packs three pairs of running shoes, six pairs of spandex shorts, sports bras in four colors, and enough BodyGlide to lubricate an entire Tour de France cycling team.

Then there's the food bag. Ana insists I bring a box of calorie-free sweetener for coffee, low-carb cocoa packets, mini Hershey's bars in case of chocolate cravings, roasted almonds to stave off over-eating, and pre-run oranges.

In preparation for the trip, I spend more time packing an emergency appetite stash than I do selecting color-coordinated sweater sets or budgeting my travel expenses.

My plane lands in Albuquerque, where the earth is as dry as a day-old scone and the color of clay. The sun is so deliciously strong, I wish I could stretch out on a rock like a lizard.

From my rental car, I call the inn where the workshop will be held for directions.

"A major snowstorm just came through," the receptionist says. "Be careful driving through the mountains."

"I'm Minnesotan," I say. "I think I can handle it."

I head north on the highway. The cars that pass me are caked with mud; the cars going south are packed with snow. Though the roads turn treacherous the closer I get to my destination, the stubborn Scandinavian in me puts the pedal to the metal—which, in a Chevy Cobalt, isn't saying much—and perseveres.

I pull into Taos—a town known for its eclectic art galleries, superb skiing, and historic Pueblo reservation—at dusk. The mountains loom before me, mere shadows in the darkening sky, layered on top of one another like a double-exposed photograph.

I want to feel at home in my new surroundings and to circumvent any uneasiness before it avalanches into an anxiety attack, so my first stop is the grocery store.

There aren't many blond, aspirin-skinned women like me in sight; the locals glare at me like an alien. The men hide their stares under brims of cowboy hats and the women peer at me beneath bright blue eyelids as I load up a basket with bananas, mixed nuts, and granola.

With a bag full of groceries safely tucked into the trunk, I drive through the main street of the city. Though this trip is an adventure, I don't feel adventurous yet. Dinner on my first New Mexican night is a Caesar salad—hold the Caesar—in an abandoned Wendy's parking lot. I've come all this way and Ana's still up to her old tricks.

I awake the next morning resolved to squeeze every last juicy drop from this experience. My classmates won't arrive until this evening, so I have a full day to sightsee.

I stop for lunch at Bent Street Café, a quaint corner eatery with a glass dome patio.

"All by yourself, honey?" a waitress asks as she hands me a menu.

"I am," I say. The odd part? I'm not the least bit lonely. In fact, I'm exhilarated by the potential for reinvention this week. No one here knows me; more important, they don't know about my fucked-up friends Ana and BB. This is my chance to try out life sans eating disorder.

I scan the menu. This is my first test as an ordinary eater. What would the average woman order?

House salad, fat-free French dressing on the side, Ana instructs.

But I'm on vacation! I snap back, surprising myself with this feisty new attitude. *And what I really want is a hamburger.*

"I'll have the Taos burger," I say. Ten minutes later, my beefcake tower—piled high with guacamole and Monterey jack cheese—arrives. After the first bite, I'm deaf to Ana's voice. I devour the entire burger, bun and all, plus a plate of fries.

"Somebody was hungry!" the waitress exclaims when she clears the table. "Glad you liked it."

I not only liked my lunch—I enjoyed it without guilt! Though it was only one meal of moderation among months of dysfunctional eating, I feel triumphant. For the moment, I am free from Ana's grasp!

As I pay the bill for my burger, I notice a stack of freshly baked cookies next to the register.

Chocolate chip; our favorite! BB rejoices. *Let's binge!*

No, thanks, I reply. *I'm full.*

That's never stopped us before . . . BB says.

BB has a point, but I'm aware of a new sensation in my belly: satiety. I ate what I wanted, I quelled my hunger, and now I'm ready to move on. I want to explore, not eat until I'm sick.

I still have an entire afternoon to wander, so I walk around the plaza and into a bookstore. I scan the spines of the memoirs and consider the authors, many of whom are B-list celebrities, corrupt politicians, and formulaic writers who pop out books faster than third world countries do babies. Rather than inspiration, my biblio-browsing incites envy. Why haven't *I* tried to publish my writing yet?

Because you've been busy doing other things, Ana says.

Yeah—like eating and exercising my life away.

I suddenly realize how much energy I've invested in keeping Ana and BB alive—while my mind, body, and spirit have been on hold. I decide, then and there, that I'm going to ignore Ana and BB, if only while I'm in New Mexico. I don't know how I'll cope all week without my bosom buddies, but I'll fake it till I make it. I'm on a mission to reclaim the passionate, feisty, fun-loving me I lost so long ago. Nothing—especially a petty obsession with weight, dieting, and exercise—is going to stop me.

"It's not easy to get to Taos," Natalie says during the welcome session of the workshop. She's not talking transportation. Taos, as a fellow workshop attendee explains it, is known for cracking people open; this town is the geographical equivalent of the big bad wolf that huffs and puffs and blows the fence of phoniness down.

I'm not immune.

Now that I've declared myself on sabbatical from the eating disorder, forces align to support my transformation. Because of a shared bathroom, there's not enough privacy for laxative abuse. The companionship of my roommate—ironically, a dietician from New York—distracts me from binges during the delicate hours of 7:00 to 10:00 P.M. Even my frantic urge to exercise dwindles, and I call it quits after only an hour of cardio and a few ab exercises.

It also helps that the inn's cuisine is the best I've ever eaten. Each meal is a homemade, healthy, organic feast. The kitchen staff doesn't believe in the Eat to Live mantra; food is not just fuel. Food is a spiritual experience, the communion of the writing community.

I surprise myself most in the mornings; while back at home, my usual breakfast is light, bland, and boring, I now spoon up heaps of spicy scrambled eggs, sausage links, sweet potato pancakes, and fruit soaked in maple compote. Lunch and dinner include fresh greens, five-bean soup, and lamb kebobs. And the desserts—the desserts are in another category of culinary ecstasy altogether.

"I've never had a cream puff," I say one evening as I lift one of the pastries to my mouth.

"It's too bad this is your first," another writer says between gooey bites. "Because this is no ordinary cream puff. You'll never eat another one this good."

I hold the pretty pastry before me, terrified. What if this single taste turns into a lifetime addiction? My worries dissolve along with the pillowy dough on my tongue. Whipped cream spreads across my lips like a smile. It is like eating a sugary cloud.

"Wow," I moan, my eyes widening as much as my mouth as I take another bite.

Not one of the writers around me can think of a better word to describe these cream puffs.

I devour one—and then I'm done.

What is the secret to my newfound moderation? I rack my brain, insistent on identifying the culprit so I can replicate the conditions back home.

Maybe the key to control is pleasure. I'm content with less food because every bite is so flavorful. Maybe I don't molest my New Mexican meals because I can taste the chef's love infused in every entrée. It's as though these meals demanded respect. As sinful as the desserts taste, bingeing on them would be sacrilege.

I observe others eating and imitate their behaviors; I notice that obeying my hunger cues and feeding myself—without overdoing it—actually feels *good*.

The most amazing side effect of renouncing the battle of the bulge is . . . I lose weight. In a matter of days, my waistbands go slack, my tops flutter over a flattened tummy, and my thighs are trimmer. My whole being—heart and soul—feels lighter.

As for the writing part of the workshop, Natalie Goldberg turns out to be as much of a foodie as me. One day, she assigns us a writing exercise, though she waffles on what the topic should be. Natalie paces the classroom, then suddenly raises a finger in the air and says, "Tell me everything you know about ice cream. Twenty minutes. Go!"

With food as my focus, I write like a maniac, the words spilling effortlessly from deep inside me and onto the paper unedited. This isn't the fluff I thought I might write; this is raw and real. It's my authentic author emerging from within.

On our second day, Natalie asks for volunteers to read aloud. I raise my hand. Natalie nods in my direction and I begin my piece, which veers away from ice cream to working at TT. When I arrive at the section about one of my on-the-job binges, I pause for a moment, then turn the page, continuing with my "safe" ice cream material. I've been successful at maintaining my shit-together façade so far; it's too early to introduce my demons to my classmates.

When I finish reading, I look up, as eager as a puppy for praise. Natalie's gaze is fixed on the floor and her brow is furrowed.

Oh, no, I think. *I'm a failure. I'm the worst writer in the world. I didn't deserve that scholarship.*

Natalie lifts her head and looks at me with her intense brown eyes.

"You skipped something," she says.

"Only out of respect for time," I lie.

"Nuh-uh," she says. "No editing allowed. Read it again— *everything*."

Thirty-two faces turn toward me. My journal shakes in my trembling hands. Am I ready to expose BB? Before I can debate, my mouth opens and the words tumble out. Though my cheeks are blazing and my voice wobbles, I read my confession of how I used to chew and spit over the sink at TT. When I finish, I gently fold the soft leather covers of my journal together. The silence in the room is suffocating.

"Haunting," Natalie says with a bowed head. "Very powerful. Thank you."

Now that BB is out of the bag, I feel liberated. Finally, I have a more important project than my body! I possess talents more powerful than ripped biceps. The other women aren't sizing up my figure—they're sizing up the writing we read in class. My motivation to produce an "ah-ha"-worthy piece is greater than the urge to squeeze into skinny jeans.

My classmates are so genuinely supportive, it's easy to open up and socialize again.

"You can't hide in a small town," one student—a resident of Taos—tells me. In my case, that's a good thing. It means no self-imposed imprisonment in my room. I'm expected not only to show up but to show *off* the glittering personality that Ana and BB have buried. For the rest of the week, I speak without instant self-recrimination and listen without planning my next line. I smile, I flirt, I laugh so hard I guffaw.

When the workshop ends, I tearfully say good-bye to and exchange contact information with my new friends. As my plane departs from the Albuquerque airport, I say a prayer: "May BB and Ana be gone forever. May the new me return to Minneapolis alone."

JOURNAL ENTRY

I don't remember the last time I ate so well, laughed so easily,
breathed so deeply. I'm afraid to go home and face the depression
lurking in Mom's basement. I wish I could fake my own death,
disappear into the mountains with a backpack and my laptop,
and live happily ever after as a hermitess.

As soon as I step into the dark dungeon of my bedroom back in
Minnesota, I sense the ominous presence of the eating disorder waiting to pounce on me. There's the fridge that I once filled with tubs
of peanut butter, there's the unmade bed where I spent so many
nights thrashing in agony after a binge, there's the torturous treadmill that demanded I run ten miles at a time.

My environment hasn't changed—but I have. There is something
palpably different about me; I feel like I'm enclosed in a protective
bubble. The ghosts of Ana and BB still lurk in the air, whisper in
my ear and try to seduce me back into their arms, but I refuse to
listen.

After I unpack, I join my mother and daughters upstairs to tell
them all about my trip. Instead of a hearty "Welcome home!" my
mother greets me with a litany of complaints.

"Wait till I tell you about the misadventures here," she says.
"We've had an ear infection, pink eye, and a sprained ankle."

Kill my vacation buzz, why don't you? I think.

I fan out my vacation photos on the kitchen countertop for all to
see. To this audience, my pictures aren't worth a thousand words; in
fact, they don't appear to be worth the paper they're printed on.

My mother glances at a few of the photographs and nods indifferently. Lola picks up the prints and shoots them like boomerangs
through the air.

"I guess you had to be there." I sigh.

No image, no matter how well captured with an expensive lens, could do justice to the Southwestern experience that helped me shed my chrysalis and encouraged my new self to emerge.

Julia studies a photograph of me with two of the other workshop attendees.

"You went away to another family," she says, looking at me with wide, sad eyes. "I missed you so much. Don't ever leave, okay, Mommy?"

A flood of happiness hits me. All this time, I thought I was expendable. But the look in Julia's eyes is so sincere, I am suddenly aware of how important my presence in her and Lola's life is.

"Mommy always comes back," I reassure her. "Always."

I don't expect my family to understand this massive upheaval taking place inside me, but I know I need support to stay positive, so I schedule an immediate session with Shania.

"I think you fell in love with Taos," Shania says after I recount my trip to her.

"I want to re-create what I felt there," I say. "But since I've been home, I feel so closed off. I need to open this up."

I sweep my hands across my collarbones.

"You realize what that is, don't you?" she asks.

"My pecs?"

"Your heart. You need to open your heart, Erica."

"How do I do that?"

"Yoga."

I've always discounted yoga because as a form of exercise, it sucks. I tried it once at the Y and didn't even break a sweat. The teacher even talked funny.

"Mov*ing* the feet into Mountain Pose . . . hing*ing* from the hip joint . . . Lift*ing* the rib cage . . ." She reminded me more of a flight attendant than an enlightened yogini.

Every pose we did was about being something else—a Swan, a Monkey, an Airplane (flight attendant theory confirmed!). Halfway through the class, I rolled up my mat and slipped out the door as the rest of the students folded into Downward-Facing Dog for the hundredth time.

Now, however, my goal is not to get ripped. Instead, I'm seeking quiet contemplation. Though I'm doubtful that headstands can heal, that striking Warrior Pose can make me stronger, or that twisting myself into a pretzel can release years of psychological buildup, I'm more flexible—literally and metaphorically—since my trip to Taos. I'm ready to try something new if it means maintaining the peaceful state of mind I found during my week amongst the mountains.

The Y offers only Fitness Yoga, and while there is plenty of heavy breathing in that class, it isn't the meditative kind, so I do a Google search for local yoga therapists. The first practitioner I find is Aaron, a mellow-looking man who combines meditation, yoga, and spirituality. We exchange e-mails and arrange for a private session.

Aaron's studio is situated on a quiet corner in my native south Minneapolis neighborhood, where remnants of the only snowstorm this winter still coat the curb in foot-high piles outside. As I walk to the front door, the doubt begins to nag again. I stop dead in my tracks. I don't really want to do this, do I? What could a stranger tell me about myself that I don't already know? I've been in therapy on-and-off for over a decade; I've analyzed every event in my life tenfold.

A shadow moves behind the massive windows of the center. Aaron must have seen me. There's no turning back now.

When I open the door, I almost knock Aaron over.

"Erica, I assume," he says, pushing a rug sweeper in brief, exacted swipes. "I was just tidying up for you."

Aaron fits my stereotype of a modern yogi: He is short, slim, and sturdy. His hair is excusably unkempt, as though he'd just dismounted from a handstand. A single line of facial hair divides his chin in half and gold hoops dangle in each ear lobe.

I stomp the snow off my shoes and slide them into the metal

rack. The center is really one large, open room, awash in an odd smell, like the odor of damp denim. The carpet is thick and soft, and the off-white walls are mostly bare.

I change into stretch pants and a sweatshirt in the bathroom, unable to shake the butterfly-like flutters in my stomach. It's not as if you're going to have *sex*, I say silently to myself. But when I step into the large open room, I feel naked.

Aaron sets up a folding chair for me and he settles atop a mountain of cushions on the floor. My height is suddenly unnerving, making me ultra-aware of my body. I feel big and awkward opposite this little lotus flower of a man.

"What brought you to yoga?" Aaron asks.

The pressure to be "on" infects me and I smile too big, nod too enthusiastically, and start to explain with the labels—anorexia and depression, with a side of anxiety. And then something inside me stops. I take a breath, and before I can edit myself, I spew forth a verbal diarrhea of truths.

"This might sound odd," I say. "But I have an inexplicable urge to get very quiet."

Aaron nods like a therapist who's seen it all before and can't be surprised by any client, no matter how crazy.

"Just to be clear," he says. "This isn't about fitness. My goal isn't for you to be able to reach your toes. I'm about going deeper."

"That's what I want."

"So why not take a class?" he asks.

"I don't like group activities," I say, imagining my forehead branded with the warning: "Does not play well with others."

What I don't say is: I'm embarrassed by my body; I don't trust it to follow instructions anymore. What if my tight calves prevent me from getting into a pose? What if my knees crack? What if, God forbid, I *fart*?

"I've also heard that some people can become very emotional doing yoga," I say.

"I've had students cry before, sure," he says. "I even had a woman faint once." I must look surprised, because he adds, "I'm not trying to scare you. She probably just had low blood pressure—but you should know what could happen."

When Aaron asks me about the eating disorder, I rattle off a well-practiced account of anorexia.

"I was anorexic, too," Aaron says.

He's got to be kidding.

"I got down to eighty-nine pounds."

Now I believe him—only true body-image obsessives would share such a sickly weight with a stranger.

"Wow," I say, unsure whether I'm praising or pitying him. "You were *really* skinny."

Skeletons out of the closet, we start with the basics— breathing.

Aaron demonstrates a full body breath in which his stomach puffs out, his ribs expand, his chest lifts.

"Can you see that?" he asks.

I stare at him, aghast, and nod. To experience deep breathing is one thing; to see someone do it, up close, is amazing. I want my body to be that powerful.

"Now you try," he says.

I do, and the rush of air, the feeling of being so full of breath I might burst is like an elixir, extinguishing the unrelenting ache inside. No wonder I've felt so stressed—my body has been in a state of oxygen deprivation.

We continue with a series of exercises that vaguely resemble a childhood game: We rub our palms together, then hold them slightly apart to feel the tingly current of energy. We kneel and curl our chests over our thighs, foreheads to the mats. Blood rushes to my brain, light shimmers behind my eyelids, and my ears fill with pressure. It's like a pleasant panic attack.

Aaron and I take on Tree Pose facing one another; my skin flushes when our eyes meet.

"I have to look at your body," he says. "For positioning purposes. Are you okay with that?"

"Yes," I say. No, I think. My tank top is riding up, my stretch marks are shining in the sunlight, and I think I feel the strings of my yellow thong rising out of my pants like the golden arches of McDonald's.

Next, Aaron gets down on his back and demonstrates Bridge Pose. I try to imitate by levitating my pelvis and tightening my glutes, but I don't feel a thing.

"I'm going to adjust you," Aaron says. He guides my hands to intertwine beneath my butt, taps my lower back up, and presses my knees together. My body snaps into place.

"Do you feel that?" he asks.

Heat rushes through me like a flame. My back arches and my entire torso expands like a balloon.

My chest—no, my heart—opens.

"Oh, yeah . . ." I say.

"Cleansing, isn't it?" he says as I take three delicious breaths. "Like brushing your teeth."

When we finish, Aaron and I step outside into the lull of late afternoon, and still I can't kick the feeling that we've done something subversive, that we have engaged in a sacred, secretive ritual that only an awakened minority knows about. We stand for a moment outside the door with subdued smiles, drinking in the unseasonable warmth.

Is small talk a sin in Hinduism? *Are* there sins in Hinduism?

"See you Thursday!" I say, much too chipper, and scurry off to my car.

There must be some lag time between doing yoga and experiencing the increase in positive energy. Just days after my first session with Aaron, I receive the dreaded rejection letter from the U of M stating that of two hundred applicants, only twelve were accepted into the MFA program. I am not one of them.

To numb the disappointment, I binge on half a box of Golden Grahams, a loaf of spinach feta bread, a quarter tub of Jif, and a bag of Turtle Chex Mix while my mom and the girls are swimming at the Y.

There is, however, a slight change in my self-destructive routine. Though I've broken Ana's dietary rules once again, I don't feel the usual shit-faced shame. I don't berate myself for the binge. I simply observe my emotions like clouds passing overhead in the sky. I am, as Aaron calls it, The Witness and not the behavior. Is this detached reaction an improvement? Or, because I don't punish myself with the usual Correctol chaser, will it be harder to resist a binge next time?

When my stomachache subsides, I practice yoga. I breathe. I repeat—and almost believe—the healing affirmations that Aaron assigned me.

The next day, while I'm reading an article in *Yoga Journal* about specific poses for depression, Julia plops down next to me on the couch.

"What's that girl doing?" she asks, pointing at a woman seated in lotus position with her eyes closed.

"She's meditating," I say. "It's when you sit very still and be very quiet."

Julia folds her legs beneath her and tries very hard to look like a little Buddha.

"That's it!" I say.

"Shh," Julia whispers, holding a finger to her lips. "I'm medi-dit-ting."

Ah-ha, I think to myself. *Imitation works both ways!*

If I model healthier behaviors, perhaps my daughters will, too.

* * *

At the start of our second yoga therapy session a week later, Aaron asks how my week went.

"Good!" I say, still too shy to reveal how bad the bingeing got.

"Anything in particular you want to focus on today?" he asks.

Without elaborating on the details, I tell him I've been overindulging on junk food.

"Yoga can help with that," he says.

For the next sixty minutes, my lesson is on how to eat. Aaron reaches for a container of raisins nestled next to his CD collection of Indian chants. He sits on a Zafu, his legs folded into lotus position, across from me.

"Can you handle three raisins?" he asks.

"Sure," I say.

Oh, no, says Ana.

Outside, I am cucumber cool. Inside, total pandemonium. The raisins, barely heavier than pebbles, should be No Big Deal. Instead, they are as loaded as a grenade set to explode in my hand. My thoughts churn, multiply, and fester.

Raisins are high on the Glycemic Index, they are on my forbidden food list, they are too easily stuffed by the fistful in the mouth during a binge. I think of the Raisin Bran that my father ate for breakfast when I was a child, I think of the yogurt-covered raisins that my mother bought me at the co-op after doctor's appointments, I think of Raisinets at the movies with Dave, I think of the mini boxes of Sun-Maid raisins that Julia ate every day for an entire summer. I think of the time I frantically pulled off the freeway to throw away an oatmeal raisin cookie I couldn't trust myself to resist. I think of the cinnamon raisin bread that I binge on when my mother runs out of M&M's.

Aaron drops the raisins in my hand.

"Just look at them," he says.

As I study each individual raisin, the practice of purposeful attention alarms me. The three wrinkled nuggets in my palm are remarkably unique: One is sphere-shaped, another is flat as a finger-print, and the third resembles a cone.

"Feel the raisins in your hand," Aaron says.

One is oily, another is flaky, and the third is firm. My eyes shift from the fruit to my gangly hangnails. I put a manicure on my mental to-do list.

"Stay with the raisins," Aaron says.

How does he *do* that? Aaron has such an astute sense of when I have drifted from the present moment.

"Keep your eyes on your own raisins!" I want to say.

"Hold the raisins up to your nose and inhale," Aaron instructs.

A pungent promise of sweetness shoots up my nostrils.

"Breathe in the perfume of the fruit."

I wiggle my bottom in frustration; I can't be present with the raisins. The more I think, the less I smell.

"Focus on your image of joy," Aaron says.

We've done this part before, recalling a moment when I felt completely at peace and bubbling over with happiness.

I can't explain why, in all my memories of motherhood, this random moment surfaces: Lola, in her car seat, a lilac Winnie-the-Pooh hat hanging low on her forehead, obscuring her bright blue eyes. She has a devilish expression on her face.

That is my image. One split-second of my daughter's life that sends shivers of love down my spine.

"Now look at the raisins and transpose your image of joy onto them."

I picture Lola's face like the sun baby that orbits over Teletubby Land, giggling and gurgling, yellow rays of light shooting from her white blond hair.

"Now put a raisin in your mouth."

I am going to eat Lola's head. Sorry, daughter, down the hatch you go. I lift my palm to my lips and allow the raisin entry. The taste explodes on my tongue.

"Close your eyes," Aaron says. "Bring the attention inward."

As soon as the eyelids slam down, Ana erupts.

It's not time to eat. How many calories are in a raisin? So much sugar. Bad carb. Bad carb!

I must annihilate the raisin.

I chomp down, break the skin of the raisin, and shred the tough outer layer between my teeth. I want the rush of saliva beneath my tongue to dissolve every granule of sucrose.

I swallow. The raisin rolls like a rock in my gut.

"Swirl the raisin around in your mouth," Aaron says. "Feel the texture."

Whoops. I've already jumped ahead. Now not only am I in a panic about unplanned calories, I have embarrassed myself in front of my guru.

"Now, swallow."

I swallow a slug of spit audibly so he does not know I have cheated.

"Let's repeat with the next raisin."

I do. BB adds her two cents to my thoughts.

Raisins taste best in trail mix. Maybe we could stop by the grocery store on the way home, buy a bag, and chew-and-spit it in the bathroom.

"Last raisin."

My stomach growls.

"Notice the flavor of the raisin."

Aaron's voice is muted, as though talking to me underwater.

"Last swallow," he says.

Hallelujah. It's over. When I open my eyes, I find Aaron smiling in that enlightened yogic way.

"How were your raisins?" he asks.

"Good," I say.

"Did you notice anything?" he asks.

"Yes."

Aaron waits with raised eyebrows.

"Would you like to share?"

I hate this sharing stuff. I want to shut down, not share.

"I wanted to get that raisin out of my mouth," I say. "As soon as it went in, my instinct was to get rid of it by any means necessary."

Aaron nods. This must be that nonjudgment thing we've been talking about.

"Anything else?" he asks.

"I couldn't taste it," I say. "Once the thoughts started, my taste buds turned off."

"Understand that those are just thoughts. When you have them, it's important to simply notice them, to breathe, and to let them pass."

Easier said than done.

"Food is neutral," he continues. "It's our thoughts that give it meaning. We can work with that frantic feeling. If we can slow the process down, we can replace the frenzy with joy."

Does Aaron ever get flustered? Does he ever lose control? Or does he just sit like a frog on a lily pad with that serene smile on his face all day?

"More raisins?" he asks, lifting up the Dole container.

"I've had enough, thank you."

The next morning I eat breakfast slowly, mindfully. I notice the grainy edge of a sliced strawberry sweeping across my tongue, the tart squirt of a grape against the inner edge of my cheek, the tear of blueberry skin between my teeth, the smooth spoonfuls of yogurt swirled with a thin dusting of cinnamon. I set my spoon down between bites. I do belly breaths. When I am satisfied, I stop eating. The Buddha would be proud.

"I've been meaning to tell you," my stepfather says one night after dinner. "The past two weeks you've looked . . ." As he searches for the right word, he gives me a hard shoulder squeeze. "Better."

"That's weird," I say. "Because I feel worse."

Later I reflect on my response and revise it in my mind. No, I don't feel worse; I feel *more*. More sadness, yes, but a sharper sense of joy, too. I experience every sensation with a novel, delicious depth. I feel lighter and tighter. Free.

chapter twenty-nine

Welcome Back, Womanhood

Apparently all that yoga jangles something loose in my womb. One night, as I settle into my favorite recliner to read, a slimy squirt seeps out between my legs.

Aunt Flo has come home.

I scuttle off to the bathroom, drop trou, and there, embedded in the crotch of my brand-new ivory panties, is the signature scarlet stain. Before I know it, I'm bleeding through pair after pair of panties, two layers of bed sheets, and my favorite Gap pajama pants.

Like a squirrel searching for her Tampax brand acorn, I slide open and slam shut the drawers of the bathroom vanity. Mascara, lip gloss, hairbrush. No tampon.

Even if I find one, it's probably no good. It's been a year and a half since I've had to use them. Everything expires these days—even bottled water. Do tampons shrivel in old age? Do plastic applicators disintegrate on their own? Can Kegel muscles atrophy after months of neglect?

Off to CVS to stock up on supplies. Since the last time I shopped for feminine products, most of them have changed. Tampons are now scented, color-coordinated, and categorized by activity. What the hell is Tampax Pearl? Do they come with bejeweled appliqués? Maxi pads have evolved, too: there are innumerable absorbencies, exclamation point shapes to accommodate thongs, even pads with cleansing towelettes attached.

Back at home, I unwrap a pad but can't decipher which side goes in front and which goes in back. After securing the dry weave wonder into my panties, I can't figure out how the wings work. It's like learning to be a woman all over again. If periods are like bike-riding, I'm flattened facedown on the sidewalk.

Little by little, it all comes back to me: The reason why women shower behind the privacy curtains at the gym, the tiny metal boxes in bathroom stalls for discreet disposal, why women freak when the toilet paper runs out.

Forget sexy panties. No more running commando. Life, as I knew it, has changed.

While Aunt Flo's return was inevitable, I'm unprepared for the emotional mayhem that accompanies the bloody deluge. My missing period was "proof" that Ana was still active inside my body. Now that I'm menstruating again, I can't hide behind the anorexic label. The jig is up. The eating disorder has been exorcised from inside me.

"Amenorrhea made me feel special," I lament to Shania at our next session. I wipe my weepy face with a tissue, unsure if my tears are due to a hormonal imbalance or the end of Ana's residence in my womb.

"Menstruation is the female body's barometer," Shania says from her armchair across from me. "Amenorrhea meant you were unhealthy."

"It meant I was a serious athlete. Now I'm just fat."

"Erica, I have known you for a year now, and you have never been fat. Ever."

I run a finger around the waistband of my size 4 jeans. "Okay, maybe I'm not fat, but I'm not thin, either. I'm normal. And I've failed at anorexia."

Part of me worries that without Ana, I'm nobody. Another part of me, however, is finally free. I'm no longer entangled by the eating disorder and its energy-draining behaviors. The return of my period is a confirmation that my body is coming back to life.

I hate going to the gyno, but I'm officially fertile again, so I schedule a long-delayed Pap smear with Dr. Mauer. On the day of the appointment, I hem and haw up until an hour before about whether I will show up for the stirrups. The tiebreaker comes in the form of writer's block; unable to compose even one miserable paragraph, I decide that an annual exam is a preferable form of self-torture.

I do have one ulterior motive: I want my Wellbutrin back. Because Dr. Swan knows all about my relationship with Ana, she won't prescribe it.

But I'm sure my OB/GYN will.

The top of my intake form reads: *Concerns you would like to discuss today*.

I should write *18 months of amenorrhea*.

I should write *STD testing*.

I should write *Breast exam*.

Instead I write "Wellbutrin refill."

I answer honestly on the health history section until I reach the *Bulimia/Anorexia* box. Do I own up to Ana? If I do, and the doctor actually reads it, she might deny me the antidepressant. If I fib and the doc checks my file online, she'll find the Mendota Hospital Assessment.

I reluctantly check the box *yes*.

"Wellbutrin, sure," Dr. Mauer says as I fidget on the table after my exam. "No problem."

She pulls up a screen on her computer. "Two times a day?"

I don't remember my former dosage—it's been over a year since I last popped one of the pills.

"Sounds good," I say. The more, the better. Bring on the happy drugs!

Dr. Mauer cocks her head.

"I mean: yes."

"Tell me about the depression," she says.

I've memorized the checklist by now. Though I don't have all of the symptoms, I report exhaustion, apathy, trouble concentrating, low mood, and overeating. Dr. Mauer nods excessively with an exaggerated frown on her face.

"And the eating disorder?" she asks.

Spin time.

"Short-lived."

"Anorexia or bulimia?"

Trick question. If I report excessive exercise or laxative abuse, she will identify me as at-risk for a seizure.

"Anorexia," I say.

"How thin did you get?"

Ana is so proud that she blurts out the stats before I can stop her.

"One hundred and four," I say.

Dr. Mauer swivels toward the wall and traces her finger across a weight and height chart, calculating my former BMI. Her finger travels to the far edge of the margin.

"That's scary skinny," she says, turning with a spooked-owl expression. She studies my face as though imagining how bony I must have been back then. "How did *that* happen?"

"I took the baby weight loss thing too far."

"Did you lose your period?"

"Yes."

"And how have they been since?"

"Regular," I half-lie. The one period I had *was* regular and I have no reason to believe the subsequent ones will be any different.

Dr. Mauer awaits more information.

"Twenty-nine-day cycles," I say, recalling the facts from my married days.

"How do you feel about your weight now?"

Ana jumps in again. "It's too high."

"What would you like it to be?"

My default answer is ten pounds—always has been, perhaps always will be—but Ana wants to be unique today, so I say, "Fifteen pounds less."

Dr. Mauer swivels back toward the wall and her finger traces the chart. "That would be all right," she says, nodding.

My eyebrows shoot up: A doctor endorsing weight loss in a former anorexic?

"How many calories did you eat back then?"

"Eighteen hundred."

"And you lost weight?"

Is Dr. Mauer evaluating me or fishing for diet tips?

"You must have done a lot of exercise," she says.

I shrug. Ana made me fudge the numbers on my intake form, reporting sixty instead of ninety minutes daily.

"What kind of exercise do you do?" Dr. Mauer asks.

"Running!" I say too enthusiastically. "I mean . . . I do a little of everything. Running, biking, elliptical, whatever."

The less rigid I appear, the less disordered I'll seem.

"Good for you!" she says. "It's a struggle to get most of my patients to exercise."

I cross my ankles and swing my legs back and forth beneath me.

Prescription, please.

"So what pharmacy should I send this to?" she asks with her fingers poised above the computer keyboard.

"Walgreens."

Clickety-click.

"You're all set!" Dr. Mauer stands and shakes my hand. "I can tell you're recovered by your openness and honesty."

I smile and thank her.

"But if you ever have trouble with the"—she leans in and whispers—"*eating thing* again, give us a call."

By "us" she means the healthcare conglomerate she works for that is on the brink of opening a new inpatient treatment center. Anorexia is big business in the Twin Cities and a regular feature on the front page of the *Star Tribune* newspaper.

"I'll switch with you."

"Excuse me?"

I lean over the counter of Walgreens where a pharmacist with stick-straight hair down to her waist rings up my Wellbutrin.

"I'd like to switch insurance plans with you," she says as she hands me the crinkly prescription bag. "Yours is so much better than mine. No co-pay. Okay, here you go: two tablets a day, ninety-day supply."

I'm pleasantly surprised. Dr. Mauer really came through for me.

"That *is* your prescription, right?"

"Yeah, yeah," I say, suddenly eager to get the goods and run before someone at Blue Cross Blue Shield realizes they've just approved 180 tablets of Wellbutrin for a former Ana devotee.

In the car, I unfold the drug information sheet and read the warnings. Side effects include the usual: dizziness, nausea, weight changes, worsening depression. And then, smack in the middle of the paper, it reads: DO NOT USE IF YOU HAVE OR HAVE HAD AN EATING DISORDER (ANOREXIA, BULIMIA).

I shake the canister in disbelief.

This medication could kill me.

Or bring me back to life.

JOURNAL ENTRY

Depression has overlooked me lately; was my trip to Taos, the yoga lessons, or Wellbutrin the magic bullet? I'm not sure, but

I'm afraid to question too much. Perhaps it is better to accept the calm when it comes and not analyze. Some things cannot be explained and even if they could, shouldn't. Whatever the reason, I am thankful for the reprieve.

"What are you looking for?" my mother asks one evening as I work my way through a cardboard box. Piles of stained clothes, unread books, and raggedy shoes surround me.

"Nothing," I say. "I'm just getting rid of all my shit."

In the six months since I moved in with my mother, I haven't unpacked all of my belongings. But I've crunched the numbers and—barring a financial miracle—I'll be living in her basement interminably. So I make peace with my living space by purging—without Correctol and a toilet bowl.

Within days, my shoes are lined, heel to heel, in seasonal order, across the back wall; my sexy date clothes, which had been crumbled in the corner of a box for months, are washed and dangling on their hangers; the eight-by-ten portraits of the girls and me are matted and framed and proudly displayed on my night stand.

"Good job!" my mother cheers as I heave bag after bag of stuff to the garage for the Vietnam Vets pickup. "Feng shui!"

Is it feng shui or pharmaceuticals? Does it matter?

"Mom?" I ask.

"Yes?"

To my surprise, my voice trembles and my eyes fill with tears when I ask, "How long are you willing to let me and the girls live here?"

"Forever," she says.

In our cheesiest mother-daughter moment thus far, we both start crying.

*　*　*

Who knows how I ended up at this particular Caribou Coffee; perhaps one day I had a caffeine craving between my yoga class and picking up my daughters from daycare and stopped in. Now I'm not only addicted to the java, I'm in love with the location.

The café is the ideal creative haven, where I can write all day by the windows and warm my legs in the sun like a lazy cat. I'm a fixture at the coffee shop, my presence as predictable as the morning rush of men in business suits.

"You're not homeless, are you?" one man asks me after crossing paths at the counter a half dozen times.

With a setup like this, who needs to go home? The café is attached to Great Harvest Bread Company, which supplies me with the essential writer's fuel: gooey cinnamon swirl bread, hefty pepperoni rolls, massive bags of trail mix, monster cookies, and mud bars. Since Subway opened a few doors down, I don't even have to leave "campus" for lunch. I never knew a strip mall could feel so cozy.

There's no shortage of witty repartee with the fellow Caribou customers. There are days when I look up from my laptop and realize with a satisfied smile that I can identify every customer and employee in the café. It's a Generation Xer's version of *Cheers*; same sense of inclusion, different addictive substance.

The morning flow of customers is comforting in its regularity. The group of raucous retirees saves a table for me until I arrive at nine. Then there's the bearded minister and his wife, who share big belly laughs and small miracles with a rotating cast of congregants. The glamorous grandmothers always have at least one toddler in tow. Toothpick-thin Sam scribbles on yellow legal sheets by the fireplace while gray-haired Jerry clambers by with his cane. Josh with the red sporty Saturn sips a cold press and nibbles on two-foot-long cheddar breadsticks while reading the *Star Tribune*. Delilah in the powder blue Beetle with GoJesus license plates pulls in around 11 A.M. James, the roofer in holey jeans, pops in for free refills all day long. Bud and Sherry, the brother and sister pair, catch up at the café on the weekends.

Then there's the manager. Every writer requires eye candy for those stints of wall-staring that are part and parcel of the creative process. Mine is Sasha—a man as pretty as his name implies—and my favorite table provides me with an unobstructed view of the Nick Lachey look-alike as he prepares drinks behind the bar.

"I've got a trivia question for you," I say to Sasha one morning with caffeine-induced courage.

"Oh yeah?" he asks, sliding a ChapStick around his luscious lips.

"How many cups of coffee will I have to drink before you ask me out?"

Apparently, a lot. Five hundred cups later, give or take, and I'm still waiting for a date.

In the meantime, I keep writing.

Now that I've found my coffeehouse-away-from-home, the muse is more productive. I sit still and finish what I start instead of free-writing aimlessly. I finally dig up the essays that have been festering in my laptop; soon they're edited, proofread, and sent out with impressive cover letters. So what if I receive rejection letters? At least my writing is in circulation.

"Finally, a bite!" I exclaim.

Fifteen faces turn toward me. It is the second session of freelance writing class at The Loft Literary Center in Minneapolis. The other students and I are taking turns reporting on our progress since the last session. I haven't done my homework—to pick the brain of a published author—but I've done something even better.

"I submitted an article to the *Star Tribune*," I say. "And it's going to be published next week!"

A cacophony of congratulations fills the room.

"What are you going to do to celebrate?" my instructor asks.

Go for a run, Ana says.

Binge until my stomach bursts, BB says.

"I'm not sure yet," I say. "I'll decide when the article comes out."

"Make sure you do!" the instructor says. "It's your first published clip; that's a big deal."

You wouldn't know it from my family's reaction. On the morning of the publication, I race to Babb's for the paper. The cashier doesn't blink an eye when I request ten copies of the otherwise unremarkable Wednesday edition of the *Star Tribune*. Back in my car, I rip to the South Section of the paper.

There is my smiling mug—in color!

As I read on, I realize the photo is the only untouched part of my article.

The name of my essay has been changed. The words have been rearranged. I recognize bits and pieces, but my voice has been muddled by the extensive editing. My piece has been butchered down from artistic to informative.

Later that morning, I e-mail a link to my writer friends with the subject line, "I see now why they call them 'clips'!"

Bill Addison, a food critic I met in Taos, is the first to reply. "Welcome to newspaper freelancing, baby!" he writes.

Bill's is the most enthusiastic of the handful of reactions I receive. When I walk into Caribou, I half expect a thunderous round of applause from the regulars. Not one person approaches me.

When my mother comes home that evening, she has two copies of the paper—still tightly folded—beneath a stack of mail. She's more engrossed by the Verizon Wireless bill than she is in my first newspaper column.

"Um, Mom, did you read my article?" I ask without removing my eyes from the computer screen.

"I bought it," she says. "But I haven't read it yet."

I practically have to unfold the paper for her and point out my picture.

"Nice," she says after a quick scan. "Jay? Did you see Erica's article?"

"That was today?" he asks as he flips hamburgers at the stove. "I totally forgot."

This is the extent of discussion about my article. My mother launches into a description of her dental appointment and shows her new filling off to her husband.

I recall one of Natalie Goldberg's refrains: "No one is standing over your shoulder to make sure you write."

Apparently, no one is at the newsstand to make sure you're published, either. I write from passion, not a need for notoriety, but I would like to be *read*. I don't know what's worse—having forgetful parents or apathetic ones?

Don't I deserve at least a moment of recognition? A pat on the back? A celebratory burrito? *Something*?

The only familial props I get are from my brother when he stops by for a hot-tub.

"Now you're published, too!" he says.

"Excuse me?" I ask. Since when is my dyslexic brother a writer?

"Remember?" he says. "I wrote that poem in sixth grade about Dad mowing the lawn . . ."

My little bro has just compared an article in the largest newspaper in the state to a poem published in an elementary school journal.

My family may not acknowledge my writing talent, but the literary world does. The nibbles come, one after another: I publish an essay in a breast cancer anthology and poems in literary journals and a writer's magazine.

I even make some money.

Come summer, the *Star Tribune* publishes my essay about my beloved Caribou.

On the day of its publication, I turn into a modern-day papergirl, stopping into all my favorite hotspots **with copies** of the *Star Tribune* folded beneath my arm.

"Shameless self-promotion!" I trill as I slip the article across countertops everywhere.

The Glamorous Grandmothers post a copy of the article on bright red construction paper in the café. Strangers approach me and gush about how entertaining my writing is. Sasha greets me with a gushy smile and heartfelt thanks. Though he doesn't treat me to a cup of coffee, he points me out to customers who comment on the article. "There's *the author*," he says with pride.

In twenty-four hours, I am catapulted from overcaffeinated café loner to small-town celebrity. Where I once felt invisible, I see familiar faces everywhere: in the weight room at the Y, in the dairy aisle of Babb's, at the gas pump at Super America, in the checkout line at Walgreen's.

It's been so long since I felt at home—in or outside of my body. Ana and BB used to be my only friends, my sole source of warm fuzzies—when they weren't wreaking havoc on my body, that is. The recognition from the fellow Caribou customers reassures me I've emerged from the anorexic rabbit hole. Now I belong to a community. I've been reborn into society and have found my calling at last.

JOURNAL ENTRY

Life is finally on the upswing!

chapter thirty

Your Brain on Anorexia

It always starts like this. One day you put on those skintight stone-washed jeans—or at least, you try to put them on, but they don't make it past the knees without a struggle—and your thighs look as disgusting as the sausages you haven't eaten in years. And that day, as the pants cut off your circulation from the waist down, you flip the switch and turn off your appetite.

You're on your third round of recovery now and you've learned how to relapse without being noticed. You've mastered the tight-rope walk between scary skinny and just a-little-too-thin.

You start by cutting out the junk food—the *real* junk food—the cookies, the brownies, the frappuccinos. The first three days are hell, when your mouth salivates at the sound of a blender in Starbucks, when your eyes have to avoid the bakery case or you might maul it like an angry gorilla at the zoo.

But once you make it over the hump, an amazing thing happens. The cravings abate, and it is suddenly all too easy to subsist on salads and boiled eggs.

It's fun at first, these daylong dips into the eating disorder. You put off eating for as many hours as you can, until the floaty feeling overtakes you. That ferocious hunger returns, and you revel in the feeling of pining for something, for the occupation of obsession. You remember the caloric arithmetic the way you remember your Social Security number.

Not-eating opens up so much time in your schedule, time for all those mundane tasks you've been neglecting, the ones that require little brain or body power. You do your laundry. You shred bank statements. You file tax returns. You catch up on your reading. You sleep. You wait for your body to turn bony.

"I haven't had sugar in two weeks!" you trill to your therapist. "I've stopped bingeing! I'm back in control!"

She sips her lemon tea across from you.

"You realize what 'in control' means, don't you?" she asks.

You shake your head no.

"That the eating disorder is back."

You scowl. You scoff. You wave off her so-called expertise. You pick lint off your turtleneck.

"Your energy is low today," she says.

You blame it on the weather, on your overscheduled afternoon, on your new medication. You blame the energy drain on everything except anorexia.

"Would you like to do something different when it comes to food?" your shrink asks.

"No," you say.

"Even if it might make you feel better?"

"No."

"Why not?"

"Because eating never makes me feel better."

You've been there, eaten that. You added the whole grains and the omega 3s and all you got was fat.

You've tried the other coping mechanisms—the journaling, the meditation, the movies—and the effects are short-lived.

But anorexia is on-call 24/7 and it makes you feel orgasmically good.

So this is why you come back: Feeling thin trumps every other feeling in existence. Feeling thin is better than the deepest massage, the most heavenly facial, the prettiest mani-pedi. Feeling thin is better than acceptance into a well-respected MFA program, better than seeing your poems in print, better than being recognized all over town from your picture in the paper. Feeling thin is better than successfully seducing an inappropriate older man, better than falling in love after heartbreak, better than the first quickening of a baby growing in your belly, better than your preschooler whispering, "I love you, Mommy."

Most of all, feeling thin beats any taste you could put in your mouth.

"You seem lonely," your shrink says.

"I am lonely. All the time."

You do not have a best friend, a boyfriend, classmates, or colleagues, but you have size 1 jeans that zip up again.

"This is not working for you," Shrinky-dink says.

You are too busy to respond. You are rolling a tissue between your fingers until you make a Kleenex joint. Then you unroll it and fold it instead. How many imaginary objects can you create with one tissue while you get your head examined? Look—an envelope! Look—a diamond! You are a Kleenex origami expert.

"What are your plans for this weekend?" Shrinky asks as you roll off her couch.

You squint. You shrug. You sigh. "I don't know."

But you know. You are going to spend your weekend being skinny.

You rush out to your car to eat a cheese wedge. Laughing Cow brand. Ha ha, who's laughing now? Such a cute little snack, wrapped like a present in silver packaging. You love this stuff. No refrigeration required and so satisfying on a single Rye-Krisp cracker. You flip the package over to check calorie content for the hundredth time: 35 calories? That's it? There must be a mistake; so much cheese, so little damage.

And that's when anorexia sounds the siren inside you. You must get the hell out of here now! You are going to *explode*! You start up the car, head onto the highway, miss one exit after another, unsure of where you're going.

Wait. Let's be clear. *You* are unsure where you are going, but anorexia knows exactly where you are headed. The YMCA. You must move your body, must burn off the cheese before you turn into a cow, must exorcise whatever ambivalence you're feeling before it festers and forms a moldy growth on your soul.

Before you have time to catch your breath, you're in your racer-back Speedo in the pool. Move over fatties with floaties! Move over blue-haired ladies! You need to be cleansed from the act of eating.

Back and forth. Breaststroke, backstroke, doggy paddle, whatever works to get the monkey off your back and the flab off your stomach. When you reach the edge of the pool, you grasp your glutes to make sure they're working, wondering if you can squeeze your cellulite away.

Back and forth. How many miles do you swim? Where in the world are you swimming *to*?

Your thoughts race with every stroke. Is this dysfunctional? Is anorexia back?

You cannot feel anything; an exercise epidural. You swim and swim and forty minutes later, you still don't feel like you've worked out.

That is, until you stand up. Then the world turns into a tilt-a-whirl, each step a will-you-or-won't-you gravitational debate. You waddle to the whirlpool without falling on your face. The other swimmers stare. You don't know why. You're nowhere near stare-worthy skinny yet.

In the dressing room, you pause as you pass the mirror. Every rib on the front and back of your body is on display. Each vertebra, from neck to coccyx, is visible, like beads on the fraying hemp string of your spine. You palpate the beginnings of a six-pack beneath a fanny pack of fat. You may be dead on your feet but seeing your skeleton beneath your skin makes all the work worth it.

"What is your ideal weight?" Aaron asks me during a follow-up yoga session.

"Ten pounds less than I am now," I say.

"Exactly ten pounds? Or is that your knee-jerk response?"

"I just want to be thinner," I sigh.

That's the rub of anorexia. I'll never lose those last ten pounds. Deep down, I know: I could be as shapely as a coat hanger and every item of clothing would still make me look fat. I could be on the brink of death and I would still slap my stomach and pinch my thighs and examine every inch of my evaporating ass. I could be skin and bones, prostrate in a casket, and still not be thin enough to satisfy Ana.

"How long is this going to take?" I ask Shania as we approach our one-year treatment anniversary. I've been through so much therapy I could've earned a counseling license via osmosis. I've tried every selective serotonin reuptake inhibitor (SSRI) under the sun. I've done the meal plans and support groups.

"Seven years," she says without hesitation. Clearly, she's answered this question before.

My jaw thunks as it hits the floor.

"Seven years?"

Seven years to recover from a diet gone dangerously wrong. Seven years to learn a skill as intrinsic as eating. Seven years to shed the skin of incessant thoughts, urges, cravings, craziness.

Seven years. The amount of time to complete two master's degrees.

Seven years. One for each lover thus far.

Seven years. The time it took to date, marry, reproduce with, and divorce the father of my children.

Seven years. My daughters' lifetimes combined.

If recovery were measured like days in the week, no wonder I'm down: it's only Monday. The hard work has barely begun.

"How do you think you can turn things around?" Shania asks. These fill-in-the-blank interrogatories are getting old.

"I already know how," I say like a tape-recorded self-help guru: "By respecting and listening to my body."

Shania smiles encouragingly.

"But," I add, "knowing and doing are two different things."

"You do well when you treat yourself well," Shania says. "Can you do that?"

"Can I? Yes. Do I want to? Yes. Will I? I don't know."

It is the stupidest psychological riddle: I have the awareness, the knowledge, even the motivation, to change. My sole instruction is to be kind to myself. And yet this is the hardest homework assignment I've ever had.

I could put a sexy spin on my disorder, call myself melancholic or athletic. I could hide behind the label of an eccentric artist. I could claim that life is too hard to live without an addiction. To get through the day, some people smoke, some people drink, some people fuck themselves silly. I starve. Maybe this is just how I deal.

What brings me back to earth and eating is that I get sick and tired of being sick and tired. Over time, the tedium of being disordered proves greater than the monotony of being normal.

I caterpillar-crawl to the realization that all the time I spent on my body is nonrefundable. I can't file a grievance with God for the energy I used planning and preparing meals, for the money I wasted on binges and refrigerator purges, for the hours whittled away at the gym.

While I've been running in place, my friends and family have moved up in the world, buying brand-new sports cars, launching businesses, mortgaging homes, getting engaged, having babies. If there's one thing I can't stand, it's being left behind in the game of life.

"You have to put the eating disorder out of a job," my former therapist Garrison once told me.

His words come back to me and I have a mini epiphany: Recovery isn't a condition—it's a decision. The only way to get better is to get busy. I scrounge around for abandoned talents, seek out forgotten friends, surrender myself to faith.

I don't transform overnight; my healing comes in waves. Taos may have been the spark, the Wellbutrin gave me the oomph to continue, and yoga changed my relationship to my body. Like the initial onset of anorexia, I don't fall headfirst into ordinariness. I start with observation. I watch an attractive woman eat half a cinnamon roll, tuck the leftovers in a cardboard box, and sit with it beside her as she sips her regular vanilla latte sans fancy instructions and sugar-free syrups. She looks serene. I want to be that woman.

I stock up on corny Melody Beattie books. I treat food as my medicine and take balanced dosages every three hours. I serve myself without an arsenal of measuring spoons or scales and resist estimating calorie contents. I savor my supper without my conscience kicking in. I remind myself that this is not my last opportunity to eat. I stop repenting for imagined indiscretions with laps around the lake.

I remarry my battered body in a private psychological ceremony: *I promise to respect you, nurture you, and care for you, in sickness and in health, all the days of my life.* At first, my body and I cohabitate like newlyweds—arguments abound and compromise is commonplace—but I trust that we will, eventually, enjoy each other again.

I strive to arrive at an ordinary place. And that place, let's be honest, is mind-numbingly boring. I arrive on time to my therapy appointments, I schedule dental cleanings, I read *Goodnight Moon* three times in a row if my daughters flash me the puppy-dog eyes.

Exercise still feels amazing and food will always taste great, but seeing my daughters' sparkling smiles every morning is even better.

JOURNAL ENTRY

There's too much to stick around for—if not in the pursuit of happiness, then at the very least out of stubborn curiosity.

Anorexia kept me alive—until it almost killed me. By keeping my mind on my body, Ana and BB distracted me from depression. But eating disorders are a dangerous game, one you can't win without dying.

I never truly wanted to commit suicide. What I wanted was to be exceptional at something, and I happened to stumble upon starvation. The restricting, the exercise, the bingeing and purging were all defense mechanisms—albeit maladaptive—that preserved what little self-esteem I had. To leave Ana and BB behind, I had to realize that I didn't need a complex psychological diagnosis to prove I was special. The happiness I sought for so long couldn't be found in a supermarket. It was buried deep inside me all along, but nowhere near the stomach.

Rereading my journals and writing this memoir brought back many painful memories, memories of an Anorexic Erica who would have done anything to be good enough, to be deserving of love. I wish I could take the emaciated me in my arms and say: *Your body is not your enemy; it is your ally. It will carry you into the future if you nourish yourself well for the journey. Your most valuable traits cannot be measured, weighed, or graphed. Your power comes from passion; feed your dreams and you will thrive.*

If I could go back in time, I would tell her: Exercise less, write more. Kiss your kids at every opportunity. Remember that your daughters are paying closer attention than you realize. Now get out there and take a bite out of life!

chapter thirty-one

The Present

"I want to recover," I once told Shania. "But I can't imagine what that would look like."

Now I know.

Recovery is waking up, sans alarm, seven days a week. It is drinking coffee at the kitchen counter while my daughters have breakfast. It is eating three meals a day, whole grains included. It is snacks when I want one. It is obeying cravings and indulging often.

Recovery is hosting a potluck dinner every Sunday as a way to make peace with and appreciate food. It is preparing and eating the feast at my dining room table, as a family, to make up for all the unshared meals of my childhood.

Recovery is running ten miles a week—total—instead of ten miles a day. It is replacing ab exercises with legs-up-the-wall meditation. It is banning one-night stands and taking a dating hiatus until I am ready to fall in love again.

Recovery is gloating over Julia's perfect score on her math homework. It is displaying Lola's latest artistic creation with pride on the living room wall. It is giggling over Julia's Kanye West crush when his latest song comes on the radio. It is cheering Lola on as she pedals, Lance Armstrong speed, down the street on her bike.

Recovery is leisurely nature walks with our new poodle. It is admiring the horse ranch we pass on the way to school and visualizing ourselves owning such a home someday. It is raucous birthday parties at Chuck E. Cheese. It is an ice cream cone enjoyed while admiring the sunset.

Recovery is not always rose-colored. Recovery is also the unsettling stillness that I have yet to get used to. It is the longing that rarely lets up but fuels my writing.

Recovery is me, sitting at my desk while the rest of the world is asleep, bathed in the halo of light from my desk lamp, staring at a blank computer screen, grasping for words to fill the page. It is the rush of wind that makes the curtains tremble and announces the arrival of my demons. It is a phantom Ana and a bossy BB knocking insistently on the window, begging reentry into my life. Recovery is the wallop of loneliness that brings me to tears when I recognize that I cannot reunite with my imaginary companions.

In those moments, before self-pity and despair consume me, inevitably my daughters call out for me down the hall. I kneel at their bedsides, stroke their chestnut brown and straw blond locks, and marvel at how, without words, my presence is enough to put them back to sleep.

I am grateful that Ana and BB abducted me as a young mother. Without my daughters, this book may not have had the hopeful ending it does. I now understand and respect the awesome responsibility of motherhood. My wish is that my daughters, and little girls everywhere, live as long, as healthfully, and as happily as possible.

This book is more than a cautionary tale; it is a thank-you letter to Julia and Lola for bringing me back to life.

If just one message arises from the anorexic muck, I hope it will be this:

The only people who can fill you up are family. The only substance that can satiate your hunger is love. Tend to your hearts, Daughters, and the rest will take care of itself.

About the Author

Erica Rivera is a former guest columnist of the *Star Tribune*. Her writing has been featured in *Writers' Journal*, *Moon Journal*, and LaChance Publishing's *Voices of Breast Cancer* anthology. She has worked as a counselor in a residential treatment center for adolescents, and she lives in Minnesota with her two daughters. Visit the author's website at www.ericarivera.net.